DATE DUE

HERE TODAY, GONE TOMORROW

The stage is set, and the dancers commence the daily ritual of the ballet class. In a few hours performers and audience will be transported to the world of the performance, and, when it's over, the stage empty, the lights dimmed, nothing remains – except the memories.

HERE TODAY, GONE TOMORROW

A LIFE IN DANCE

CHRISTINA GALLEA ROY

Book Guild Publishing
Sussex, England

First published in Great Britain in 2012 by
The Book Guild Ltd
Pavilion View
19 New Road
Brighton, BN1 1UF

Typesetting in Garamond by
MRM Graphics Ltd, Winslow, Bucks

Printed and bound in Spain under the supervision of
MRM Graphics Ltd, Winslow Bucks

A catalogue record for this book is available from
The British Library.

ISBN 978 1 84624 690 6

Constancy of purpose achieves the impossible

Chinese proverb

Contents

Acknowledgements

There are so many people to whom I owe a debt of gratitude – teachers, mentors, role-models, colleagues and collaborators, all of whom contributed to the extraordinary adventure which my life in dance has been. They are far too numerous to list here, and I hope that the following chapters of this book bring them to life along with my admiration and appreciation.

In the writing of this book, I must firstly thank Mary Clarke, Editor Emeritus of Dancing Times, who gave me the opportunity to write for the magazine and, in so doing, gave me the courage to write this book. I am also grateful to her successor, editor, Jonathan Gray for his continued support and encouragement. I owe much thanks to my two very good friends, David Bellan and Dick Coldwell, CBE, who have spent so much time reading, and re-reading the chapters, while supporting and encouraging me. David, balletomane 'par excellence', BBC broadcaster and journalist, has also punctiliously corrected my spelling and above all, my punctuation, while Dick has brought his academic and analytical mind to bear to make me check and re-check dates and places as well as giving me insight into a layman's reaction to the book. Ex-company member Emma Payne has made an incomparable contribution when, after her career as an exuberant Puck and an imaginative Alice, she spent many weeks compiling an archive of the company's history. From this I could trace where the company was on any given day over the past thirty-five years, what programme was performed and even who was dancing.

I must also acknowledge the assistance given to me by all the photographers and the curators of the dance archives, worldwide. I am especially grateful to Geoff Howard, who having photographed the company on-stage and off-stage over many years, has been a constant source of help and advice in the preparation of this book.

Finally, both Alexander and I owe a huge debt to our mothers, who tolerated our unconventional lifestyle, with only occasional grumbles, but who were also present to aid and abet us over many years.

Introduction

In a non-descript backstreet behind the Olympia exhibition centre in West London is an imposing, red-brick Victorian building, a former post office of the Royal Mail, now used by the Victoria and Albert Museum to house some of their most valuable collections. Installed on the first floor is a treasure trove, an Aladdin's cave of memorabilia, an irreplaceable and invaluable collection documenting the most ephemeral of all art forms – the V&A's Theatre Collection. Until 2007 the London Theatre Museum was situated in Covent Garden's former flower market, serving as a showcase of theatre history in the heart of London's Theatreland. Its closure was undoubtedly a sad loss for theatre lovers, but a permanent exhibition has now been moved to the stately setting of the Victoria and Albert Museum. The collection is far too extensive for all of it to be on show and the former post office headquarters in Earl's Court have proved to be an ideal home.

In majestically high-ceilinged rooms, carefully controlled at the desired temperature, lit with subdued natural light filtering through the tall windows, this remarkable collection is carefully conserved to withstand all but the inevitable fading of time and is meticulously archived to allow access by students, scholars and theatre lovers. There are records of Britain's greatest performers, as well as the writers, directors, designers, composers, impresarios – so many who have contributed to the country's rich theatre history going back several hundred years. The Theatre Collection also includes a major dance collection containing many fascinating objects: from the mid nineteenth century there are Marie Taglioni's pointe shoes, with their tiny hardened pointes, shiny satin, still pristine pink; from 1924 there is Picasso's huge and magnificent stage curtain for *Le Train Bleu* created for the Diaghilev Ballets Russes; and there are the original costumes from Nijinsky's *Le Sacre du Printemps*, the colours looking as fresh and vibrant as at that scandalous premiere in 1913.

It was, therefore, something of a surprise to hear from Sarah Woodcock, the Theatre Museum's irrepressibly enthusiastic former dance curator, that the museum would welcome anything and everything Alexander Roy and I could give it to create an archive documenting the ballet companies we had created and directed over a period of some thirty-seven years. This included our earliest attempts at self-sufficiency, a recital programme for two dancers which gave Alexander Roy his first opportunity to choreograph. With *Soirée de Ballet*, we toured throughout Europe for two years, then expanded in 1965 to form International Ballet Caravan, a small peripatetic group based firstly in Paris, moving a year later to London. By 1974, the company had become firmly established in Britain, increased in numbers and was working twelve months of the year, much of it in the United Kingdom. It seemed that a change of name from one recalling strolling players was needed, so the company became Alexander Roy London Ballet Theatre. Over the following twenty-five years the company, made up of never more than twelve to sixteen dancers, created its own repertoire, nurtured several generations of dancers and performed in many of the major capital cities, as well as in thirty-one different countries throughout the world. Alexander Roy created around fifty ballets for the company, both one-act ballets and full-length works, often also arranging musical scores and designing the scenery.

'There is so little information about the independent companies' – Sarah Woodcock's words rang in our ears. It had never occurred to us that our companies, deliberately founded and zealously promoted as personal entities, could find a place within a national institution of such importance as the V&A Theatre Collection. Independent we had always been; free of the restraints of boards and committees, ignoring tradition and hierarchy, able to exist without relying on subsidy or outside funding. We needed to be in charge personally, to be flexible enough to adapt to new opportunities and, above all, free to work and create in conditions of our own choosing. Independence has its advantages and its pitfalls, obviously; it was not without a struggle, often it was a battle just to survive, and always a challenge to meet those standards which we set ourselves. However, survive we did, and the rewards and the highlights are what we remember and cherish.

'Here today, gone tomorrow' can perhaps best describe the transient quality of our art form; more than any other art, dance is the most difficult to record and to preserve. Photographs show only one second of a movement, a single glance of a performer, while written observations remain within the eye of the beholder. Flickering black and white film gives us some idea of Anna Pavlova's art and mostly amateur film-makers have left us some souvenirs of companies such as the Ballet Russe de Monte Carlo from the 1930s and 1940s, but most of what took place in the dance world before the 1970s remains unsatisfactorily recorded. This is all the more so for a small independent company without the resources and staff to collect and preserve those items which could be of interest for the future. It was certainly the case with our companies; the first video camera was a borrowed, second-hand one which produced some fuzzy recordings of performances from the late 1970s; it was well into the 1980s before we were able to make recordings of rehearsals and performances which could be put to practical and lasting use. For all the progress, a filmed performance still does not replace the real thing, it does little to explain how a performance comes about or how and why a company exists. In our case, 'today' has become 'yesterday' and 'tomorrow' has been and gone, so it is all the more reassuring to know that a shelf of archive boxes packed with photos, programmes, press cuttings, and all the memorabilia of a professional lifetime's work can be found in the V&A's Theatre Collection as witness to this time.

As for this book, I must hope that it will provide a record of those years, of both the background of the two artists who brought it all to life and of the work; the ballets, the dancers, the tours and the performances. I also wish to pay homage to those teachers and mentors, the choreographers, directors and dancers we met and worked with in the early years whose influence and inspiration continued to guide us. Many of these have faded from view without being filmed, satisfactorily photographed or their work being well recorded. Continuing the theme of 'Here today, gone tomorrow', I must also include the theatres, the towns and countries we visited, all of which have changed so dramatically during the same period of time. Sometimes the subsequent story can be best told by notes from a diary, a tour itinerary or a magazine article and these are included along with tour snapshots, and studio and stage photographs where they seemed to best illustrate events. This has been an extraordinary voyage commencing with two dancers in an overloaded Volkswagen Beetle evolving into an international ballet company performing to audiences throughout the world. It all took place during an exciting period of dance history and I believe our very individual contribution to dance is an unusual one and perhaps because of this, it is unique.

Jane Pritchard, curator of dance (Theatre and Performing Collections), Victoria and Albert Museum, at Blythe House.

chapter
one

Beginnings

How many times have I woken, chinks of light peeping through the blinds or shutters of a hotel room, and waited for the first signs, the first sounds or voices which would give me a clue – which country am I in? Which town? What am I doing here? What's in store today? It could be the insistent drone from the air conditioner of an American motel, or the lively bustle of early-morning workers in a French city; perhaps the roaring, hooting, screeching of Asian rush-hour traffic, or the unmistakable smell of frying food seeping up the stairs of an English bed and breakfast. Sometimes I feel that my whole life has been a voyage, or rather that I have been a traveller all my life; it has become a part of me and has become inexorably entwined with another part of myself, which is dance. I can remember planning this as far back as memories will take me. My grandparents had a huge, leather-bound set of the *Encyclopaedia Britannica* which I would pore over, engrossed in the intricate engravings and the dull grey photos of the Victoria Falls, the Great Wall of China, headhunters in Sarawak or huskies pulling sleds in the Arctic Circle. I knew then that I had to see all this and much, much more.

As well as deciding that Australia could not keep me away from the rest of the world, I also resolved, aged about six, to become a ballerina, even to have my own ballet company with which I would travel around the globe. The main inspiration for this ambitious project came from the huge, glossy souvenir programmes of Colonel de Basil's Ballets Russes which my mother had kept from the company's visits to Australia. The Russian ballerina Irina Baronova became my role model as she looked about the size I might grow to, while I also hoped I might become as pretty as she was. In the event I did dance one of Baronova's roles, in the ballet *Le Beau Danube*, under the direction of the choreographer Léonide Massine; this was in the same year when Alexander and I married, setting forth on a journey together whereby my childhood dreams became a reality. A few years later with our own ballet company, we performed not only in London, Paris, Berlin and New York, but also in places as far off the beaten track as Alaska, Ecuador, Trinidad and Taiwan.

Our beginnings couldn't have been more different – Alexander's in Central Europe, where he survived the almost total destruction of his home town, Magdeburg, growing up without any hope of a normal childhood. Twenty thousand kilometres away, in Australia, a country comparatively unscathed by the horrors of war, I spent an uneventful, if unconventional, childhood. However, there were similarities; we were both only children born of parents in uneasy marriages which did not last. For differing reasons there was little contact with any extended family members, leaving us often alone as children, and to our own devices. Unperturbed by this, we created imaginary friends and playmates, and invented our own games; through this we acquired lively imaginations as well as developing self-sufficiency and resilience, attributes which were to become essential in the years ahead.

In a city still lying in ruins, Alexander spent the last days of his childhood hanging around the Russian army camps where he could wash the soldiers' horses in the nearby River Ehle in return for a bowl of borsch; occasionally there might also be a chunk of hard black bread to take back home to his family. But it was difficult to resist joining the older boys who gathered on street corners having discovered easier ways of eking out a living on the black market; a single bottle of vodka could be magically swollen to produce three bottles to resell to the Russian soldiers, and American cigarettes, smuggled across the already existent West–East divide, were worth even more. Alexander's father took precautions, finding him work as an apprentice in a pharmacy, where he spent his days dusting shelves and rows of bottles, or

2

Irina Baronova, baby-ballerina of the Ballets Russes as The Queen of Shemakan in
Le Coq d'Or, c.1938.

Alexander's father, Herbert and his mother, Hanna, performing in variety performances in Magdeburg just after the war.

decanting cough mixture into small containers, with occasional welcome sorties to accompany an older person home with their heavier purchases.

His father was a keen musician, an accomplished pianist and accordionist, skills which were to serve him well during the post-war chaos of Germany when there was little other work available. His mother also had a natural stage presence, winning some success as an actress, and performing in variety shows, without ever being able to consider a career as a professional actress in the very conservative restrictions of German family life. It was during his time at the pharmacy that Alexander started taking ballet classes with a local Russian-born former ballerina. Using his lunch hour to cycle through Magdeburg's rubble-strewn streets to the local ballet school, he took classes in an unheated room, in shorts and bare feet as practice clothing and ballet shoes were, at that time, unprocurable items. His lunch on a typical day would have been a pocketful of carrots, one of the few food items the family had managed to obtain during the immediate post-war years of deprivation and even near starvation. The ballet classes, which had been recommended by the family doctor who feared the pale-faced teenager might have a weak heart, brought out a natural aptitude for dance. However, it was after seeing a performance by a Russian folk dance ensemble that Alexander's interest in dance was awakened, and he visited the nearby city of Halle, where he had heard a new ballet academy was opening. Here he met the choreographer and director Gertrud Steinweg, who offered him a scholarship to study with her.

Alexander aged about 14 – his first 'big leap'.

Steinweg had been a pupil of Mary Wigman at a time, in the 1920s, when German modern dance was enjoying much respect and popularity. Wigman was a great star performer and ran a school in Dresden which produced a whole generation of major dance performers and creators, some of whom, notably Hanya Holm, travelled to America to make a huge impact on the development of American contemporary dance. Steinweg decided early on in her career to concentrate on choreography, becoming dance director at the opera house in Aachen while moving on later to the more prestigious theatre in Mannheim. During the Nazi regime she would have been forced to relinquish modern dance, to improve her knowledge of classical ballet, adapting her choreography in order to remain an active professional, as modern dance was considered 'improper'. After the war, in East Germany under the Soviet regime, classical ballet was enthusiastically promoted, bringing Steinweg to settle in her home town of Halle teaching classical and contemporary dance, while looking for work in a theatre. A highly intelligent, cultured woman, she was fired with energy and ambition and it was not long before she was appointed ballet mistress, or director of dance, at the opera house in Leipzig, and planned to take Alexander with her. There was, however, one problem: the young dancer needed a diploma in order to work professionally.

Mary Wigman in *The Devil's Dance* (1920s).

Gertrud Steinweg c.1925.

Alexander tried everything to be accepted for the necessary examinations which were already scheduled, as in a country where even window cleaners need diplomas, there was no way around this. Managing to complete the theoretical papers dutifully embroidered with the Soviet-style political 'correctness' of the day, he squeezed himself into the ballet studio on examination day, where the lack of the obligatory number on the back of his practice clothes soon became obvious. However, he was allowed to remain, and following the technical examination was requested to present to the examiners a Spanish solo dance. The pianist burst forth with the lively accompaniment while Alexander desperately attempted to recall an item, 'Impressions of Spain', given during a recent performance by a well-known solo dancer in Halle, Georg Groke. He stamped his feet as hard as he could, clapped his hands, thrashed his arms through the air, undulated his torso enthusiastically and, to his amazement, won a burst of loud applause from the visibly amused examiners. Diploma in hand, he could join Steinweg at the Leipzig Opera House.

A particularly successful production of the Polovtsian Dances from *Prince Igor* took the Leipzig ballet company to perform in East Berlin where

Alexander was spotted by the direction of the Berlin State Ballet and offered a contract with what was, and probably still is, Germany's most prestigious opera house. Here he was carefully nurtured for principal dancer status, finally being offered a scholarship for further study with the Bolshoi Ballet in Moscow, which he declined, believing his physique was not suited to the heavy, muscular style of Russian male dancers of the day. Alexander stayed two seasons with the Berlin State Ballet, gradually advancing to soloist status, and besides taking classes with the Berlin company he was able to take advantage of the teachers active in West Berlin at the time, notably Gustav Blank and Tatjana Gsovsky.

On taking over the position of director of the ballet at the Komische Oper (Berlin's second opera house), Gertrud Steinweg was soon to offer Alexander an engagement with her company, where he danced in her acclaimed version of *Scheherazade*, and notably created a leading role in a new full-length production of *The Devil in the Village*. In the tradition of Eastern European theatre practices, rehearsals for the new ballet stretched over six months, Alexander being constantly supervised and becoming the object of consistent, if mostly constructive, criticism from the Komische Oper's famous director, Walter Felsenstein. This experience of meticulous, detailed rehearsal was to mark him deeply and affect his professional working practices throughout his future career.

Alexander at the time he joined the Berlin State Ballet.

Alexander, with Georg Groke as the devil, in the ballet *The Devil in the Village*, choreography by Gertrud Steinweg at the Komische Oper, East Berlin.

Living in Berlin in the 1950s was also a bit of luck. The four occupying powers competed at excelling each other's contribution to the cultural life of the city, which was slowly recovering from the almost total destruction of the war. In a city where the Berlin State Opera and Ballet were temporarily housed in a former variety theatre, visiting companies made do in make-shift theatres but had little trouble in attracting capacity audiences. Dance was the obvious choice to break any language and culture barriers so many of the best companies in the world appeared in Berlin during those vital years. The Soviet Union sent a group of soloists including the great stars of the Kirov and Bolshoi ballet companies, Natalia Dudinskaya, Konstantin Sergeyev and Galina Ulanova. It was the first glimpse the West had of the development of Soviet ballet, which amazed audiences with its virtuosity, as did the marvellous Moiseyev ensemble with its incomparably exciting folk dance. This visit also gave Alexander the opportunity to take ballet classes with the great Russian teacher Asaf Messerer. From Britain came the Sadler's Wells Ballet, led by Margot Fonteyn. However, it was Brian Shaw as the Blue Skater in *Les Patineurs* who was the Berliners', and Alexander's, favourite, as was Jean Babilée, the extraordinary French dancer who was the undoubted star of an already starry ensemble, Les Ballets des Champs-Elysées from France.

From the USA came the Ballet Russe de Monte Carlo led by ballerinas Rosella Hightower, Alexandra Danilova and Alicia Markova, with their partners André Eglevsky and Anton Dolin, as well as American Ballet Theatre led by Alicia Alonso, Igor Youskevitch and Nora Kaye, performing their unique repertoire of dance-dramas and Americana. New York City Ballet was another visitor, giving Europe its first view of George Balanchine's 'American' repertoire, as well as works by Jerome Robbins for the new generation of finely tuned yet athletic American dancers. Living, as he was, in the debris of a city devastated by war, Alexander was cut off from easy access to these events by living in East Berlin. However, by many often devious means, he managed to see most of these remarkable performances with their great dancers, an experience which stunned and delighted Berliners in general, and left an enduring impression on the young Alexander Roy.

The Devil in the Village at the Komische Oper enjoyed huge success, making Alexander something of an overnight star in the Berlin ballet world. With a busy schedule of guest performances and offers of engagements from several ballet companies, a sense of restlessness took over, a characteristic which marked his future career. The lure of the West was irresistible and he took the adventurous, if foolhardy, step of leaving the prestigious companies of East Berlin to work in provincial West German theatres. Alexander's first engagement was in Krefeld where, after the initial shock of finding himself in small-town Germany, he repeated the success of *The Devil in the Village* in

Alexander at the time he arrived in West Germany.

a new production. The Krefeld theatre was fortunate in having as intendant Kurt Schumacher, one of Germany's most innovative at the time, who presented the German premieres of important new plays such as Beckett's *Waiting for Godot* and Dürrenmatt's *The Visit*. He also gave Alexander opportunities for small acting roles and encouraged him in his first attempts at choreography. Moving to the ballet company in Bremen, he danced leading roles in *Pulcinella*, *Hamlet* and other created roles, but he was already making plans to try his luck further afield, possibly in Paris.

An offer to join the American Festival Ballet which was touring extensively in Europe meant leaving the security of the German opera house system, with what were referred to by professionals as 'gravestone contracts', but eager to move on, Alexander knew that this also meant leaving Germany. American Festival Ballet, directed by German-born Renzo Raiss, was led by the Bulgarian ballerina Sonia Arova. A child prodigy in Madame Preobrajenska's studio in Paris before the Second World War, Arova was smuggled out of France during the Nazi occupation to live with foster parents in England. Still a teenager she danced as a principal dancer with the International Ballet, the Metropolitan Ballet and later with London Festival Ballet. Moving to the USA, she became ballerina of American Ballet Theatre alongside Nora Kaye and Alicia Alonso, then headed the Chicago Ballet. As 'star' of the American Festival Ballet Arova added a distinct lustre to a hard-worked company, assuring, besides her polished technique, an exotic glamour to every performance. Her partner was the Dutch-American dancer and choreographer Job Sanders, who had also been a member of American Ballet Theatre and the Chicago Ballet. A strong performer, both in classical and modern ballets, Sanders had choreographed some impressive first works, both for companies in the Netherlands and for American Festival Ballet. The repertoire of American Festival Ballet included classical works, but featured ballets created for the company, much in the style of the repertoire of American Ballet Theatre. It gave Alexander his first contact with American contemporary dance and jazz and he found himself dancing, besides *Swan Lake* and *The Nutcracker*, a role in Job Sanders's jazz ballet *Streetcorner Royalty* and as a cowboy in Loyd Tygett's *Shindig*.

The company toured incessantly, criss-crossing Europe in pre-motorway days, often performing in difficult conditions, but it was a vital experience for Alexander, above all a valuable insight into the differences between an opera-house-based company and a touring company where every performance is a 'first night'. American Festival Ballet performed virtually every day, a schedule which Arova, appearing in four different roles in every performance, as well as the other dancers, was already accustomed to, from similar tours with American Ballet Theatre and Ballet Russe de Monte Carlo in the

Sonia Arova and Job Sanders, leading dancers of the American Festival Ballet, performing the
Grand Pas de Deux, *Don Quixote*.

United States. It seemed that being ill or injured was simply not 'professional' and none of the dancers would give less than 100 per cent to a performance; at the same time Arova and Sanders used every spare minute to rehearse a new ballet or work on a pas de deux. Among the other dancers there was at least one other couple of international stature, and the soloists and the corps were experienced dancers, toughened by the work ethic in the States at that time. An audition in New York, be it for a ballet company or a new musical, would have a queue of hundreds of dancers wrapping around a Manhattan block from daybreak. Jobs were always few while the demands were very high. For Alexander, used to the cushioned existence of the German opera house dancer, it was an invaluable experience. It was also in American Festival Ballet that Alexander met a young Australian dancer, who was another new arrival to the company…

With my mother, the artist, Nan Fullarton, aged about 6.

Twenty thousand kilometres away from war-torn Europe, I was born in Sydney, Australia, to an English father and a mother who was a third-generation Australian of Irish and Scottish origins. Brought up by my mother, a popular writer and illustrator of children's books, I was fortunate to grow up surrounded by books and art, as well as learning to enjoy the theatre. Having made the decision at an early age to become a ballet dancer, I dreamt of having my own ballet company, preferably with Mikhail Fokine, the Ballets Russes' best-known choreographer, as resident choreographer. Unusually for a six-year-old, I was disinterested in dancing in *Swan Lake* or *The Sleeping Beauty* but coveted such roles as The Firebird, Zobeide in *Scheherezade* or the Ballerina in *Petrushka*. In provincial, isolated 1930s Australia, the 1936–37 tour of the Ballet Russe de Monte Carlo appeared as a visit from another world. Of course others had visited Australia; Adeline Genée and Alexandre Volonine leading a company in 1913; Anna Pavlova with her world-famous company in 1926 and 1929, while Pavlova's husband Victor Dandré returned with Olga Spessivtseva heading a group of dancers in 1934. But these were really just small groups supporting star performers, whereby the quality of the Ballets Russes dancers, the richness of their repertoire, the colour and glamour of the sets and costumes were unique and unequalled in Australian theatre history. The Ballets Russes tours were also lengthy, with the original four-month tour being extended to ten months, including several weeks in Sydney. My mother, along with so many Australians, was bowled over. This great gust of art and culture from the other side of the world fulfilled all expectations of what Europe could offer, so she attended as many performances as she could. The Ballets Russes company, now billed as the Covent Garden Russian Ballet, returned in 1938; if this time she could no longer swoon over the now absent Igor Youskevitch in *Le Spectre de la Rose* or Leon Woizikovsky as The Golden Slave in *Scheherezade*, there was the excitement over the 'baby ballerinas', Irina Baronova and Tatiana Riabouchinska, as well as leading dancers such as David Lichine, Yurek Shabelevsky and Anton Dolin.

In 1948 Ballet Rambert came to Australia to be welcomed with great enthusiasm by a now badly starved ballet audience. If the British company's visit could in no way compete with the excitement of the Ballets Russes, Australian audiences responded firstly to the dancers who had managed to survive the war, continuing to perform under the most difficult of conditions, and to their special 'English' quality; their lightness, their lyricism, as well their exceptional dramatic ability. The extraordinarily varied repertoire included, besides the classical ballets, major works by Frederick Ashton, including his immensely popular *Façade*, and several key works by Antony Tudor such as *Lilac Garden, Gala Performance, Judgement of Paris* and

Dark Elegies. The more recent works included Frank Staff's much loved *Peter and the Wolf* while Walter Gore, who had returned to the company after the war, and despite war injuries had now taken over as principal dancer and resident choreographer, was creating a string of ballets, some highly dramatic and others charmingly lightweight. The tour was so popular that it was extended to six months, forcing the company to have more sets and costumes sent from England, so they could make return visits to all the major cities with new programmes. Despite the success, the tour had unfortunate consequences for the company, when their much loved principal dancer, Sally Gilmour, along with several others, decided to stay in Australia. Even more tragically, all their sets and costumes were lost on the trip back to England, and despite their success in Australia, the company arrived back home bankrupt.

Walter Gore and Paula Hinton in Gore's ballet *Winter Night* during the
Ballet Rambert tour of Australia, 1948.

16

Walter Gore, on tour in Australia in 1948.

During their stay, I was taken to see many performances and although still only a child, works such as Andrée Howard's *Lady Into Fox* and Antony Tudor's *Gala Performance* were etched in my memory. Walter Gore and Paula Hinton, performing a wide range of roles, and who were to have a decisive role in my future, had already entered my consciousness as examples of a new type of dancer – actor-dancers, to which I already very much aspired.

17

With virtually no government funding for the arts, Australia was fortunate to have the Borovansky Ballet, the country's only major professional ballet company. Edouard Borovansky, who had been a member of Colonel de Basil's Ballet Russe de Monte Carlo, along with several other dancers, had chosen to stay in Australia at the end of the company's last tour at the outbreak of war in Europe. Edouard Borovansky, or Boro, as he was universally known in Australia, was a Czech-born dancer who had been a member of both Anna Pavlova and Serge Diaghilev's Russian ballet companies. He joined the Ballets Russes in 1932, becoming a valued character dancer, creating many important roles for choreographers Mikhail Fokine and Léonide Massine. As a director, Borovansky was, however, a monster. He was rude to the point of being abusive, even generally loathed by most of his dancers; all the same, most of these could fall under the spell of his easily manipulative charm to support him and the company. He was also a notorious lecher causing most of the girls in the company to battle to escape his advances. Australians in general loved him. They loved his hard-working, plain-speaking, expletive-laden ways and admired his determination and guts in creating and sustaining the company in what were always extremely precarious conditions. This appreciation was always demonstrated when Boro appeared in the only dancing role he sustained over the years, the Strong Man in *Le Beau Danube*. He had created the role in Massine's enormously successful ballet in 1933 and was an immediate success, often stealing the scene from Massine himself, as the Hussar, and Alexandra Danilova, the Street Dancer. He was very good and very funny and continued to perform the role well into the 1950s, invariably receiving an ovation. He formed the Borovansky Ballet in 1940, gathering together young Australian talent and the more experienced European dancers to perform a repertoire of ballets very similar to that of the Ballets Russes. Besides performing the traditional classical ballets the company excelled at works such as *Petrushka*, *Scheherazade*, the Polovtsian Dances from *Prince Igor*, *La Boutique Fantasque*, *Le Beau Danube* and *Graduation Ball*. It was a tried and successful repertoire, the dancers competent, sometimes brilliant, especially when in the 1950s the younger Australians, such as Kathleen Gorham and Vassilie Trunoff, had become experienced artists and guest stars were brought from abroad.

At ten years of age I finally started ballet classes at the Frances Scully School of Dancing, considered to be the best school in Sydney. As Miss Frances Scully was no longer teaching, Miss Kathleen Danetree now directed the school. A typical English woman of her generation, with tightly curled grey hair, pearls and a twinset, Miss Danetree's rather strict demeanour could be terrifying to a young student. The studios were on the third floor of the narrow, dark building reached via a small backstreet. The lift, with its double

Eduard Borovansky in 1944.

doors of decorative wrought iron, was manned by a grubby if suited man smelling strongly of tobacco, who literally pulled the lift up manually with a huge rope passing through the lift cabin. There was then a long narrow corridor to negotiate where the polished dark wood panelling disappeared into an unlit ceiling, before one reached 'The Office' and the studios. Fortunately, these were large and bright, the school always busy, and filled with children's voices and music. The primary class which I joined was full of six-year-olds practising walking and running to a tinkling piano, making it obvious that I had waited too long to start ballet classes. (For some reason, my mother had been advised by an elderly Russian ex-dancer that ten years of age was the perfect time to commence.) However, I was soon promoted straight into Grade 2 and could start to study seriously, but had to work hard to catch up.

The school's teaching revolved around the curriculum set down by the Royal Academy of Dancing (RAD), leading to the dreaded examinations which took place every two years when the RAD would send out examiners to the extremities of the British Commonwealth. These formidable women, ex-dancers from another era, wore long, black dresses and still flaunted

Pavlova-style classical hairdos. Their remoteness and foreign English accents led the students to see them as direct ambassadors from the Queen, rather than from a dance academy, and the two weeks spent examining were dreaded. Lines of children would wait their turn, standing shivering in the darkened corridors in uncomfortable tutus, borrowed for the occasion, to be given fifteen minutes to show 'the 2nd Adage Enchaînement' or 'the 4th Allegro'. On one such occasion, having spent two years working on the Grade 4 examination syllabus, I was so paralysed by the tension that it was impossible for me to remember what the 4th Allegro Enchaînement was. Fortunately, the examiner was sympathetic enough to prompt with 'the one that begins with glissade, jeté'.

Kathleen Danetree had a good reputation as a teacher; Elaine Fifield and Rowena Jackson had studied with her before travelling to England where they were, at that time, principal dancers with the Sadler's Wells Ballet. One of my contemporaries, although a couple of years ahead of me, was Lucette Aldous, who, after winning the Frances Scully scholarship to study at the Royal Ballet School, went on to make a remarkable career as principal dancer with Ballet Rambert, London Festival Ballet and finally The Royal Ballet, where she established a successful partnership with Rudolf Nureyev. If Miss Danetree's talents as a teacher were restricted by the obligations of meeting the RAD requirements, with the pressure of assuring that sufficient students successfully passed the examinations, the school certainly instilled in the young dancers an exceptional will and ability to work.

Once a full-time student, having persuaded my mother to let me leave school, with which I had become sadly bored, I often took four classes daily including pointe work, repertoire classes, character dance classes, besides the obligatory classical ballet class; apart from these, I would have to battle with the others to find space in any studio which might be vacant in order to practise on my own. However, the ultimate goal of dancing on stage appeared to be unattainable. Miss Danetree considered school performances 'vulgar', disapproving of those other Sydney schools who gave an annual school performance; admittedly it was usually those who offered classes in 'tap, toe and ballet' and who allowed children onto pointe at a much too early age or pushed young limbs into the splits. However, there were secret arrangements among the older girls, for some of them were appearing as extras during the Borovansky Ballet's Sydney season. The perfect opportunity presented itself to me when a replacement was needed urgently for the countess's daughter in the crowd scenes in the ballet *Petrushka*. Surreptitiously I was taught my minor role, but as the performances were already running a stage rehearsal was not possible. I presented myself at the stage door of the His Majesty's Theatre at the appointed time and took my first steps backstage.

The extras' changing room was under the stage, almost adjoining the orchestra pit, but separated from it by a partition wall. Trestle tables were set up with light globes hanging like garlands across the ceiling. There was a table mirror at each place with the huge, colourful costumes hung on rails behind the dancers. It was hot and stuffy under the stage and the heat from the lights intense. The smell from the Leichner greasepaint was a heady perfume and the air was filled with the sounds of the orchestra warming up; the violins tuning together, trills from the woodwinds and the gentle thumps from the drums sending vibrations through the crowded room. It was quite the most exciting thing I had ever experienced, but I also felt totally 'at home'. On stage, as part of the bustling crowd in Alexandre Benois's set of a Russian village fair, it was as if I was drowning in the waves of Stravinsky's extraordinary music – sounds such as I had never heard before rising from the orchestra pit. And then there was the drama of the final scene with Petrushka's death; there was no need to act, I couldn't help but be part of the drama taking place right in front of me. Being backstage brought about numerous advantages: it was possible to watch the rest of the performance from side-stage, and in fact I managed to squat down in the downstage wing, almost enveloped in the huge red velvet house curtain. Arriving early enough at the theatre I could watch the company at class, or in rehearsal, and once the *Petrushka* performances were over, and although it was a little more difficult, there was a way, past the stage door manager's office, creeping low enough below the counter to remain unnoticed, to find my way backstage to watch rehearsals or even performances.

I would have continued the traditional path of a would-be ballet dancer, progressing by the regular examinations, had I not, by chance, or rather, 'just for the experience', joined an audition for a new ballet company to be formed by Walter Gore and his ballerina wife, Paula Hinton. They were, of course, already well known in Australia from the lengthy tour of Ballet Rambert, and they had returned briefly to join another Rambert dancer, Joyce Graeme, then directing a short-lived Australian National Ballet: here I had seen them in an unforgettable performance of *Giselle*. Against all expectations, I was chosen for the new company, to be called Australian Theatre Ballet, and which included other very young dancers straight out of school, as well as several experienced soloists.

Rehearsals started a month after the audition in a large church hall in the suburbs of Melbourne. There were just three male dancers and seven females, the ballet master, Cecil Bates, an experienced soloist from Ballet Rambert, as well as Gore and Hinton. The dancers came from different states in Australia, and from differing backgrounds. All were very young, although having just turned sixteen I was the youngest, and most had had no professional

Aged sixteen, at the time I joined Australian Theatre Ballet, photographed in
Collins Street, Melbourne.

experience. Gore and Hinton had been brought to Australia thanks to a local
ballet society, directed by two elderly women, who were obviously totally
unaware of the immensity of the project they were proposing to bring to life.
Gore and Hinton's London Ballet had recently closed in the UK, they were
heavily in debt, and doubtless they were glad to be offered work in a country
they already knew well, where they were greatly liked and respected. They
had three months to turn a ragbag collection of eager but naïvely unprepared
youngsters into a professional ballet company. They did it very seriously with
strenuously demanding daily classes and long days of repetitive rehearsals. It
was a tough and painful apprenticeship for most of us, who suffered physically
from the pains of under-trained bodies and mentally from the stress of the
demands put upon us.

I was totally in awe of them both; fascinated by Paula's tiny, taut and
muscular body, her wide expressive face with its high cheekbones and heavily
mascaraed eyes, and by Gore's quizzical expression, where his eyes appeared
to be speaking for him while he remained mostly silent or gave instructions
in a gentle mumble which one could only guess at. But mostly I was shocked

by the demands of the choreography. For the first time in my life, I heard music by Poulenc, Ibert, Chabrier and experienced how the choreography matched the speed, the lightness and the quirkiness of those composers. There were rhythms I couldn't hear, counts I couldn't follow, and steps and more steps I struggled to memorise. We were also learning 'Little Swans' from the excerpts of *Swan Lake* which we were to perform, and I had been entrusted with the role of Carlotta Grisi in the romantic ballet *Pas de Quatre* with its long, controlled solo. Gore cast me in the principal role in his ballet *Hoops* which meant working with props – there were already balls and skipping ropes to tussle with in *Street Games*, and now there were hoops to cope with, to turn pirouettes inside of, huge hoops, small hoops and great bundles of hoops to hang on to while being lifted on to my partner's shoulder. It was a nightmare, often leaving me in tears and despairing as to whether I would ever succeed.

In Gore's ballet *Street Games* – I am on the left.

After three months of rehearsals the company set off on tour, visiting twenty-five towns throughout the state of Victoria. If the Australian country towns in the 1950s were not quite the Wild West, there were some on the itinerary with a single main street, and with a sole pub-hotel, which we would have to share with drunken sheep shearers. Performing in town halls, school halls and the occasional theatre, conflict with the management began early on. The dancers remained ignorant of all the details, but Gore and Hinton had obviously committed themselves to a project which was neither professional nor viable for the major artists they were. There were several times when they were on the point of quitting, leaving the dancers unsure of their loyalties, and threatening to break the company into different groups. However, for these simple country audiences, where there were sometimes no dressing rooms, small stages with insufficient stage lighting, and little time for preparations, Gore and Hinton continued to perform as if their lives depended upon it.

They would dance Gore's pas de deux *Tancredi and Chlorinda*, both technically and dramatically demanding, on the better stages, and Andrée Howard's lyrical and tragic *Death and the Maiden* on other occasions. Paula's dramatic intensity was both deeply felt and highly controlled. If her technique was not that of a classical ballerina, she had unique talents in her lightness, her elevation, and a steely strength within a body of exceptional flexibility and expression. As well as being principal dancer for Ballet Rambert, Paula had also appeared as guest artist for London Festival Ballet, scoring a success for her interpretation of *Giselle*, as well as dancing in Anton Dolin's *Pas de Quatre* besides international ballerinas such as Alicia Markova. She had also danced in Paris with Les Ballets des Champs-Elysées, and with Jean Babilée's company. With us, on the tour in Victoria, she and Gore also performed his charming pas de deux, *Pastorale*, where the closeness of their relationship was evident, and they performed together with the company in *Light Fantastic*, revealing a delicious sense of fun and a subtle humour.

In the meantime, we were all appearing in at least four ballets at every performance, learning slowly but surely to become professionals. The dancers' relationship with Gore and Hinton was tenuous, varying almost daily – reflecting, no doubt, the pressures everyone was under. Paula could be warm, amusing, entertaining; she could be helpful with technical problems, with make-up and hair-dos – and indeed her experience was essential to us, the inexperienced members in the company. But she could also be harshly critical, while Wally remained quiet and reserved, leaving any unpleasant or unwelcome decisions to be announced by the ballet master, Cecil Bates. It was Cecil who held the company together during those difficult early days of the tour, as is so often the role of a company ballet master.

This was the first ballet magazine I ever bought and it featured Walter Gore and Paula Hinton performing with their company, the London Ballet. It seemed impossible to believe that little over a year later, I would be working in their new ballet company in Australia. They are seen here in Gore's ballet *Light Fantastic*.

Musical accompaniment for the performances was provided by a single piano and it proved a constant struggle to provide a decent instrument in an acceptable state during the tour. On one fateful occasion, when the piano was being moved so Veronica, the pianist, could have a much needed view of the stage, the lid fell loudly and firmly on Veronica's right hand. Similar incidents do invariably happen in the life of a touring company, but the chances of finding a replacement pianist capable of sight-reading multiple scores at a few hours' notice, in the depths of the Australian countryside, seemed remote. However, as fate would have it, a good pianist was expected among the audience that night and the unfortunate woman was virtually held hostage on arrival and forced to start rehearsing. In the event, Veronica was able to accompany her with her left hand, saving the situation for the evening. Gore wrote afterwards in a magazine article that that was the performance the company came of age, when the extra collective concentration and involvement needed to bring about a successful performance overcame the dancers' nerves, complexes, self-doubts and hesitation to make a major step forward into professionalism.

The Borovansky Ballet was still highly active in Australia and there appeared to be little hope of the new company having a chance in the major cities without a struggle. But an invitation for a season in a small but professional theatre in Adelaide was a major boost. The company spent several weeks rehearsing for a two-week season while Gore swiftly produced two new ballets; the gentle and lyrical *Soft Sorrow* (later re-mounted for Ballet Rambert), which gave me an important solo role, also making a first commission to the stage designer Barry Kay, who was later to make a brilliant international career. Needing a new closing ballet, he created *Musical Chairs*, a crazy, inconsequential piece enjoyed by everyone, which opened with Paula, as a society matron (presumably inspired by some of our hostesses at post-performance receptions), singing 'The Last Rose of Summer' in a forceful soprano. Gore needed to include himself in the cast and chose me as his partner, giving me a first experience of dancing with a choreographer who, in the rush to complete the work, often doesn't remember his own choreography. The effort of the rehearsals also brought on troubles with Gore's war injuries, leaving him gasping with pain as I tried to steer him around the stage. However, both Wally and Paula (as we were now comfortable in calling them) were happy and relaxed in Adelaide and the performances were well received. A further season in Melbourne followed, attracting good audiences and excellent reviews.

It seemed as if the company had made it; it had reached an acceptable professional standard and was ready to go on to bigger and better things. However, there was nothing in sight. Presumably the management had expected bookings to come flooding in; although there were many signs of interest, funding had also run out, and the dancers' contracts had come to an end. There appeared to be no room for two major ballet companies in Australia at that time, while it was clear that Wally and Paula could not be satisfied with a company permanently touring the smaller venues in the countryside. Everyone started to make plans for the future; the Gores were to return to the UK, while the company was disbanded, leaving little to show for a year of intense work and effort from the enthusiastic organisers, as well as from the company members.

At a final get-together, Wally and Paula joined us at the home of one of the dancers. We had a picnic in the garden where I was amazed to find Wally devouring a plate of sandwiches which my mother had prepared. I had never seen either of them eat before, although they would often be seen on tour with a plate of lamingtons, a typically Australian cake, and a cup of tea. The dancers had decided that they did actually exist on this limited diet. Knowing that I was planning to travel to London, Cecil Bates pulled me aside with a list of useful addresses and whispered, 'I'm sure you'll be working with Wally again. He's very fond of you.' I was totally dumbstruck, knowing that I had caused so much trouble with my inexperience, my lack of technique, my tears and tantrums, feeling that I was more of a liability, in spite of remaining totally in awe of him and his work.

A few months later Wally wrote of the company in the English magazine, *Ballet Today*, 'The eight-month period I would welcome again for the happiness and satisfaction it gave me – provided I could start with the same dancers, pianist and stage director.' If only we had known! Despite the brevity of the company's existence, the experience was to leave a lasting impression on all the dancers, and more than half the company went on to make careers in international ballet companies: Robin Haig went to the UK to dance with the Royal Ballet and the Scottish Ballet, Barrie Wilkinson and Mel Clifford danced with London Festival Ballet, as well as with the Gores in the re-formed London Ballet, and Barbara Krouthen and I were to meet up again in Germany. I had found a mentor in Gore and this experience confirmed my long-held ambition to travel to Europe.

I arrived in London on my seventeenth birthday. It was a dark, damp, fog-filled day in midwinter. In the 1950s there were still bomb sites in the centre of London and accommodation was difficult to find, with luxuries such as central heating and private bathrooms virtually unknown. My mother, who had accompanied me, brought with her a drawing board and trunks full of artists' materials and reference books. She needed to continue working to support us both, and we needed to find accommodation urgently. With no understanding of the enormity of the city, nor the differences between the 'good' parts of town and the less desirable ones, we rented a flat in Turnham Green in West London. At that time, this was at the end of the Tube line which meant long, tedious trips into town and, as our flat was situated almost next to the River Thames, the famous London 'smog', which we experienced almost immediately, was at its thickest. The next move was to the centre of London, in Charing Cross Road, directly above a West End theatre. Presumably this was considered convenient for visiting the theatres, and the ballet studios, but it proved to be dark and airless as well as constantly noisy and dirty. Finally we found the perfect place, in Pembridge Gardens, Notting Hill Gate, two steps from the Tube station and the busy shopping centre. Notting Hill Gate, at that time, had none of its present celebrity status; but the proximity to Kensington Church Street, with its famous antique shops, and to Kensington Gardens, couldn't be bettered.

The size of the city and the wealth of history to be discovered, the amount of galleries and museums to be visited, and above all, the variety of theatre and dance performances to be seen, was overwhelmingly exciting. We experienced the first visit of the Bolshoi Ballet, with Galina Ulanova and Raissa Struchkova leading a company of dazzling star dancers in sumptuous productions. My mother and I joined the hundreds who formed a queue day after day outside the Royal Opera House in Covent Garden, having travelled into town with the city's office cleaners on the first Tube. We were greeted by the porters from the fruit and vegetable market which then surrounded the opera house, and settled down with rugs and a thermos flask for the long wait for the box office to open. Eventually, small numbered tickets would be issued, while the wait would continue with ever increasing tension when returned tickets arrived back at the box office; finally, standing room tickets would be sold. We were always lucky, sometimes being seated high in the gods but preferably standing at the back of the stalls, from where I saw the sublime performances by Ulanova and Struchkova in *Giselle* and in *Romeo and Juliet*.

Following their appearances at the Royal Opera House, the Bolshoi gave a short season in Croydon with a programme of pas de deux and excerpts from their repertoire. It was an opportunity to discover their extraordinary virtuosity, and the first chance to see those works which were already standard gala performance items in Russia. It was also a welcome opportunity to see the company at close quarters in the smaller auditorium, and in a more relaxed atmosphere. Works such as the *Spring Waters* pas de deux, with its acrobatic lifts, would be encored not just once, but twice, as would the amazingly exciting solo from *Taras Bulba* with the character dancer Georgi Farmanyants soaring, head high, out of the wings. But most exciting of all were the appearances of Raissa Struchkova with her husband, Alexander Lapauri, in the *Muszkowski Waltz* and *Walpurgis Nacht*, performances full of the joy of dance, reaching out to the audience in a manner which must have done more for Russian–English relations than any politician.

Another exciting company was the Ballets de Paris of Roland Petit. We caught the night Zizi Jeanmaire, having quarrelled with Petit, walked out, leaving Violette Verdy to dance her first *Carmen* in a programme already packed with French drama and surprises; it included Buzz Miller and Veronica Mlakar in a thriller-ballet, *La Chambre*, and *Le Loup*, again with Verdy and Petit. The Spanish dance companies of Antonio, José Greco and Luisillo were regular visitors and favourites in London as was the Indian dancer Ram Gopal. However, I was unexpectedly disappointed with the newly titled Royal Ballet, which seemed to me to be so restrained and refined to be dull and uninteresting. Looking now at Baron's famous photo books of dance of that era, the immaculate lines of Wilis in the Royal Ballet's *Giselle*, the charming fairies in *The Sleeping Beauty* and the beauty of Margot Fonteyn or Svetlana Beriosova, I wonder why this was so. Perhaps it was the fact that I was seated so high in the gods looking down through the chandeliers, the gilt and the red plush, with so much expectation, that disappointment was inevitable. But Fonteyn and the other ballerinas seemed strained and tense, the company lacking in vitality, leaving me unmoved by most performances. There were exceptions – the Russian ballerina, Violetta Elvin, was a warm and touching Giselle, and the New Zealander, Rowena Jackson, exciting in all she did.

Much more interesting to me was the Sadler's Wells Theatre Ballet, where we could afford better seats and perhaps because of that enjoyed the smaller, 'junior' company performing works such as Ninette de Valois' *The Rake's Progress* and the early ballets by choreographers John Cranko and Kenneth MacMillan with an intensity and vitality I found lacking in the larger Royal Ballet. Also performing at Sadler's Wells, Ballet Rambert's repertoire still included major works by Antony Tudor, which were dutifully revived for London seasons, but in order to survive, the company spent many months touring the provinces performing the always 'safe' nineteenth-century classics, *Giselle* and *Coppélia*.

At the Royal Festival Hall, London Festival Ballet had established a successful recipe of classical and modern ballets in the new, modern theatre, which seemed to assure a freshness and vitality. Thanks to an Australian friend and colleague of my mother's, the artist Eilean Pearcey, who specialised in drawing dancers, I had an introduction to another artist with a commission to draw and paint the Festival Ballet during their London season. This gentleman, a Polish count, no less, had an unlimited source of free seats as well as access backstage, and offered to take me to performances. This was obviously a huge advantage as I was able to see several performances from the best seats, but I thought it safer to keep it from my mother that the agreed meeting place before our evenings spent at the ballet was in Soho, in a somewhat rundown building where on the third floor the count had his studio. The premises were shared with a photographer and the walls were covered with photographs, drawings and paintings of naked young women in what seemed to me extraordinarily 'rude' positions. When, after a few visits, the count suggested that I might like to pose for him, I knew that it was time to forego the free tickets. However, there was real excitement seeing Toni Lander, Flemming Flindt and John Gilpin in *Etudes*, the Australian ballerina Marilyn Burr and the very English Belinda Wright at the peaks of their careers, with an array of international guest artists in programmes which were always enjoyable. There was more ballet, with more ballet companies, to be seen in a week in London than there was in Sydney in a year, and I would have been happy to be able to dance with any of them.

London also offered a huge choice of teachers for an eager dance student. I had arrived too late to find the famous teachers of the West Street studios, including, notably, the Russian Vera Volkova, but Anna Northcote, an ex-member of the Ballets Russes, continued the tradition in the studio in West Street, in the heart of Covent Garden, teaching the Legat method with four classes a day packed with students and professionals. Other former ballerinas then teaching included Kathleen Crofton and another of Pavlova's 'girls', Cleo Nordi, each with their own studio and their own following. Wally and Paula had given me, along with innumerable addresses and recommendations, a letter of introduction to Audrey de Vos, a teacher of great individuality who had considerably influenced their own work.

De Vos's studio was in one of Notting Hill Gate's tree-lined streets, in a former artist's studio. This was reached down a narrow garden path and entering the studio was almost like coming into a temple. De Vos liked to think of her studio as an oasis of art and learning, tucked away and sheltered from the outside world. She was fortunate in having a bright and airy studio, better than most at that time, although the changing rooms were just a space behind a curtain or the piano. Visitors were received on a small gallery from where one could look down upon the studio and where one could catch a glimpse of Rosie, de Vos's companion, who took care of the books and the accounts, served coffee to visitors, and tended her charge with regular doses of Sanatogen. De Vos's teaching was unconventional, in fact regarded suspiciously by many, including Ninette de Valois, who forbade the Royal Ballet company members from attending her classes. However, Royal Ballet ballerina Beryl Grey took daily private lessons and others, including Nadia Nerina and Maryon Lane, were frequent visitors, as were many dancers from London's Festival Ballet and Ballet Rambert.

De Vos's 'method' was based on a holistic approach to training, individually tailored to each dancer, taking into account their physique and temperament. Her classes included modern dance, body-conditioning, improvisation classes, as well as classical ballet, and there were many parallels

Audrey de Vos (c.1960) in her studio in Notting Hill Gate.

in her teaching to the Martha Graham technique, or even the teachings of Joseph Pilates. Little is known about her background, but she was a pupil of the famous Serafina Astafieva (teacher of Alicia Markova, Margot Fonteyn and Anton Dolin) and Laurent Novikoff in London; apparently she opened her own school in Weymouth in the 1920s, but eventually settled in London, where, besides teaching during the war, she drove an ambulance during the Blitz. It appears she developed her 'method' way ahead of its time and quite on her own. She aimed at producing dancers who danced without strain or visible effort, and yet who were knowingly in control of their technique, mainly through perfecting the 'placing' of the body while strengthening the all-important centre and pelvic muscles. Ideally, released from tension and technical worries, one would then be free to express oneself creatively and artistically; Paula Hinton was probably the best example of this teaching.

Perhaps De Vos did sometimes take the importance of 'placing' too far; as students we would always try to peep through the dressing room curtains to watch the regular daily private class de Vos gave to ballerina Beryl Grey. At one time they were working on Grey's forthcoming performances of *The Sleeping Beauty* with the Royal Ballet. The most challenging technical section

31

of the ballet is no doubt the Rose Adagio, when the ballerina dances with four would-be suitors, needing to hold balances on one leg while changing partners. With de Vos taking the role of all four of Grey's partners, they worked on the balances, de Vos having almost scientifically reduced the danger element of losing balance down to the need to hold the position with a muscle around the right rib cage. We all got tickets for *The Sleeping Beauty* at the Royal Opera House and eagerly awaited the moment when Beryl Grey made her first entrance, radiant and confident in a rose-coloured tutu, to greet the row of suitors. The music for the Rose Adagio built to a huge climax as the balances became more and more challenging, excitement filled the auditorium and Grey, ever more and more the perfect ballerina, held the rock-steady balances, finishing with a triumphant long, long arabesque and a brilliant, flashing pirouette. In the interval we met up with de Vos, rosy with success: she greeted us excitedly – 'Did you see her right rib?' Maybe she was right, but I suspect Beryl Grey would have held those balances anyway.

Audrey de Vos was, however, highly possessive of her younger students, disapproving of them taking classes with other teachers and always unwilling to consider them ready for professional work. Ballet masters and ballet company directors such as John Taras or Nicolas Beriosoff would call regularly at the studio looking for dancers for their companies, and occasionally one of the older dancers would be engaged for companies in glamorous sounding locations, perhaps Helsinki or Zurich, even for the Grand Ballet du Marquis de Cuevas, while we younger dancers would remain in the cloister-like surroundings of the studio awaiting the next visit from what seemed like outer space. She must have suspected that I took advantage of the Saturdays, when she did not give classes, to go to elsewhere, and indeed it was to Anna Northcote's studio, where I would be challenged by totally different, and fiendishly difficult, classes. On a Monday morning de Vos would, on seeing me at the barre, exclaim, 'What has happened to you? You were dancing so well on Friday, and now you're all over the place.'

After a year in London, Walter Gore came back into my life with an offer to join him at the Frankfurt Opera House, where he was to become ballet director. Wally made the proviso that I should take classes with Stanislas Idzikowski in order for me to build up more strength and stamina than de Vos's classes could give me. 'Idzi', as he was generally known, was a great Polish-born dancer who had danced with the Diaghilev Ballets Russes. The daily class was given in a church hall near Kensington Church Street which was shared with the local Women's Institute, Sunday school, and the Boy Scouts. His day inevitably started with the routine of meticulously sprinkling water over the dry wooden boards which formed the dance floor. Resin was strictly not allowed to combat the floor's naturally slipperiness, and on arrival one would find Idzi with a watering can already busy at work. There followed a ritual whereby he would stop to greet one with a handshake and a kiss, leading one to Madame Evina, already seated at the piano, probably wearing a small hat fringed with rather faded fabric flowers, while arranging sheets of music. Madame Evina had also been a dancer with Diaghilev and shared her life with Idzi, although, I believe, they never married; again a handshake and a kiss, after which Idzi would then lead the way to the changing room. He had been a pupil of Enrico Cecchetti, the great Italian dancer and teacher at the Mariinsky Ballet in Saint Petersburg, who then followed Diaghilev to France, becoming a stalwart of the Diaghilev Russian Ballet Company. Cecchetti had trained Idzikowski not only as a dancer, but when they both lived in London in later years, as a teacher of his method.

It was an extremely tough and demanding class, with a rigid structure of certain exercises always repeated on the same days of the week. The initial barre exercises were the same every day, but once in the centre, Idzi, dressed dapperly in a suit, with highly polished street shoes, would demonstrate them. At sixty-five, and without any apparent warm-up, he could still jump a foot in the air to show a *changement* and one could easily imagine the dancer he had been – a rival to Nijinsky in his virtuosity, but his small stature and restrained personality had limited his range of roles. The class was exactly sixty minutes in length, after which the ritual of handshakes and kisses was repeated, along with commiserations to Madame Evina at the state of the piano following the last visit of the Boy Scouts to the hall. Walking up Church Street afterwards one felt as if on a cloud, the most extraordinary feeling of levitating a foot off the ground, full of energy and ready for the day ahead. No doubt Maestro Cecchetti had planned his class just this way for the hard-working dancers of the Diaghilev company who took their daily ballet class at nine o'clock with a day of rehearsals ahead of the evening performance.

In the weeks leading up to our departure to Germany, Paula and I would often take class together with Idzi while Wally would collect us at the end of class to walk together back to Notting Hill Gate, all of us full of growing excitement about the move to Frankfurt, and with Wally entertaining us with his plans for what promised to be an exciting year ahead. It was hard to break the news of my impending departure to de Vos and she took it badly, believing no doubt that I needed several more years' tuition under her guidance. In fact, although I continued to take classes with her until leaving London, she did not speak to me for three months.

Frankfurt was not an attractive city in the late 1950s. Scars from the extensive war damage were much in evidence; almost the whole of the medieval city centre had been flattened, leaving vacant allotments throughout the city. Rebuilding had obviously taken place urgently with huge, heavy, grey concrete blocks housing what were for me the heavy, grey-clad burghers of Frankfurt. Evidence of war injuries could be seen on the streets, men with missing legs, some with a wooden leg, missing hands or arms and terribly scarred faces. The people seemed dour and rough, pushing their way onto the trams or to the front of a shop counter; the effort that had been needed to survive and to rebuild their lives had formed their behaviour. At carnival time they came to life, when the inns and cafes would fill with lively groups downing the local apple wine while rocking from side to side, singing ever more loudly. Carnival floats rolled through the streets sporting their grotesque, crudely made displays, ruddy-faced musicians and oversized bar-maids weighed down with trays of steins of beer and apple wine. It was a folklore that was hard to appreciate, its pagan roots lost in the past, but it seemed a necessary ritual to celebrate the approach of spring and to let one's hair down generally.

Coming from Australia, London had seemed backward and old-fash-ioned, but Germany in the 1950s was perhaps more so. In the rented accom-modation I shared with my mother we had only cold running water, while heating involved battling with a troublesome coal stove after lugging buckets of coal up from the cellar. The kitchen contained a bathtub which we were allowed to use once a week and had to share with the landlady, a typical middle-aged hausfrau who appeared to check the state of our part of the apartment daily. Passing through our living room she would plump up the sofa cushions, clucking disapprovingly and reminding us forcefully *'Nicht für Arsch!'* (Not for your backside!). No doubt at the end of the war there were, as throughout Europe, many women left alone with no choice but to share their homes with strangers. It was surprising that there appeared to be no post-war resentment towards us, or towards the British, and we were con-stantly taken aback to receive little presents from staff at the theatre.

Working in a German opera house was a totally new experience. The the-atre was huge, the stage the size of a football pitch, and the building so full of rooms and offices of every kind that finding the ballet studio, or indeed the stage, was a problem. The dancers were included in most of the operas and the operettas and if dancing on stage, already well filled with scenery and singers, could be frustrating, it was an essential education for me to learn more about music and opera. The musical standard in Frankfurt was high; conductor Georg Solti had been musical director for many years, so after a year without performing I joined in enthusiastically, kicking my legs as high as possible in the can-can in *The Merry Widow*, sitting on the tenor's knee in *Rigoletto* or painting myself green for the triumphal march in *Aida*.

The company in Frankfurt was very typical of a German opera ballet company of the time. The only really well-trained classical dancers were the principals, Maria Fris and Rainer Köchermann, both from the Berlin schools of Tatjana Gsovsky and Gustav Blank, and both former principals of the West Berlin ballet company. Maria Fris had also spent some time in Paris where she danced with Janine Charrat's company, notably creating the major role in Charrat's ballet *Les Algues*, dancing with fellow German Peter van Dyk, both winning international acclaim. Extremely good-looking, elegant classical dancers, Fris and Köchermann were, in the tradition of the provincial opera houses, used to arranging and choreographing their own appearances in the opera and even in ballet productions. This was obviously not acceptable for Gore and he appeared to challenge them by setting fiendishly fast and difficult enchaînements in the opening ballet to music by Rossini, but excluding them from the more important works. Much more to Gore's taste was the excellent Yugoslav character dancer, Ivan Sertic, who later made a good career as choreographer and director in Germany, while he appeared to enjoy working with the mature group of dancers who formed the company. These typically German dancers disguised their technical shortcomings with dramatic intensity and years of experience. Gore overlooked the row of beer bottles piling up in the ballet studio, and even gave way to the accepted practice of the girls being allowed to take a few days off at 'that time' of the month.

If communication with the German dancers was limited by language problems (fortunately, I had had a couple of years of German at school), contacts and friendships were soon made, as they are everywhere in the dance world. Our fellow dancers were extremely welcoming to the three of us who came from London that season; they helped us with the essential rounds of the police, the tax office, the insurance office, in finding accommodation, and above all, in 'force feeding' us with the choreography of the dance scenes in the operas and operettas which we had to learn in one or two rehearsals, while then hissing instructions to us on stage. We were surprised to find that some of them were married, some had children, and that they enjoyed four weeks' summer holidays, on full pay, with many other 'perks' unheard of in the British theatre at that time. They also constantly discussed their future after dance, and above all, their pensions, a subject which at eighteen years of age had never crossed my mind.

The numbers of staff on hand in the theatre seemed amazing; there were people to put on our make-up (a service I soon dispensed with); others to arrange our hairdos and the many wigs we wore; we had dressers, of course, but also an army of quick-change dressers in the wings who would manhandle one to rush out of one costume into another.

The theatre had its own huge scenery and costume workshops as well as its own shoe and boot makers who even produced the dancers' pointe shoes. These were obviously made with durability in mind, and in fact, I had one pair which lasted for five years, but they sounded and felt more like wooden shoes than ballerina's slippers so I soon arranged for mine to be sent from Freed in London.

The change in Wally and Paula from those difficult days in Australia was tangible. They enjoyed the comfort of a new apartment which Paula busily decorated when she was not needed for rehearsals, turning up the next day with speckles of paint in her hair, and Wally displayed his good spirits by wearing to rehearsals a canary yellow top with his usual black trousers and fluorescent pink socks. Initially fired with enthusiasm with what appeared to be ideal conditions, he was inevitably irritated by being called out of rehearsal for a directors' meeting, or even at losing most of the company for a morning's stage rehearsal of an opera where we were little more than extras. Ballet was still the Cinderella of the arts in a German opera house so Gore had to fight hard to stage those works he wanted, and above all, to get a reasonable number of performances for the ballet. His first plans to stage *Les Sylphides* for the opening of the season, in the tradition of the Ballets Russes, was rejected by the music director as he disapproved of orchestrating Chopin's piano score; *The Nutcracker* was likewise discarded as being too old-fashioned, and a production of *Confessional*, one of Gore's most successful dramatic works for Ballet Rambert, turned down for fear that its religious overtones might offend the city's Catholic citizens. However, he did create one of his most enduring ballets, *Eaters of Darkness*, for the opening programme, giving Paula one of her greatest roles, and successfully revived the charming *Light Fantastic*. The whole programme was designed by the theatre's resident designer, Hein Heckroth, well known at the time from his work on the ballet films *The Red Shoes* and *The Tales of Hoffmann*. The performance was well received, although it appeared that Fris and Köchermann may have undermined its success to some extent through their closer relations with the local press.

The German public, perhaps more interested in seeing foreign ballet companies, and sceptical of the standards of their resident companies, seemed hungry for dance performances, and during my stay in Frankfurt we were treated to a row of visits from international touring companies. The French-based Grand Ballet du Marquis de Cuevas gave two performances with a programme of classical works. This privately run company, financed by the Marquis' American millionairess-wife, toured incessantly in France as well as undertaking occasional foreign tours. It boasted excellent principals, including

Paula Hinton in Gore's ballet *Eaters of Darkness* with Harry Haythorne. This photo is
from the 1962 London Ballet revival.

Rosella Hightower, Nina Vyroubova and Serge Golovine, performing a repertoire very similar to the original Ballet Russe de Monte Carlo, but adding
original works by contemporary choreographers such as George Skibine and
John Taras. If the general standard was often criticised, the de Cuevas
company did retain a certain glamour, fulfilling an essential role in bringing
dance to audiences far and wide across a Europe which was still struggling
out of the greyness and shortages of the post-war period.

Maurice Béjart's Ballet-Théâtre de Paris made one of their first foreign
tours to Germany and visited Frankfurt, where they presented Béjart's very
original choreography to 'concrete' music by Pierre Henry, performed by
glamorous, long-legged French ballerinas and sexy half-naked men. The
Yugoslav dancer Milorad Miskovitch came with his Paris-based company,
performing a programme of contemporary works, to the nearby town of
Offenbach, and American Ballet Theatre, making a rare European tour, performed in Wiesbaden. This was my first view of this remarkable company
and the programme I saw included Agnes de Mille's ballets *Fall River Legend*
and *Rodeo*, as well as *The Nutcracker* pas de deux danced by the incomparable
pairing of French ballerina Violette Verdy and the superb Danish dancer Eric

Bruhn. More than anything, this programme gave me the reassurance that ballet could be a major art form and a powerful theatre experience.

Seeing Nora Kaye, American Ballet Theatre's most famous dramatic ballerina (notably in *Fall River Legend*), made me inevitably compare her with Paula Hinton, generally considered Britain's greatest dance-actress. Although Paula was irrefutably the holder of this title, the American Nora Kaye had a steely classical technique and could hold her own besides illustrious ballerinas such as Alicia Alonso in American Ballet Theatre. Paula excelled in the romantic repertoire, performing works such as *Giselle* or *Les Sylphides*, but thwarted by a too-late start as a dancer, was the first to admit she was terrified at the prospect of turning a double pirouette on pointe. Nora Kaye appeared to be very consciously in control of her emotions in works such as Tudor's *Pillar of Fire* or de Mille's *Fall River Legend*. She did this superbly; her fury as Lizzie Borden in the latter work was totally convincing and terrifying. Paula, on the other side, could be considered a 'method' actress, immersing herself in her roles. Tears would roll down her face in performance in emotional scenes while even in rehearsal she could weep uncontrollably. Playing opposite her one would feel guilty at concentrating on getting the steps or the timing right, or even being aware of the grimy surroundings of a rehearsal room. Wally called her his Stradivarius (or more affectionately 'Strad' when referring to her in letters to Marie Rambert), and she was his most precious instrument, and most valued interpreter. Nora Kaye was also fortunate in being the supreme interpreter for Antony Tudor (she and Paula had in fact danced in the same works, albeit in different productions, in different countries, notably in *Lilac Garden* and *Gala Performance*) and also for Agnes de Mille and the young Jerome Robbins. There are no champions in dance, and it is impossible when discussing artists of this stature to say that one is greater than the other. However, observing Nora Kaye at this time was a valuable lesson for me, showing that there are different ways and techniques in expressing drama through dance and that Nora Kaye's way, born of technique and control, could be just as valid as Paula's intuitive riding on a wave of emotion, albeit with skill and talent.

No doubt it was because of these performances that I felt a restlessness for change and for the more intensive work as a part of a ballet company. I approached Wally for his advice about moving on and amazingly, he proved to be more than helpful. He wrote to Marie Rambert recommending me for Ballet Rambert, and arranged auditions for me with Nicolas Beriosoff in Stuttgart as well as with the Ballet der Lage Landen (Ballet of the Lowlands) in Amsterdam. Interestingly, Rambert replied that I would be welcome to audition but as she had only two paying contracts at that time I should better look elsewhere if I needed to earn my living. In hindsight this seems an extraordinary situation for a company as prestigious as Ballet Rambert, but it was, of course, in the 1950s, still very early days for public funding of the arts in Britain. Beriosoff was having a much easier time in Stuttgart than Gore in Frankfurt. The city and the theatre had a long tradition of dance, allowing the company a busy schedule of performances. He offered me a contract for the following season, but with the arrogance of youth I thanked him, saying I would first try the company in Amsterdam, as this was a 'real' ballet company. Amazingly, our paths crossed on many occasions in future years and although we never did work together, 'Papa' Beriosoff always remained interested in my professional progress.

The Gores were to remain just one more season in Frankfurt and I moved to the Ballet der Lage Landen in Amsterdam, a company which had become something of an outpost for British choreographers. There were several works of Gore's in the repertory, including a production of *The Nutcracker*; Jack Carter had created his successful ballet *The Witch Boy* for the company as well as mounting his own productions of Act 2 of *Swan Lake* and a full-length *Coppélia*; Michael Holmes had mounted much admired productions of *Les Sylphides* and *Le Carnaval*, while there were works by Andrée Howard, Peter Darrell and Denis Carey. The company, directed by Mascha ter Weeme, was a hard-working one, constantly producing new works and performing ceaselessly throughout the Netherlands. It gave me a useful opportunity to learn the classical repertoire, to work with a variety of choreographers, while taking over more and more important roles.

Coming to Amsterdam from Frankfurt was almost like emerging from a tunnel into the sunlight. I arrived in the summer, when the town was at its most lively and friendly, the canals busy with boats and barges, the streets packed with city workers, students and children on bicycles, and a sense of enjoyment in the air. The company was more than welcoming to me, as the only foreigner in their midst, but everyone spoke English so well that it was difficult to learn any Dutch. I had started a couple of months earlier than planned to replace a dancer who was injured, so spent many hours daily working alone with the English dancer and company ballerina, Angela Bayley. Angela had been with the company for some years, after working with Ballet Rambert, and must have memorised every ballet in the repertoire. She taught

Mascha ter Weeme, director of the Ballet of the Lowlands, in Amsterdam,
with Walter Gore, c.1960.

me the corps de ballet choreography of Act 2 *Swan Lake* in a day, *Les Sylphides* and *The Nutcracker* in two or three days and even all three acts of *Coppélia* by the end of the week. I was eager to learn and even more eager to dance these ballets, gradually taking over solo parts.

The Dutch dance companies had to work hard to earn their subsidies, travelling throughout the country, but usually returning to Amsterdam at night, following a long day which might include one or two school matinees, as well as the evening performance. Salaries were low but rents and general living expenses were cheap. In contrast to the German dancers, the Dutch seemed to be unperturbed by the comparatively short life of a dancer, for several were already choreographing, teaching and taking advantage of the government's generous support of further study for career changes. If the standard in the Ballet der Lage Landen was generally just competent, with several exceptions of real talent (some did go on to dance with Ballet Rambert, and with the Harkness Ballet in the USA), the company was homogenous and very committed to their work. However, and more than ever, I was constantly aware that my initial classical training had been short and intermittent, and I longed for a further period of study, and in particular, with the teachers in Paris of whom I had heard so much.

The 'great' days of Olga Preobrajenska, Mathilde Kschessinskaya and Lubov Egorova, the émigré ballerinas from Russia's imperial theatres, who dominated the teaching scene in Paris for so many years, were over, but there were a dozen first-class teachers to chose from; Russians such as Victor Gsovsky and Nora Kiss, and French teachers, mostly from the Paris Opera Ballet, such as Serge Peretti and Raymond Franchetti. I chose to work with Nora Kiss, a diminutive but formidable woman of Georgian origin, known universally as Madame Nora. She was teacher to many of France's leading dancers, her reputation attracting dancers from all over the world to her studio at Salle Wacker. The studios, impossibly small by today's standards, would be packed for three or four classes a day and one could find oneself at the barre wedged between luminaries such as ballerinas Rosella Hightower and Violette Verdy or competing at fouettées with Paris Opera Ballet stars Josette Amiel and Jacqueline Rayet. Madame Nora was, however, a teacher with a personal interest in each dancer, eager to keep up with their career moves, their personal lives and their daily problems. Not unlike Audrey de Vos, she had evolved a personal 'method' which eliminated strain and encouraged natural movement, as well as a willingness to attempt the unconventional.

I was both intimidated by, and eager for, the challenge which I felt was necessary to make the next step forward in my career and following the season in Amsterdam, planned to spend some months working with Madame Nora. However, as so often during my career, chance played an unexpected role; in this case I was picked out of the class by a visiting dancer and choreographer who was in Paris looking for a dancer to join an American company on tour. The visitor was Job Sanders and I left Paris with him the following day to join the American Festival Ballet, then in rehearsal in Augsburg, in Germany.

chapter two

The Partnership

A German dancer meets an Australian ballerina in an American ballet company, rehearsing in Germany, prior to a tour in Spain. It was an unlikely event, but it was also a suitable introduction to a partnership where dance and travel were intrinsically interwoven. We had both joined the American Festival Ballet replacing dancers who had fallen out during the company's German tour, and had but a few days to learn a variety of roles. Alexander was engaged as a principal dancer and I was initially in the small corps de ballet, although within a couple of weeks I was called upon to dance the grand pas de deux from *The Nutcracker*, as well as taking over several solo roles. Rehearsals continued day and night, and we even took advantage of breaks on the long bus journey across Europe to reach the opening city of the Spanish tour, Santiago de Compostela, to learn more of the repertoire, dancing on the pavements, the village squares, even the filling stations along the way.

The tour, which was organised by the National Tourist Office of Spain, brought the company along the endless dusty roads from one region to another in the height of the Spanish summer.

On the road with American Festival Ballet – Job Sanders rehearsing and Sonia Arova at the border of France and Spain.

Dancers from American Festival Ballet backstage in costume for *Shindig* – from left: Loyd Tygett, Sonia Arova, Christine Hennessy and Job Sanders.

Spain was an exciting, exotic, sometimes frightening country at the end of the 1950s. The huge barren centre was home to people living in Third World conditions; small farmers inhabited mud and wattle huts, the women did their washing in the trickle of a stream; a shepherd travelling with his flock would huddle under a huge black umbrella to avoid the scorching midday sun; in the cities the crippled, the maimed, the blind, some with huge gaping holes where their eyes had once been, lined the pavements. Beggars gathered on the steps to the churches and cathedrals where many churchgoers did hand them a few pesetas. Whether this destitution was the result of the not so distant Spanish Civil War, or of the resulting years of poverty and oppression, we did not know. But for visitors to Spain, before the onslaught of mass tourism, the hotels offered huge, almost luxurious rooms with vases of flowers and plates of fruit; the restaurant meals were generous to the point of being excessive, and ridiculously cheap.

Travelling as we were during July and August, the heat in the non-air-conditioned bus was almost unbearable, and the endlessly long drives were interrupted almost daily when the tyres exploded under the strain. Fortunately, we rarely performed on a travelling day, and so had time to explore the cathedrals of Burgos and Santiago de Compostela, to see the treasures of the Prado, the wonders of Córdoba and Seville and were able to wander around the streets of many towns and cities, sometimes able to peep into an interior courtyard where the women would gather to shelter from the heat under a bower of bougainvillea or around a miniature fountain. We performed in open-air venues, from the bull ring of Pamplona to the elegant parks of Madrid, but never before eleven o'clock in the evening when the heat would finally subside, and the towns would come alive at the end of a long baking day.

As outsiders in an otherwise American company, Alexander and I soon found a natural empathy, in time beginning to talk of the future, our plans and our dreams. He had already made his first essays at choreography in Germany, and was even thinking of forming a small group of dancers – an idea which immediately appealed to me. During that long tour of Spain, and the following months touring with American Festival Ballet, a partnership was born, with a commitment to work together.

The subsequent tour in Germany brought home to me the extraordinary number of theatres which existed in Germany; every small town, every city, had a municipal-run theatre with a busy programme of performances. The company performed in every size of town and in every imaginable type of theatre, taking us once from the town hall in Dinkelsbühl, in southern Germany, to perform at the opera house in Düsseldorf, in the north, the next day. We spent many hours in the bus, some of the dancers even stretching out on the floor, and several, complaining that they had seen enough scenery to last a lifetime, pulled a cap down over their eyes. There was a good selection of books lying around, where I discovered many of the writers of that period – Jack Kerouac, Saul Bellow, James Baldwin – and the hours passed by pleasantly enough. There were always pointe shoes to darn, tights to mend, letters to write, and with the two ballerinas' poodles on-board, bus stops happened with some frequency.

During the following four years Alexander and I moved from company to company, constantly restless, impatient to dance more and more important roles, while enriching our experience working with different choreographers. This led us to ballet companies in several different countries, working with choreographers in varying styles. From American Festival Ballet Alexander was the first to leave, to work with Kurt Jooss in his version of Purcell's *The Faery Queen*, with the company at the opera house in Essen, in Germany. Jooss had been a leading figure in the German dance world from the 1920s working in a style which fused classical ballet and German modern dance (he had worked extensively with Rudolf Laban in Germany and had studied

Alexander backstage in Essen with Kurt Jooss.

46

ballet with Lubov Egorova in Paris). During his tenure at the Essen Opera House in the 1930s he created prodigiously, winning international recognition for his powerful political dance works *The Green Table* and *The Big City*. In 1933 Jooss was forced to leave Nazi Germany spending the years to 1947 working in England. By the late 1950s, as director of the Folkwang School in Essen, he had become a respected and respectable elderly gentleman who silently watched rehearsals while his assistants slowly and painstakingly patched together the choreography, using the Laban notation method.

Alexander was happy to have the opportunity to meet this 'giant' of the then meagre roster of internationally renowned German choreographers, and Jooss, taking an interest in the obviously ambitious younger man, advised him, if he seriously wanted an international career, to leave Germany and to cut all his ties. Obviously, twenty years later, the situation would have been very different, with a former student of his own Folkwang School, Pina Bausch, becoming an icon in the dance world and the ballet companies in several German cities including Stuttgart, Hamburg, Frankfurt, Munich and Berlin all attaining international standards.

I stayed several more months with American Festival Ballet when Gore came to the company to mount *Eaters of Darkness* and *Peepshow*. The Gores were proving to be somewhat 'difficult', a label which was often given to them when working with companies; they did not turn up as expected, and remaining totally incommunicado, left everyone ignorant of their whereabouts. Finally, they did arrive, giving us just two weeks to mount both ballets, while we rehearsed other new works by Job Sanders and Lyod Tygett. Rehearsal conditions in a gloomy hall on the outskirts of Salzburg, reached through kilometres of shoulder-high snow, were far from perfect. Gore complained that the company was not compliant to him – they were just overworked and not being paid – but Job, Sonia Arova and I did our best to placate him.

It was also a danger to mount such an important work as *Eaters of Darkness*, demanding a high level of intensity and concentration, on an unfamiliar company, and we had no idea if it would be successful. The first performance was in Vienna, with Paula dancing the leading role, and, as in Frankfurt, I recreated my role of 'the girl with the doll'. At the opening of the ballet Paula was virtually thrown through the huge metal door at the back of the stage and, as the first of the inmates of the asylum in which she finds herself, I came onstage with my hair wildly brushed up, my cheeks hollowed and eyes blackened with make-up. An audible gasp of horror came from the auditorium, and the rest of the ballet was performed as if the entire audience was holding its breath, as were we, until showers of applause proved it to be a huge success. I had another role to enjoy in Lyod Tygett's new piece of Americana, *Box Lunch Picnic*. It was in no way as successful as his Wild West ballet,

Shindig, and my role as Freckle Faced Maud was as naïve as the ballet itself, but it gave me the first opportunity to play comedy on stage. Despite the serious lack of rehearsal time I was able to experience the great feeling of communication with an audience when they are laughing with, and at, you.

It had been planned for the Gores to come with the company on our subsequent tour of Portugal and Spain, but Paula caused unexpected problems by demanding to be flown to Paris every morning to take class, and then transported to the performing venue. Obviously, they just did not want to come, and so after the season in Vienna, Sonia took over the leading role in *Eaters*, proving to be effectively dramatic if obviously, because of her taller stature and sultry looks, lacking Paula's air of vulnerability. Those following months with American Festival Ballet were instrumental, above all, in increasing my admiration of Sonia Arova. A bad foot injury meant I could dance only the character roles at that time so I spent the first half of the programme in the wings watching Sonia, in *Swan Lake* Act 2 or the *Don Quixote* pas de deux, as well as taking in all the details of her rehearsals before the performance – notably of the Black Swan pas de deux. She and Job Sanders rehearsed this pas de deux for several weeks but never felt convinced that it was ready for performance. They continued, therefore, to perform the *Don Quixote* pas de deux, where their insistence on perfection never faltered. I must have watched the pas de deux at least a hundred times and never once, no matter how difficult the surroundings or awkward the stage, did either of them ever fluff a pirouette, mistime a lift or, in particular, did Sonia do less

Sonia Arova and dancers from American Festival Ballet in *Eaters of Darkness*, 1960.

than hold incredibly long and secure balances. She was also an invaluable travelling companion, speaking not only Russian, Bulgarian, French and English as first languages, but also fluent Spanish, Italian and German. She had a constant source of remedies for anything from stomach troubles to blisters as well as tips on coping with touring life.

At that time, before linoleum dance floors in transportable rolls had been developed, dancers had no choice but to dance on the bare boards of the stage floor. The stages of the opera houses in London and Paris and other major cities would have been constructed with dancers in mind, but dancing in a variety of theatres and halls, as we did every day, caused considerable problems. In Germany and Switzerland a clean floor also meant a waxed and polished one; a deadly combination for dancers, where a firm grip on the floor is essential. In France and Italy the stages would usually be freshly washed but the floorboards could be a hundred or a hundred and fifty years old, dry, splintery and possibly dotted with holes and lumps, even metal rails which could be removed to slot in pieces of scenery. Powdered resin, made from pine resin, is the usual treatment providing a non-slip surface for a ballerina's satin pointe shoes, but this can also form a gluey mass which traps a man's shoe and stops his pirouette mid turn. Compromises had to be reached and more solutions tried, from scrubbing with household cleansers to sprinkling with Coca-Cola. But for a ballerina executing a highly difficult classical variation it remained treacherous. Sonia solved the problem by having a thin rubber sole glued to the sole of her pointe shoe as well as darning the tip of her shoe, which we all did in those days. This stopped the satin being torn off but Sonia had a special trick in sewing to build a bigger platform on the tip of the shoes to help hold a balance on pointe – a tip passed on, apparently, from the great Russian ballerina, Anna Pavlova.

The winter tour to Spain and Portugal commenced in February 1960 and was planned to last for several months. However, someone had overlooked the fact that by the time we reached Spain it was carnival, with Lent to come, and audiences in strongly Catholic Spain had other plans during the frantic carnival period, while they were not permitted to go to the theatre during Lent. The company spent the final evening in Valencia where the performance had been cancelled; we were all feeling rather dazed, not knowing what the future of the company would be or if and when we would be paid. Leaving Renzo Raiss and Job Sanders almost having a fist fight on the steps of the hotel (we presumed that the principals had not been paid), I remember walking through the streets of the town centre of Valencia with Earle Sieveling, a recent arrival from the States. With the carnival in full swing, it was an unreal, even surreal, sensation forcing our way through the thronging crowds, everyone high on the excitement, the music, the dancing, which filled the streets, while we just felt the need to find a quiet corner to take stock of things. In retrospect it seems a pity to have missed out on the carnival, but as the youngest members of the company, ambitious and very earnest, it seemed important to us to spend a couple of hours drinking coke, discussing our profession and our aspirations. Earle stayed for a couple of seasons with American Festival Ballet and then returned to New York to join New York City Ballet, where he became a successful soloist. In the 1970s he set off on a new career and became one of New York's most popular chefs and restaurateurs.

From Spain the company made its way back to Switzerland where the director had quickly booked a series of performances. However, the situation did not improve, audiences were meagre, and the company was struggling to survive. We, the dancers, were paid just ten Swiss francs a day, leaving us with the choice of paying for a hotel room for the night or having dinner. In midwinter the coach was too cold an alternative to spend the night in, but it was sometimes possible to stay in the theatre dressing rooms, sleeping in chairs or on table tops. There was little choice but for the company to make a break and I left to join Alexander in Essen. American Festival Ballet did

Sonia Arova with Rudolf Nureyev in Anthony Crickmay's studio before their performances of *Swan Lake* with The Royal Ballet in 1962.

re-form and continued to exist for another few years before finally settling in Rhode Island, giving up its international ambitions. Sonia Arova revived her earlier partnership with Eric Bruhn, and together with Rosella Hightower and the newly arrived Rudolf Nureyev, formed a quartet for a series of performances. Sonia also appeared with Nureyev as guest artist, with The Royal Ballet, subsequently rejoining American Ballet Theatre, and became director of the Norwegian National Ballet in 1966. In 1970 she took over as director of the Hamburg Ballet, and later moved to the USA to continue a successful career as director and teacher. Sonia Arova died in 2001 after a long battle with illness.

The following season Alexander and I joined the Amsterdam Ballet which proved to be a rewarding move. At the time when I first worked in the Netherlands, with the Ballet der Lage Landen, the country had four full-time professional ballet companies – the Netherlands Ballet based in The Hague and besides the Ballet der Lage Landen, the Netherlands Opera Ballet and the Scapino Ballet in Amsterdam. All were hard-working companies with busy performance schedules and were constantly adding new works to their repertoires. The Ballet der Lage Landen worked with many British choreographers, but the Netherlands Ballet and the Opera Ballet, besides performing the classical ballet repertoire, looked to France for their choreographers, and had acquired a number of ballets by Serge Lifar, as well as works by more contemporary choreographers such as Jean Babilée. These companies were also the starting point for the Dutch choreographers Rudi van Dantzig and Hans van Manen, both of whom were to make major contributions to European dance during the future decades. The Amsterdam Ballet was formed by the amalgamation of the Ballet der Lage Landen and the Netherlands Opera Ballet, in an attempt by the city government to economise on subsidies, and two years later the Netherlands Ballet was also incorporated to form Het National Ballet, which, after a difficult first couple of years, became an internationally acclaimed company under Rudi van Dantzig's directorship.

Our year with the Amsterdam Ballet was a difficult 'political' one for the company, with director Mascha ter Weeme almost excluded from company affairs by an administrator from the city council. Mascha ter Weeme was one of a band of remarkable women who, during the 1930s and 1940s, founded, nurtured and supported dance and ballet companies virtually single-handedly, several of these becoming major international dance companies. These women include Ninette de Valois and Marie Rambert in England, Lucia Chase and Ruth Page in America, Mary Wigman in Germany, and others include Dulcie Howes in South Africa, as well as Hélène Kirsova and Gertrud Bodenwieser in Australia. In the Netherlands, it was thanks to the Polish-born Sonia Gaskell and the Dutch former dancer and teacher Mascha ter Weeme that interest in dance was born in the 1940s, resulting in the lively dance scene which now exists in the country.

Mascha ter Weeme, in Amsterdam, together with Vittorio Rossi, the Italian stage designer and impresario, Pieter van der Sloot, the Dutch choreographer and René Bon, the French dancer and teacher.

The season in Amsterdam was packed with new ballets and good roles for both of us. I created the leading role in Belgian choreographer Robert Kaesen's ballet *The Chameleons*, in which he was experimenting, with some success, in working with modern dance movements learned by watching films of Martha Graham's company. Michael Holmes re-mounted his exemplary production of *Les Sylphides*, the result of extensive study with Tamara Karsavina, who was in the original cast in 1909, giving me the chance to tackle the very challenging fast tempi he had learned from Karsavina and insisted upon for the waltz. Next, Léonide Massine chose me as 'The First Hand' in his famous Johann Strauss ballet, *Le Beau Danube*. Working with Massine was something I never dreamed could happen. I already knew so many of his ballets from seeing them innumerable times with the Borovansky Ballet – *Le Beau Danube, Symphonie Fantastique, Le Tricorne, La Boutique Fantasque* – and *Le Beau Danube* is one of his most successful. In London, I had also caught up with *Mam'zelle Angot* with the Royal Ballet, and best of all, had seen Massine perform himself in *Le Tricorne* with the Netherlands Ballet in which, although well over sixty, he was still an exciting dancer.

In *Le Beau Danube*, I did covet the role of the Street Dancer, but Massine brought with him a very young, attractive Italian girl for the role. However, I was more than happy to be cast as The First Hand, the role created by Irina Baronova, my childhood idol from those old programmes of the Ballets Russes performances in Australia. Massine's wife took the first rehearsals, teaching us the choreography. There is one great hurdle for The First Hand, quite as bad as for the Black Swan – she has twenty-eight fouettées (continuous turns on the same leg on pointe) to turn in the finale of the ballet, centre stage, surrounded by the entire cast. Pirouettes, above all, fouettées, were never my strong point; I came to them too late, only learning to enjoy them much later on in my career. Anyway, with help from all the ballet masters and diligent daily practice, I mastered them and by the time Massine came to rehearsals was quietly proud of my achievement. During the first rehearsal he clapped loudly to stop the pianist and shouted – 'You are turning just fouettées! Baronova, she turns one tour attitude and one tour à la seconde!' Disaster! Massine then showed us a flickering, greyish film where Baronova is clearly seen turning fouettées, but she does lift her arm on every other one, so it could look like an attitude. 'Ah – she did not do it right that day.' But he agreed that I could do them the same way. My relationship with Massine did improve, however, when for the final week of rehearsals he would sit on the floor directly in front of me as I turned the fouettées, now calling encouragingly 'Plié, plié' which became my mantra when turning them on stage. However, no one had prepared me for the fact my costume was made up of three petticoats under a large, gathered skirt, and I had a bonnet to cope with. After the opening performance, Massine put his head round the dressing room door – 'Not bad' he muttered very seriously. That was good enough for me and the elation was heightened when the local Amsterdam paper wrote that I 'went off with the honours of the evening'. And perhaps so I should have; I had been 'studying' Massine's choreography for more than ten years.

It is a great pity that his ballets fell out of fashion and most have not survived; apart from the wonderful lighter works of his early years, Massine also created the first 'symphonic' ballets, using music by Tchaikovsky and Brahms for more serious ballets which have since been considered master-pieces of the time. But it was also perhaps his fault that companies became reluctant to agree to his exorbitant fees and hefty royalties, as Massine had become a rarity in the dance world – a businessman–choreographer, amassing a serious fortune, helped by his involvement in the ballet films *The Red Shoes* and *The Tales of Hoffmann*. Besides other homes, he also bought an entire Italian island, later acquired by that other dancer with business sense, Rudolf Nureyev.

In Robert Kaesen's ballet *The Chameleons* with the Amsterdam Ballet in 1960.

Sonia Arova, as guest artist with the Amsterdam Ballet, in Job Sander's ballet *Bacchianas Brazilieras* in 1961, seen here with Job Leering and Alexander (back).

My childhood dreams come true – dancing 'The First Hand' in Léonide Massine's ballet
Le Beau Danube, in 1961.

During his stay in Amsterdam, Massine, who looked after himself with great care, could be caught in the early mornings backstage at the opera house doing his daily barre exercises, dressed in tight black trousers, an immaculate white shirt and, incongruously, a thick hairnet. Before leaving the city, he invited all the company to a reception at the best hotel in Amsterdam, next to the theatre. Naturally, we were all delighted with this generous invitation and took advantage of the drinks and canapés being passed around; Massine made a short speech thanking us all for our hard work and departed. However, when we followed him shortly afterwards, we were surprised to be presented with a bill – Massine had just paid for his glass of milk before leaving.

That season I also danced Sonia Arova's role in Job Sanders' beautiful short ballet *Bachianas Brasileiras*. Alexander and I both worked with choreographers Jack Carter, Hans van Manen, Joyce Graeme, Pieter van der Sloot and Walter Gore, whose path crossed mine yet again when he came to create *Parade*, a large scale classical work. Presumably he was asked to give the company a suitable opening ballet for a mixed programme and it fulfilled that purpose without becoming one of Gore's important works. Paula had accompanied Wally to Amsterdam, sitting in on all his rehearsals. It was really the first time I was able to chat with her freely, without inhibitions on my side, and Paula was warm and communicative. We discussed the state of dance in general and the problems we all had in finding companies we enjoyed working with. Usually, I felt much more at ease with Wally, although he hardly spoke at all, and on occasions when Paula was not present in rehearsals during our time in Frankfurt (she spent several weeks dancing with Jean Babilée's company in Paris) we all enjoyed a much more relaxed and productive working atmosphere. Paula had become extremely protective of Wally, and of his work, and in her efforts to assure that he was always accorded the respect that was his due she could create an air of tension, even conflict. However, at that time in Amsterdam, they were planning to restart their London Ballet and both were optimistic and confident about the future.

Another highlight of that season in Amsterdam was the arrival of the American ballerina Rosella Hightower as guest artist to appear in a series of performances. Not unlike Sonia Arova or Paula Hinton, she was a totally individual dancer, not the stereotypical classical dancer, but one who had attained the stature of a great ballerina through intense hard work combined with a total commitment to the life of a dancer. Once on stage she assumed a brilliance and star quality which was supported by a keen intelligence, backed up by her many years of international experience. I first 'discovered' Hightower while in Frankfurt when she came to the opera house on tour with the Grand Ballet du Marquis de Cuevas. Rosella shared the role of *Giselle* with Nina Vyroubova and when not dancing that role would perform the Black Swan pas de deux in a lengthy programme which also included *Le Beau Danube*. Fascinated by the possible contact with so illustrious a ballerina, I had crept into the darkened auditorium to watch her practising on stage during the afternoon. The small, slight woman in her mid thirties, in nondescript practice clothes, worked on her own and without music. Rosella was practising the solo variation from the Black Swan, possibly the most challenging solo in the classical repertoire. She commenced taking the preparation for the difficult double pirouette in attitude en dehors, and fell off pointe; unperturbed she tried again, managing a single pirouette, but again falling off pointe. Next she tried the equally tricky double pirouette à la seconde, which proved to be just as disastrous. Falling off balance she appeared to give up halfway, leaving me to feel quite ill with fear on her behalf. I knew Rosella had recently given birth to a daughter and presumed she simply wasn't really back in shape. Hoping there might be a replacement for the evening's performance, I left the auditorium rather disappointed.

That evening I witnessed for the first time the metamorphosis of which Hightower was capable. The opening bars of the Black Swan pas de deux are among the most exciting in classical ballet as Siegfried sees Odile for the first

Rosella Hightower as guest artist with the Amsterdam Ballet in *Soirée Musicale*, choreographed by John Taras.

time and ballet lovers register the excitement that lies ahead. Glittering in black and gold, Hightower was transformed into a swan-woman, teasing and seductive. She hardly needed assistance from her partner, but flew through the air using all her technical expertise as well as her dramatic powers to astound him and the audience. As the solo began I held my breath as she rose on pointe from the preparation, sailing around with two perfect pirouettes in attitude, resting on pointe before using her skills and musicality to chase the music in order to immediately repeat the challenge. There was more to come when she completed not two, but three turns à la seconde, then darted forward in a triumphant relevé arabesque to claim her victory. It was a quite extraordinary performance, made all the more so when the following evening she danced *Giselle* in a totally contrasting style, a charming simple girl in the First Act and an ethereal ghost-like Wili in the second act. Photos of Rosella Hightower tend to be very posed and glamorous, giving little sign of the drama and humour she was capable of, while as with Arova and Hinton, there are virtually no films to record her achievements.

As a guest artist with the Amsterdam Ballet, she was again to perform the Black Swan pas de deux and John Taras's charming *Soirée Musicale*. Again, there were worries on hand: on arrival in Amsterdam Rosella realised she had left all her pointe shoes in France, while her partner, the former Paris Opera Ballet principal dancer Alexandre Kalioujny, had not danced classical roles for some years, having recently retired from performing to teach. However, Rosella took all this in her stride, found she could use the Amsterdam Ballet's ballerina Angela Bayley's shoes, allowing her to work with Kalioujny almost non-stop for three days, after which they produced an astounding series of performances. Czech-born Alexandre Kalioujny had been a pupil of Madame Preobrajenska in Paris, soon becoming a leading dancer at the Paris Opera Ballet, notable for his outstanding technique. It was fascinating to watch how he regained these skills during those rehearsals in Amsterdam, finally challenging the conductor during performances to follow him, as he soared higher and higher with the final series of entrechat six at the end of his Black Swan solo. Instigated by Nureyev, today's dancers tend to change the original choreography of these classical variations at their will, claiming that the original is not interesting enough. But I suspect that a series of fourteen entrechats six is too demanding for many, and to jump these so high as to 'stretch' the musical phrase demands a different sort of expertise and stamina than one sees today.

Alexander and I were fortunate in having as company teachers not only Michael Holmes, but also the French dancer and teacher René Bon, and the Australian ballet master Harry Haythorne. For Alexander the year in Amsterdam was like going back to school. Although an established principal dancer in Germany and well able to hold his own among the American dancers, he was aware that his classical technique was the product of a typical German schooling based on strength and force rather than control. Germany had virtually no real tradition of classical ballet and those teachers active in the 1940s and 1950s had learned by imitation rather than by true knowledge. He knew if he was to be truly successful dancing in Western Europe, and further abroad, he would have to 'relearn' his classical technique and he was fortunate in having those three ballet masters on hand to help him.

Michael Holmes taught an extremely demanding technical class, based on the Cecchetti technique, while René Bon was able to pass on much of his knowledge which had formed his own extraordinarily virtuoso technique. René, who had been a pupil of the revered Parisian teacher Leo Staats, and had danced with the Opéra Comique and the Paris Opera Ballet, was a principal dancer with Marquis de Cuevas's company as well as with the companies of Maurice Béjart and Janine Charrat. His small stature had limited his roles, but he was an unbeatable technician; although no longer dancing regularly he could still turn fifteen pirouettes immaculately and jump sixteen double *tours en l'air* consecutively. Harry Haythorne's teaching had roots in Paris, as well as in London, where he had studied with many of the 'greats' – Stanislas Idzikowski, Audrey de Vos and the German modern dance teacher, Sigurd Leeder. His teaching was enhanced by great musicality.

For Alexander, as well as taking advantage of this intense work as a dancer, living in Holland, for a German, was not without problems. Anti-German feeling was still high following the terrible years of occupation during the Second World War and it was essential for Alexander to learn to speak English, and to do this well, as fast as he could.

Just before leaving Amsterdam we found time to get married, much to the relief of our landlady, who had enquired when we rented the apartment 'Are you a "real" couple?', and we felt never really believed our stuttering reply in the affirmative. Making for Paris in search of new work, our goal was to dance with one of the many small companies which were based there. These were mostly directed by dancer-choreographers such as Jean Babilée, George Skibine, Milorad Miskovitch, or Janine Charrat, very much the sort of small, personal, creative company we dreamed of forming ourselves. However, it

A very '60s' wedding.

was summer, holiday time, and there was no sign of any of these in Paris when we arrived. In the event, we accepted an engagement for the following season with the Ballets de l'Opéra de Marseille, directed by the French choreographer Joseph Lazzini, considered by some as the 'new Béjart'.

Coming to Marseille after cosy, friendly Amsterdam was a total shock. The city felt as if it belonged more to Africa than to France, the heat shimmering along the long straight streets which reached down from the train station to the city centre and the port. The city was populated by a mixture of races and nationalities such as we had never experienced; Africans from the French west coast colonies, Vietnamese, Chinese, and above all Algerians who had fled their country during the lengthy and bloody civil war. Accommodation had been booked for us in a small hotel directly next to the opera house, a few steps from the Vieux Port. The hotels adjoining ours, which wrapped right around the opera house, were obviously busy 'working places' for the numerous prostitutes in the area, while the steps of the opera were occupied, when there was no performance, by a number of 'clochards', some of the many living rough in the city. They would carefully line the steps with

60

cardboard or newspapers before spreading out their evening meal, made up of scraps from the city's rubbish bins, as well as small donations from the local shops. Sometimes the meal would be disturbed by the attempts of a fellow *clochard* to share the meal, but once it was cleaned up they would settle down on the stone steps for the night. No one seemed to find this unacceptable, nor did anyone protest at the comings and goings of several gentlemen, some of them in important positions in the city, into our rehearsals, which would often continue until late at night. After a few whispered exchanges, one or two of the dancers would then leave the rehearsal and depart with the gentlemen. It was as if a Degas painting of a top-hatted gentleman charming a *'petit rat'* (the name given to the nineteenth-century Paris Opera Ballet corps de ballet dancers) had come to life, leaving us dumbstruck. The explosions which took place at night also alarmed us – the *'plastiques'* of the Algerian war sympathisers which would rock the hotel on its foundations in an attempt to blow up a neighbouring newspaper office or a government building. Warily we explored the city, imagining we were being followed in the cramped and messy streets of the Arab quarters, or being propositioned by drug dealers in the Vietnamese areas, but it was easy to enjoy warm, sunny Sundays along

Dancers from the Ballet de l'Opéra de Marseille. Alexander is second from the left.

the Corniche where the water was, in the 1960s, still crystal clear and full of brilliantly coloured plants and fish.

The opening programme of the season included works by Lazzini in a typically Béjartian neo-classical style and also *Giselle*, with guest artists Rosella Hightower as Giselle, Milorad Miskovitch as Albrecht, and with Alexander in the role of Hilarion. Lazzini's production of *Giselle* was a traditional one, learned presumably from the Ballet Russe de Monte Carlo version. The corps were a mixed bag and the girls had neither the physiques nor the technical standard for the second act Wilis, so possibly because of this were costumed in long, flowing shifts. These looked suitably ghost-like and disguised a lot of their technical inadequacies. Hilarion, in the tradition of the Ballets Russes, was given a more important role than is usual now, with a short solo in Act 1 and a substantial one in Act 2, when he is attacked by the Wilis; both of these were taught to Alexander by Rosella. This caused a stir at the final dress rehearsal when Milorad Miskovitch made his Act 1 entrance as Albrecht, resplendent in a feathered hat and flowing cloak (no comparison to the excessively long, trailing black velvet one in which he made his entrance in Act 2) to find Alexander/Hilarion on stage. The conductor was ordered to stop while Miskovitch, taken aback, queried what Hilarion was doing on stage at the moment of 'his' entrance. Lazzini attempted to explain the dramatic advantages in having Hilarion present, but was forced to acquiesce. More problems arose when, in Act 2, clouds of smoke issued from smoke machines in the wings, filling the stage and blanketing the auditorium. Rosella, always perfectly mannered, stopped the rehearsal this time: *'Maître,'* she called, 'I can't see where I'm going.' Finally, it was agreed to set the opening of Act 2 with a gentle gust of smoke which would then be abandoned for the rest of the act. Miskovitch was a good, attentive partner, as he had once been to Alicia Markova when he first came to prominence ten years earlier. In Marseille, with Rosella, he gave a series of rewarding performances.

Working as a ballet master in a French opera house at that time could not have been an easy task. As we had immediately noticed, it was advisable, in fact probably essential, for Lazzini to cultivate the friendship of important members of Marseille society, and local government, and he needed to encourage the company dancers to cooperate in this way, as indeed had once been the tradition of the Paris Opera Ballet. It was usual in Marseille, as in most opera houses in France, for the opera company to perform a different operetta almost every weekend, and this always involved dancers from the ballet company. Lazzini, therefore, was required to choreograph, or revive, several scenes for each operetta, usually to include a can-can, a ballroom scene, and possibly a circus or a woodland scene. Accomplishing this seemed a considerable achievement, until we realised that the choreography hardly changed from week to week, but with different music and costumes – who would know the difference? Still, this did not leave much time to rehearse for the ballet premieres which occurred four or five times during the season. It had been known for Lazzini to rehearse until four o'clock in the morning, also that his admittedly fertile imagination was possibly fuelled by substances readily available on the streets of Marseille. However, we did not have any first-hand experience of this and managed to retain an amiable relationship with him, knowing all the same that we would not want to stay much longer in Marseille.

Lazzini remained ballet master in Marseille until 1969 when he was succeeded by Rosella Hightower, followed then in 1972 by Roland Petit when the ballet company was able to break the ties with the opera house, resulting in the foundation of the Ballet National de Marseille. Under Petit's directorship for the next twenty-five years, the company attained national as well as international acclaim. Joseph Lazzini remained active in the dance world in France, directing regional dance organisations and notably choreographing a successful version of *La Fille Mal Gardée* for the Paris Opera Ballet which he also mounted for several international companies, including the Kirov (Maryinsky) Ballet.

Once the *Giselle* season was completed in Marseille we took advantage of an offer to leave Marseille, joining an Italian company as guest artists for a tour of Italy. We performed just two classical pas de deux each performance, leaving us time and the leisure to enjoy travelling the length of Italy, virtually as tourists. The company also took part in several short opera seasons where we could experience good old-fashioned productions with beautiful Italian voices. Visits to Modena, Reggio Emilia and above all Siena, full of magnificent architecture and soaked in history, were the highlights and the tour would have passed off uneventfully enough had we had not gone on to Sicily.

As we learned, every Italian town and city has an opera house, whereby the high point of the year is the annual opera season. In the smaller towns this only lasts for a few days, but generally the opera season lasts a couple of weeks, and most towns will also have their own resident orchestra and chorus, made up of local music teachers and keen amateurs. For the opera season, a conductor, soloists, principals and, where needed, a ballet group will be engaged, usually from Rome or Milan, these often including artists of a high calibre.

The Teatro del Balletto, the company we were working with, had been invited to Caltagirone, in Sicily, for performances of Verdi's *La Forza del Destino* in which Alexander and I danced a gypsy-like pas de deux. The journey to Sicily involved an all-night train journey from Rome to the toe of Italy where the train was loaded onto a boat to cross the Strait of Messina before continuing on to Caltagirone, a hilltop town in the centre of the island from where one could see, in mid February, a snow-capped Mount Etna, gently puffing smoke from its crater. Our compartment was almost full, but the train made a few stops during that long night, when we were invaded by a large Sicilian family, parents with three children and a grandmother, who settled in noisily to eat and talk all night.

On arrival in Caltagirone, around midday, the company director waved us goodbye until the next day's rehearsal, advising us not to waste time finding our own hotel accommodation. There proved to be just three hotels which were already full up with the huge influx of singers and others taking part in the opera season. We wandered through the long, narrow, deserted streets noting the posters nailed to almost every door; posters with wide black borders surrounding a large black cross, announcing the recent death of a family member. There appeared to be an unnatural number of deaths for such a small town, which made us uneasy, as did our arrival at what appeared to be the centre of town, a large cobbled square ringed by arcades. The square was full of men, small dark men in black suits, standing around, talking a little, but the whole had an air of desolation, as if some disaster had just happened. It took some courage to approach a group and to ask if they could suggest where we might find a room for our stay, but to our amazement they were immediately helpful, escorting us to a nearby restaurant. Here we found a room available, although the manager was obviously doubtful as to whether it would be suitable. It soon became obvious why he hesitated, as the room had no heating and no hot water, but we could hardly be choosy, and were glad to be able to settle in.

The main square was obviously a meeting place for most of the men of the town, who gathered there every day in the hope of finding some work. There was, basically, no work, although presumably in summer there would have been employment in the nearby fields and orange groves; this very typically Sicilian situation has always been the reason for the huge immigration away from the island. However, we soon discovered that the people were quite unique in their friendliness, their generosity, and, no doubt due to the lack of any other activity, their interest in the annual invasion of their town by the *'artisti'*. We experienced this as we were settling in for our first night;

a knock at the door brought forth an unknown man with a hot water bottle and two glasses of grappa to help fight the chill in the room. Each morning, strangers were on hand to collect us and drive us to the theatre, while at the end of the rehearsal, or after the performance, another car would be there waiting at the stage door. All the dancers had acquired their 'minders', who would always refuse any payment or offer of food or drink with great dignity.

Spending some time in a cafe near the opera house, we soon made friends with an eleven-year-old boy who appeared to be the head waiter. As we found out, he had spent some time at school, but was disinterested in continuing with this, preferring to work at the cafe from 8 a.m. until the early hours the following day. Obviously he was very bright, with lots of charm, and told us of his plans to leave for Rome as soon as he could, so he 'could earn lots of money'. For some reason he took a great shine to Alexander, making him presents of bottles of wine or spirits – which were obviously taken from the cafe bar, but which Alexander would systematically replace. We often wondered what happened to him, but there were many such young boys working in the cafes and bars, no doubt many who never went to school, leaving them little chance of bettering their situation.

A short ballet performance given at an orphanage run by the local convent proved to be a touching occasion when we performed for regimented rows of tiny children with shorn heads in nineteenth-century tunics. However, our visit to the convent did give us our first opportunity to take a shower since leaving Rome! There were other occasions to remember, such as the time we spent a Sunday afternoon at the cinema, sitting in the midst of those huge Sicilian families, watching a real Italian film packed with action – gladiators, slaves and lions. They had all brought picnics with them, passing slices of salami and chunks of bread and cheese up and down the rows of seats while shouting abuse at an incompetent gladiator, or cheering on a slave battling with a lion. It was truly as if we were in the Coliseum two thousand years earlier. However, it was with some relief when we left to return to Rome, and for us, to travel further on to Germany.

During this period our plans for a recital programme of pas de deux and solos had become more and more defined; the time felt right to make a break from working within a company to start upon an independent existence. However, a call from Nederlands Dans Theater put these plans on hold, bringing us back to Holland. It was a landmark season for Nederlands Dans Theater, a breakaway group from the Netherlands Ballet directed at that time by the Dutch choreographer Hans van Manen and the American ballet master Benjamin Harkarvy, as it was the moment when American modern dance 'arrived' in Europe. John Butler had been invited to mount his production of *Carmina Burana*, recently premiered in New York, and brought with him to The Hague the American choreographer Glen Tetley. Although the Martha Graham Dance Company had toured briefly in Europe in the 1950s, the impact of the 'new' American modern dance had been very limited. Butler and Tetley, both of whom had commenced their careers with Graham, as well as working with many other leading American companies both modern and classical, found in Nederlands Dans Theater a company ready to absorb new techniques with new ways of dancing and performing. Tetley, who after a long career as a dancer had only just started choreographing, winning enormous success with his first work, *Pierrot Lunaire*, in New York, now remounted the ballet for Nederlands Dans Theater, staying on to create several more works and ultimately to take over the position of co-director. The rest, of course, is dance history and includes Tetley's move to the UK, his subsequent collaboration with the re-formed Ballet Rambert in the mid 1960s, which coincided with the formation of the London Contemporary Dance School and the company born of this.

It was a busy season for us with Nederlands Dans Theater; besides Butler and Tetley, we worked with Hans van Manen, Benjamin Harkarvy, Rudi van Dantzig and Yvonne Georgi, and there were also ballets by William Dollar and Anna Sokolow in the repertoire. Rewarding as the work could be, it was not unlike being on a factory conveyor belt, as we often rehearsed daily with three, four or even five different choreographers or ballet masters. The working day would be divided into one-and-a-half-hour, or two-hour slots; as one choreographer finished, the next would arrive, fresh and enthusiastic to start. By mid afternoon, the dancers would be tending bruises and blisters, rubbing on more liniment and swallowing a handful of dextrose sugar tablets in order to cope. The experience of working with Nederlands Dans Theater at this time of change was invaluable to us, although it reconfirmed our desire to break away on our own independent path.

66

POSTSCRIPT

Working with Gore in Amsterdam was the last time we collaborated, although he did offer us both the opportunity to join him in the newly founded London Ballet in 1962. The company existed for a couple of years, after which he concentrated on guest choreography around the world, mostly with Paula performing. A stint of four years as director of the Gulbenkian Ballet in Lisbon was finally a rewarding and, I believe, enjoyable time for them both. Sadly, Wally died, only sixty-nine years old, while working in Spain; however, Paula continued mounting his ballets for companies internationally, often performing in them. Notably, *Eaters of Darkness* was remounted for Northern Ballet Theatre, with Paula dancing as guest artist.

Wally was given a memorial service in London at the Actors' Church, St Paul's, Covent Garden. It was a well-attended service and those ready to lead the proceedings, remembering and praising him, grew uneasy awaiting Paula's late arrival before beginning. Paula, in particular, had always been bitter at the fact that Wally's talents and achievements had not been sufficiently appreciated in Britain but perhaps this quiet and gentle man knew he was destined to be an outsider, unable and unwilling to fit into an institution where he did not have the upper hand and was not prepared to battle in order to have his way. He very nearly missed out on his memorial service as Paula, who finally appeared, was riding pillion on choreographer Jack Carter's motorbike. They had crossed London with her hanging on to him with one hand while clutching the urn with the ashes in the other. 'Wally nearly didn't make it,' she explained breathlessly, 'we nearly all went flying off coming around Trafalgar Square.' I like to think that Wally, who had a wry humour, would have enjoyed making the doyens of the British ballet world wait for him while they polished their tributes.

Harry Haythorne did join the Gores as ballet master for the reformed London Ballet, then became Peter Darrell's associate for the Scottish Ballet. He returned to Australia to direct the Queensland Ballet, subsequently spending eleven years as director of the Royal New Zealand Ballet, work which earned him a CBE and for which he remains director emeritus. Always an exceptionally fine character dancer, he still occasionally performs with The Australian Ballet, while shortly before his eightieth birthday he was to be seen performing in Sydney in a production directed by Graeme Murphy, singing while tap-dancing on roller skates – talents he had learned in his early days in variety. Harry also shares his great knowledge of dance history as a lecturer at The University of Melbourne.

Michael Holmes returned to England from Amsterdam to become a much respected teacher in London and continues his passion in reconstructing medieval dances.

chapter three

First Steps in Independence

Reviewing the first London performances of *Soirée de Ballet* in June 1964 Patricia Barnes (wife of the eminent dance critic, Clive Barnes), commenced as follows: 'One cannot help admiring the courage of Christina Gallea and Alexander Roy, two young dancers who have set themselves up as a complete evening's entertainment with only a few costume changes and props to assist them. But one wonders why they should consider it preferable to appear this way rather than with a company.' Many did wonder why we made this choice, when by remaining with ballet companies in Berlin, in The Hague or in London, we could have made our way to the top and to a reasonably secure future. However, there is no doubt that the latter path demands not only talent and hard work, but also the ability to await one's time, to allow others to decide one's future, even to be in the right place at the right time; not a route to be followed by artists with their own ideas, and impatient to fulfil them.

Publicity photos for *Soirée de Ballet*.

The concept of a performance given by a solo performer or two dancers had long been a tradition in Germany, several leading figures in the German modern dance movement, Mary Wigman, Dore Hoyer and Harald Kreutzberg among them, created major works and won considerable success as solo performers. In the 1960s there were also several dancer-couples performing successfully in Europe – notably in France, Germany and Switzerland – leading Alexander to nurture the idea of creating such a performance himself. During our string of engagements with ballet companies throughout Europe, the venture had been prepared carefully; photo sessions were organised, a brochure printed, enquiries made to agents and promoters, while we fitted in our own rehearsals around those of the companies with which we were working.

Finally, with a series of bookings, we were able to plan a tour seriously, but were held up once again when I had an accident during a ballet class with Nederlands Dans Theater. Landing badly from a jump, and on top of my foot, I heard a loud crack, but the local doctor, insisting that I would be screaming with pain if the foot was broken, left me dancing, if not performing, for a further three weeks. Obviously, he didn't know that dancers have a higher tolerance for pain than other people. Finally, demanding an X-ray for my still seriously swollen foot, the worst was confirmed, and I was sentenced to a further five weeks in plaster. Obviously, we cancelled our tour, and although most theatres were able to re-book us for a later period, the problem of finding the funds to get through several weeks without work was a real one. Our contract with Nederlands Dans Theater had come to an end, but the company generously kept me on full pay, while Alexander continued appearing in performances of *Carmina Burana*.

A short-term engagement in Paris materialised for Alexander, taking part in a television film with the dancer and choreographer Jacques Chazot, principal dancer at that time with the Opéra Comique in Paris. As a tall, good-looking man, Chazot was a favourite in Parisian society, regularly featured in the social pages of *Paris Match*, accompanying a countess or a politician's wife to a social occasion, while he was notably in demand as a partner at the annual debutantes' ball. Chazot also had the unusual talent of dancing on pointe, performing his male solo variations wearing pointe shoes, landing from jumps onto pointe and throwing in a series of fouettées and other pirouettes on pointe. This was done very seriously during his performances at the Opéra Comique, but his greatest success was in a variety turn dancing the female role in the Black Swan pas de deux from *Swan Lake* with the very small René Bon as his partner. The one blessing in what was otherwise a forgettable engagement was the chance for Alexander to work with the delightful Liliane Montevecchi, once Roland Petit's

Croqueuse de Diamants in his 1950s ballet, later becoming a successful music hall artiste in Paris and on Broadway.

Once freed from the plaster cast, I was able to join Alexander in Paris to take classes with Nora Kiss while continuing to rehearse for our forthcoming tour. Madame Nora proved to be a great support at this time, helping me during the daily classes to strengthen the seriously weakened foot, as well as spending many constructive hours chatting with Alexander about his choreography and learning what our plans were for the future. The move from Holland meant there was no fixed base for our activities, making everything extremely complicated. Friends and family in London had designed and arranged for the printing of brochures and posters, but these needed to be sent on to us in Paris, where we had to clear them through customs, repack them into individual parcels, and finally send them on to the performing venues. The costumes were being made in Amsterdam, while the music needed to be recorded in The Hague. Even finding suitable music was a matter of chance; the score of Franz Lizst's *Orpheus* was finally located in East Germany, while a piece by Jacques Ibert turned up in Rome. Telephoning abroad from Paris entailed a trip to the post office where after ordering a call there was a wait of an hour, sometimes two hours, for this to come through. Paying bills was complicated by the fact that France as well as the UK had currency restrictions in place, making it impossible to transfer money from one country to another.

As in many similar ventures, we were helped by the generosity and encouragement of friends, family and colleagues. Once the television film was finished, it was possible to move from Paris to settle in Amsterdam where Mascha ter Weeme offered us her studio for rehearsals, the wardrobe mistress from the Amsterdam Ballet continued making the costumes, while the technicians helped us set up a suitable touring sound system. It was obviously proving difficult to find an agent to take us on for this untried venture, so I hammered out letters to theatres and promoters on a portable typewriter in a friend's kitchen while Alexander continued working on the choreography for the programme. Of course, we had no experience in 'business', had little idea how to go about making contacts, and once we were successful in obtaining an engagement, how best to negotiate terms, and finalise contracts. In those days before computers and emails, even telephones were rarely used, so we relied on the post, learning to be patient awaiting replies for a week or two, or longer. These delays brought about so many complications arranging dates not only to suit the theatre's schedule, but in fitting them into our itineraries in a practical way. Above all, we still had to learn how to squeeze better terms from a promoter without losing his interest. In finalising contracts, we learned mostly by imitation, by trial and error, in several languages, and in the early days a simple letter of confirmation of the date and terms was usually sufficient. But when bookings in France came in, the contracts were several pages long written in a style, and even printed in a typeface, which seemed to come from the eighteenth century. We were aghast to learn that the terms of the contract were at our own *'risques et périls'* and that force majeure could wipe out the whole agreement, as could war, famine and riots. Optimistic as always, confident that everything 'would be all right on the night' the documents were signed and returned.

The Grand Pas de Deux, *Don Quixote*.

At the same time, the programme was taking shape. From the start, we planned that this must have, above all, variety with multiple changes of mood and of style, showing the whole range of dance, from the obligatory classical pas de deux through dance dramas to modern dance, even jazz; it needed to entertain, to hold the audience's attention – almost to trick them, with constant costume changes, but minimal breaks between ballets, that they were seeing a full company of dancers, not a single couple. It was wise to start with a pas de deux from the classical repertoire when we would be fresh at the beginning of the evening. The grand pas de deux from *Don Quixote* is perhaps

Blue Roses

Alexander in the Mazurka from *Les Sylphides*.

the most effective of all the 'grand' pas de deux; Minkus's music sweeps along, full of life and colour, whereby the traditional choreography, although challenging, is made enjoyable with the pseudo-Spanish style and is full of bravura. The *Don Quixote* pas de deux is also much easier to perform successfully than the purely classical pas de deux from *The Sleeping Beauty* or *The Nutcracker*, where perfection of line and style are demanded, and where one needs a full stage setting to do it justice.

After a three-minute break for the costume change, we continued with a version of the Orpheus and Eurydice legend to Franz Liszt's symphonic poem. The traditional story lends itself well to dance, performed in a neo-classical style with a lot of lifts, and with some ingenuity we followed the storyline so that Orpheus did not actually look at Eurydice until the tragic ending. Alexander then had another quick change into his solo *Alborada del Gracioso* (The Serenade of a Fool); a complete change of mood, where the dancing matched Ravel's humour and agility. There was some scenery to change for these short ballets; a cut-out house front for *Alborada* and some furniture for the following ballet, with which we finished the first half.

The most dramatic ballet of the evening, a piece entitled *Guilty*, was danced to some little known music by the French composer, Jacques Ibert, written on the theme of Oscar Wilde's *The Ballad of Reading Gaol*. The programme notes quoted Wilde – 'For each man kills the thing he loves', and in consequence I became the luckless victim in the ballet. The interval would be spent cleaning up, especially after some rolling around on the floor and the quite acrobatic lifts in the final ballet. We next appeared in the prelude, mazurka and waltz pas de deux from Mikhail Fokine's *Les Sylphides*, a gentle, romantic duet in the romantic classical style which we always enjoyed. The following ballet was *Café d'Illusions*, a light-hearted piece where a young man observes a girl in a cafe, his fantasies bringing her to life in different guises. It gave me a good chance to show my versatility portraying three different characters, as did the following solo piece, *Blue Roses*, to Debussy's *Reflets Dans l'Eau*; a lonely woman, lost in the shadows of her own world, imagines the visit of a 'gentleman caller'. Inspired by Tennessee Williams's play, *The Glass Menagerie*, the solo proved to be a study for a later major work, based on the play, which Alexander choreographed for International Ballet Caravan. I have to admit that by this time, my legs were in danger of failing, and my feet and above all my toes, which had been encased in pointe shoes all evening, were suffering. It was therefore a relief to change into tights and sneakers for the final *Impromptu con Spirito* a jazzy work to George Gershwin's *Three Preludes*. However, with luck, and fortunately, quite often, we would get a second wind at this point, a final burst of energy which carried us on to the end.

Becoming professional partners was not without difficulties. Although we had worked together in different companies for the previous two years, we had seldom danced together. It had been possible to snatch some time during that period to rehearse a classical pas de deux, or simply to practise lifts, but we now had to form a real partnership. Our training had been so different, although our ideals, our ambitions and even our role models were the same. Alexander's German background was based on strength and theatricality, while my British training, as well as my early experience, accentuated precision and accuracy, and my work with Gore meant that my strengths lay in speed and lightness. Audrey de Vos said that Alexander was an 'earth dancer' while I was an 'air dancer' and she felt this made for an interesting partnership. These differences could lead to stormy rehearsal sessions but with work, patience and time we reached that point when two dancers think and move as one, a sort of telepathy taking over.

The first performance of the *Soirée de Ballet* took place in January 1963 in Braunschweig (Brunswick), northern Germany. It was one of the coldest Januarys on record with a blizzard sweeping across Europe from Siberia, virtually closing the motorway from Amsterdam to Braunschweig. Packed into our Volkswagen Beetle, laden with costumes, sound equipment and a generously proportioned Dutch female stage manager, we inched our way across Northern Europe to arrive at our destination. The Sunday matinee performance was the first of a tour which took us to, besides Germany, Switzerland and Austria. The performance in Braunschweig was, as is usual in Germany, at eleven o'clock on the Sunday morning, and the central heating had obviously not been programmed for this early hour. The audience sat in their coats and hats while we fought to warm muscles which were still stiff from the long drive, and at the end of the performance the majority of the audience left the theatre in a rush following a short bout of applause. We were, of course, mortified; it was not a good beginning. However, while packing up, telephone calls came in to the theatre from members of the public, excusing themselves for having left in such a hurry, affirming how much they had enjoyed the performance, and chastising the director for the lack of heating.

We continued our tour through one of the toughest winters on record, fighting our way through snow and ice, while performing in large and small theatres, in major cities as well as in small country towns. Audiences were, on that first tour, usually quite modest, but occasionally we would amaze everyone, including the promoter, by selling out. The audience response was quite remarkable, especially in Germany and Switzerland, where we would often receive ten, twelve, even fifteen curtain calls then to be stopped in the street to be congratulated, even embraced by enthusiastic audience members. If it was greatly rewarding, it was, however, total madness: the physical demands of sustaining a two-hour programme left us exhausted the following day. Fortunately, there were very few occasions with performances on consecutive days, while after a performance day we would normally travel on to the next venue, which in pre-motorway regions of Europe entailed long, leisurely trips giving us the opportunity to gradually recover physically from the previous day's exertions. This also gave us the chance to explore Europe from northern Germany to the Italian lakes, from the Austrian Alps to southern France.

A very over-loaded Volkswagen 'beetle', 1963.

After the first series of performances, finances dictated that the stage manager be sent back to Amsterdam, leaving us to spend the day before the evening performance setting up the stage and arranging the sound and lighting with the local crews. It was a crash course in stage management, by which we learned much about backstage technicalities – hanging stage curtains, setting up 'wings' for entrances and exits, positioning loud speakers and, above all, in view of our limited stage sets, how to create an atmosphere with stage lighting. Of course, everything was so much simpler in those days when the 'flying' bars for attaching stage curtains were hauled up by hand, lighting boards were operated manually, without computers, while communication between technicians was made with flashing lights or even a healthily loud buzzer. However, stage crews were mostly helpful, if overawed by our ambitious demands; many stage technicians in the smaller venues were really just council employees more used to repairing street lights than to working on stage, and totally inexperienced with dance performances. They had to be persuaded to cooperate; we would want to 'mess up' their neatly prepared

Lighting rehearsal on tour in France.

stage curtains to widen and deepen the stage, setting the 'masking' as far off stage as possible, as dancers need space above all, with two dancers needing just as much space as twenty. Stage lighting, especially in France, usually consisted of rows of coloured light bulbs, red, blue, green and amber, with, if one was lucky, a dozen 'real' stage lamps positioned in the auditorium. Often we had to settle for the limited options of 'full up' (bright) or 'romantic' (mostly blue) lighting, which were the usual settings for dance performances at that time, and the use of a follow spot was always declined, as an inexperienced operator would have no chance of following a fast-moving dancer.

The great difference in performing this way, rather than as a member of ballet company, was the intimacy felt for the stage, the theatre and the audience. So often, especially working in an opera house setting, access to the stage is almost forbidden to dancers until a few minutes before an entrance. In a ballet company stage rehearsals are limited to one or two before an opening night, while collaboration between the backstage staff and the performers is almost unheard of. Working on our own, and later with our company, we would always spend the whole day in the theatre. Even on tours to fascinating foreign countries, sightseeing was avoided on a performing day and our days would be spent between the hotel and the theatre with a short outing to a nearby cafe or restaurant at midday. It was only in the evening after the performance when everything had been packed away that we could relax to enjoy our surroundings, the places and people around us.

It was for us both a sort of ritual to arrive at the theatre around nine o'clock, with the technicians, to inspect the stage and the auditorium in order to make decisions about the best way to hang the stage curtains, to set the stage and to light it. Many companies, and many theatre technicians, keep to a strict formula, with exact measurements, laying down the placing of their scenery so that the stage is identical every evening. We preferred to adapt to each stage; some were wide but shallow, some totally square, some with thrust stages into the auditorium, some even round; there would be problems of exits and entrances to consider, possibly the lack of height to hang our stage curtains. Inevitably there would be problems which could not be changed, and so we would have to adapt, sometimes with compromises being made. Once these decisions had been made, the truck unloaded, Alexander usually stayed on stage, unpacking and setting up the sound equipment, which was really just a chance to keep in touch with the technicians, following the activity on stage.

I would then check out the dressing rooms, unpack the costumes, sorting out those which needed washing or repairing, and hanging up others ready to be pressed by the local wardrobe mistress. I could usually hear, via the dressing room tannoy, the jovial banter of the technicians while bars were lowered from the flies and the curtains tied on, the lights adjusted. As we were in Continental Europe my language skills would be needed from time to time, so I kept in constant contact with happenings on stage while setting up my own dressing room, which would ideally be that closest to the stage. It was always interesting to wander around the theatre checking the sight lines from different parts of the auditorium, investigating the foyers which, especially in Italian and French opera houses, contained unexpected treasures; paintings and statues, little anterooms behind the boxes, or corners where sometimes stores of old programmes and posters, perhaps from the nineteenth century, could be found. We always tried to have the stage ready no later than four o'clock, when we could start our own work. During the early days of the *Soirée de Ballet* I would go through each role for myself on stage, placing my costumes and the props ready for the quick changes in the wings, as a magician must do, and only then could I feel secure on each new stage.

The evening ritual always began two hours before the performance with make-up and a final warm-up. Alexander and I would try a lift or two, a few pirouettes, he would check and recheck the tape recorder and the tapes, while we went through the running details of the first half of the performance with the local stage manager. I wonder now if we were not nervous, even frightened, when the curtain finally opened with just the two of us, alone with the audience. No matter how many times I danced the same role, there was always a nervous 'tingle' before the curtain opened, but rather than fear, there was a great feeling of anticipation after the day of preparation. One instinctively feels whether the audience has to be won over (and they are different in every performance), or if one can relax and simply give the best one can. On average I believe there is probably just one performance in fifty where there is that glorious feeling that everything has gone just 'right', every technical challenge met, the collaboration between us, the performers, has been totally successful, and that a sort of spirit has taken over the performance, sweeping it along to success. This was all a voyage of discovery for us in those early days with so much to learn, but also had so much to gain from the particular independent path we had chosen.

In expanding our 'market' to as many different countries as possible, it had been surprisingly easy to book a series of good-sized opera houses in France in June of 1963 and we set off full of optimism – although all the contracts were on the basis of sharing the box office receipts without any guaranteed fee. A theatre seating more than a thousand must surely assure us of a decent audience, and this would get us over what promised to be a lean summer season. Without any experience of the situation in France, we had no idea that, especially in those days, the theatre 'season' finished around Easter with people rarely going to their local theatres after that date – except possibly for the local ballet school performances. These took place in June, as did the school examinations, followed by holidays throughout the country from 1 July. Very few people were interested in an unknown couple of dancers appearing at their local theatre in June, so there were twenty-eight spectators in the opera house at Aix-en-Provence, forty-odd in Brest and Cherbourg and little better elsewhere. However, those directors reneged on their share of the box office receipts, giving us every franc, they fired us with enthusiasm, inviting us back again for the following season at a more suitable time.

Many of those theatres formed the basis of our future tours for many years, with the added bonus that the theatres and theatre technicians in France were used to dance performances, allowing us to learn much from them. The theatres were mostly municipal or council run, with a permanent staff including technicians who came from generations of the same family who had always worked in the theatre. Although equipment was still very basic, everything was meticulously well looked after, with the men working well and competently. They would often offer the use of their painted backdrops, which hung high up in the flies, the 'Village Square' or the 'Jardin Public', but we would disappoint them by finding these not really suitable, although sometimes there would be a well-painted 'Wooden Glade' which could serve as a backdrop for the excerpts from *Les Sylphides*. Where in Switzerland a stage manager would ask if the curtain should be wide open for 'showing our exercises', the French crews had regular contact with touring groups from Paris – Les Etoiles de Paris or Les Etoiles de l'Opéra de Paris, which were small groups of 'star' dancers who regularly presented gala performances throughout the country.

It was during this tour that we had our first experience of things going badly wrong, making us aware of just how different southern France was from the rest of the country. Of course, our experiences in Marseille should have prepared us for this. Halfway through the tour was a performance in Narbonne, in the Languedoc region, a town near enough to the Spanish border to have been a target for many of the hundreds of thousands of Spanish refugees from the Spanish Civil War of the 1930s who flooded into

Our posters on a market hall in southern France – not attracting much attention.

southern France. In June the heat was already intense, the town rough and busy, the traffic hooted and screeched around the modest hotel–restaurant where we had found accommodation. Our room was directly over the restaurant kitchen, so the added heat from the cooking, with the pungent, almost nauseating smell of the heating olive oil, filled the room. The cooks shouted at each other, the waiters yelled their orders into the kitchen, and the guests seated in the outdoor restaurant appeared to argue so loudly and aggressively to be alarming. If it hadn't been so hot, we would have been uneasy to leave the room at all.

The locals spoke a rich, incomprehensible dialect – a mixture of Occitan and Spanish – and the theatre was a rundown cinema managed by a short-tempered woman director. The fact that there had been no advance booking at all was blamed on us, although it was obvious that there were no posters advertising our performance to be seen in the town, or even in front of the theatre, which was still plastered with posters from the previous week's cinema programme. There was no choice but to cancel the performance – the first time we had faced such a disaster. However, it gave us the chance to spend the following day on the beach, on the shores of the Mediterranean, and funnily enough, this visit reconfirmed what became a lifelong attachment to

France, especially to the south. A couple of years later, there was an interesting news story which had made it into the national press. Our theatre director in Narbonne had been arrested and charged with running a drug-smuggling ring from North Africa; small boats full of tobacco, and drugs, were landing during the night at a secluded beach near Narbonne, the goods then being stored at the back of the cinema!

However, the tours so far had been successful enough for us to be invited back to most of the theatres, which entailed producing a second programme – with all the time and expense this demanded. In Stuttgart, where we had decided to settle for the rehearsal period, we found a ballet school where we could use the studio during the day, in return for some teaching of the local dance pupils in the evenings. John Cranko, from England's Royal Ballet, was now directing the Stuttgart Ballet and he, with his assistant directors Peter Wright and Anne Woolliams, was helpful and welcoming, allowing us to join the company classes whenever we liked. This was obviously a huge advantage as classes were good and the company was a lively, friendly one. The question was raised as to whether we would join the Stuttgart Ballet, but we were now totally committed to our own venture. However, we now had a real base in Stuttgart, with a rented apartment, and if funds were as precarious as ever, we were helped by Alexander's further guest performances with the ballet company in Essen. In enlarging our repertoire, Gore had given his agreement to mount *Tancredi and Chlorinda*, which would have been a powerfully dramatic acquisition, while Beriosoff had offered to teach us Fokine's *Le Spectre de la Rose*. However, with the peripatetic lives we all led, the problems of actually getting together for rehearsals remained unsolved.

Access to the record library of Stuttgart's Amerika Haus led to two unexpectedly successful finds: some rather lush romantic nineteenth-century music by Edward MacDowell which was perfect for a supernatural story of a haunted house which we called *Journey into Darkness*, but best of all was a plethora of the most delightfully lively, enjoyable music by Louis Moreau Gottschalk. A contemporary of Chopin, Gottschalk was, besides being a prodigious pianist, a prolific composer, using for the first time Creole and African American influences in his compositions. The resulting ballet, *Le Manège*, had a fairground setting, which kept us busy with multiple costumes changes, playing an assortment of characters, both performers and spectators. The major work of the second programme was a contemporary style pas de deux danced to J.S. Bach's *Partita* and *Chaconne* for solo violin. Entitled *In War with Time*, it incorporated the spoken word, chosen from Shakespeare's sonnets dealing with love and loss. It was a long work, twenty-five minutes of non-stop dance, something of a marathon and doubtlessly hard work for the audience. However, it did give Alexander the chance to choreograph an abstract, modern work and it was welcomed in the more sophisticated venues.

As well as rehearsing, performing and travelling throughout Europe there were always new plans and projects; looking back now I cannot believe how constantly inventive, or restless, we were. Although the Harold Holt concert agency in England had taken us under their wing, planning two tours for 1964, it did not seem to be possible to settle in London. Visiting Paris quite regularly to take classes, the city still seemed too expensive and too 'tough' to be a suitable home, encouraging us to continue looking elsewhere. When performing in a small private theatre in Ascona, on the Lago Maggiore, we had fallen in love with the Ticino, the Italian region of Switzerland. Many artists and writers had settled in Ascona; the town is charming, the surroundings beautiful and it is the centre of a region of lively towns – Locarno, Lugano, Bellinzona – and only a couple of hours from Milan.

The Teatro San Materno in Ascona was built for the modern dancer Charlotte Bara by her father, a wealthy German industrialist. Bara had studied dance with a student of Isadora Duncan, becoming a recitalist performing very much in the manner of Isadora with a predilection for religious and exotic themes – Egyptian temple dances seemed to feature regularly. When we met Bara, she was a tall, bulky woman, now quite elderly, but still wearing long floor-length robes and with waist-length hair. She lived opposite the theatre in a medieval castle which contained a seventh-century chapel, and although she disapproved of my dancing on pointe, she was very charming to us. At the time, it seemed a wonderful place to make our base.

Another scheme was put to us by an impresario in Salzburg who wanted us to form a Salzburg Festival Ballet Company, assuring us he could have us based at the Festival Theatre and use the Festival Orchestra – an unlikely proposition! Aix-en-Provence, in southern France, seemed another ideal setting for a ballet company, but none of these schemes came to anything while we continued our itinerant existence.

The second year of *Soirée de Ballet* brought about more performances, bigger and better audiences, and in June of that year we presented a season in London, at the Rudolf Steiner Theatre, off Baker Street. The stage proved to be far from perfect, too small, noisy and slippery, while the venue, although used at that time for small-scale performances, was not well known. However, the season had been offered to us by a successful London photographer who was starting up as an impresario, and after promoting a series of concerts he was interested to break into the dance world. Everything was very professionally done; he produced some attractive posters and flyers, and organised an effective press campaign bringing several important members of the London dance press to Baker Street.

SOIRÉE DE BALLET

The brochure for our London season, 1964.

When standing on stage at the beginning of a performance when the curtain opens, it is possible to actually 'feel' the atmosphere of the auditorium. That evening in London an icy wind enveloped us as we stood ready to start the *Don Quixote* pas de deux, which almost froze me to the spot. There were some friends in the auditorium but most members of the audience must have come out of curiosity and some even with the attitude, 'Well now, show us what you can do.' Obviously, performing in London was always going to be a totally different experience to the provincial theatres we had been visiting where audiences were often starved for dance performances, and the local critics were more likely music critics rather than dance experts. With

86

hindsight, it would have been wiser to have given a single programme, instead of attempting a change of programme for a second week of performances, choosing the strongest works from both programmes and taking the limitations of the stage into account.

However, after that first glacial encounter, the atmosphere improved, even on the first night, and by the second week, audience numbers had improved likewise. There were even a few good and constructive reviews; Patricia Barnes, after her initial query as to why we should want to perform in this way, was very complimentary of Alexander's dancing, praised some of the ballets and writes of the audience as being 'fairly enthusiastic'. Katherine Sorley Walker in *The Daily Telegraph* called Alexander 'an expressive and sensitive choreographer' and wrote that I 'could dance precisely and at times brilliantly' while Alexander 'as a performer had considerable eloquence of movement'. We couldn't really have hoped for better.

After the two-week season we were exhausted, but set off for France to a series of open-air performances, followed by a holiday period. The new season would then begin with a month's tour of East Germany; the invitation to tour the so-called German Democratic Republic had come as something of a surprise. Alexander had left East Germany at a time, before the Berlin Wall, when restrictions were lighter and permits to leave the GDR could be granted for personal or professional reasons. However, it was an action which was highly disapproved of in the East, leaving one labelled a 'reactionary' or even 'an enemy of socialism'. Despite this, an invitation for the month-long tour came out of the blue, with fifteen performances to be given in September 1964. We had both been issued with visas and all the necessary paperwork, so we could make our way from West Germany by road through the first part of the border to drive right across East Germany to Berlin. In travelling to West Berlin, it was essential to avoid stopping on the motorway, something which was forbidden. Should one be forced to do this, due to a breakdown or some other problem, one could expect to be immediately surrounded by the 'VoPo', the dreaded East German police. However, we made it safely to West Berlin, turning up on the agreed date at Checkpoint Charlie to cross into East Berlin.

The Berlin Wall was, of course, frightening; between the two layers of metres-high cement which marked the Western and Eastern sides of the wall was a grassy area, dotted with watchtowers, below which Alsatian dogs prowled on long leads between rolls of barbed wire. Passing through the barrier of the checkpoint, the car rolled over a row of cameras to be pulled up by the border police. In the shed-like building a group of officers pored over our papers, grumbling that these were not in order. Alexander, as a West German citizen, didn't need a visa – therefore, he couldn't use this border crossing, although I would have to do so. It meant that I would have to cross through into East Berlin on foot, and join Alexander, who was to drive to an alternative crossing point some distance further around the wall. It was early evening, already getting dark, as I made off following the curve of the wall in the hope that at some point I would find this other border crossing. The houses along the wall had all been boarded off, the windows bricked up, the street totally deserted, the cobbles rough and difficult to walk on. I had no idea where I was, or where I might find Alexander again. The thought crept into my mind that it could all be a ploy and that by now he would have been grabbed by the Stasi and was sweating it out under investigation. It did take an hour or so, but eventually our car was in sight rolling towards me, and with a great sense of relief we located the hotel, settling in for our month in the German Democratic Republic.

Our early arrival gave us a few days before the tour to see something of East Berlin and above all to see performances of Brecht's Berliner Ensemble, as well as those at the Komische Oper, Alexander's 'old home' theatre, which under Walter Felsenstein's direction had become recognised as a major international opera house. With a whole suite in the old Adlon Hotel (right up against the wall), we stayed in East Berlin in considerable luxury; we had rehearsal studios at our disposal, and were able to spend the evenings eating very well and seeing some marvellous drama and opera performances. All of this was in great contrast to the life around us. East Berlin was grim; around the omnipresent wall groups of people would gather, simply standing and looking westward. The shops were as good as empty, the buildings rundown and grimy, an atmosphere of gloom pervaded everything despite the huge banners hanging from the city buildings, declaring 'Joy through Work' or 'Success with Socialism'. Electricity seemed to be in short supply with most rooms making do with a single 40-watt globe, shop windows remained dark in the evenings while many basic foods – meat, butter, sausage – were still rationed.

However, as guests of the government from the West, Alexander and I were able to eat in the best restaurants where otherwise unobtainable items were available to us. We would watch guiltily the growing queues of people waiting for a table, which might take an hour or so, while some who apparently were not dressed suitably would be turned away. For those who were seated, the items they wanted to order would inevitably not be available, and we often saw an excited crowd of eager would-be diners reduced to silence with a plate of sausages and potatoes, the only items available on the menu. Those serving in shops and restaurants were apathetic and disinterested, although it soon became clear that a healthy gratuity, although strictly forbidden, brought forth wonders. We were faced with an unusual problem – we had too much money. Our earnings were good, but in East German marks, which could not be exported. Special permission to buy items which we could export, including jewellery and antiques, was agreed, but it was soon clear there was very little available.

The tour opened in a good-sized opera house in Frankfurt an der Oder, where we found, once away from Berlin, that life in the country seemed much more comfortable, the people friendlier and the shops fuller. We performed in Leipzig at the time of the Leipzig Trade Fair when the city was packed, sharing our hotel with the president, or general secretary, as he was titled, Walter Ulbricht, and a huge group of government officials. It was with something of a shock when, stepping into the lift, my handbag was wrenched away and disappeared, albeit with the assurance that I would receive it back at our room – which indeed did happen. We couldn't help wondering how they knew who we were and which room was ours. Inside the hotel women guards had been placed in the corridors every few metres, leaving us to look warily around our room for a hidden camera or microphone. At lunch that day, in the hotel restaurant where Ulbricht with the other party dignitaries were also seated, it was amazing to observe oranges, bananas, pineapples, sea food and items which no resident of East Germany born after about 1940 would ever have seen. All of this disappeared the following day, with the departure of the politicians.

With a free day in Leipzig following the performance, it was time to do some serious shopping. It seemed a good idea to buy some of those items not normally affordable for us, and I thought an electric sewing machine would be a good idea, managing to persuade a distinctly unwilling salesman to demonstrate one for us. The machine started with an alarming whir, then literally fell to pieces, wheels and screws bouncing off the counter. 'Don't try to buy anything mechanical here,' the salesman whispered to us, 'this happens to everything.' Another surprise was when I tried to buy a bra; as a dancer, obviously a small size was needed, and this was not usually a problem. Here in Leipzig, bras had obviously been made for monster-women; sizes 40 or 50 and nothing else. Again, it was explained to us: 'There has been a problem, as they had to fulfil the quota of so many tons of bras, the makers deciding it would easiest to make them BIG.' I did, however, find an attractive winter coat, which had been imported from Holland and so was on restricted sale – for foreigners only. The saleswoman willingly took it off display, helping me to try it on. Before long, I attracted a huge crowd of onlookers all admiring the coat and without any signs of envy advising me to take it – as I could, and obviously they couldn't. We even bought ten pairs of shoes between us during this shopping spree as they seemed to be in good supply, but were to regret it the next day, when returning from the theatre we were forced to take them off and walk back to the hotel barefoot.

There appeared to be very few people in East Germany who supported the regime, most being cynically resigned to the failure of the so-called socialist dream. To us, it seemed that a new kind of class society was firmly in place, whereby those in charge had become the new aristocracy, with all the privileges this meant, while 'the masses' suffered with overcrowded housing and extreme shortages, especially with food, where skin problems and rashes were obvious due to vitamin deficiencies. Our driver and the tour manager, the 'minder' who accompanied us, spoke to each other in a kind of code. One would ask the other if they had 'looked out of the window' the night before. This meant 'had they watched West German television?', and although it was strictly forbidden, many did this; indeed it became a lifeline for many to the outside world. The tour manager was a youngish woman who, after a couple of glasses of Crimean champagne on the evening we performed for the Russian officers in Potsdam, told Alexander, 'I have your file with me, you know. We know all about you and where you have been since leaving the East.'

It was also in Potsdam that I first came face to face with a Russian soldier. Like most of the lower rankings, he was Mongolian or Siberian, with a wide, Asian face and narrow eyes with which he watched us without expression or comprehension. Probably over-dramatically, I immediately recalled stories of the terror these soldiers had spread as they swept into the German towns and villages in 1945; soldiers such as this one, standing fully upright on open wooden carts at the reins of tough little ponies from the steppes. It was a picture which must have reproduced the arrival of Attila's Huns hundreds of years earlier and like those soldiers, I knew that these war-toughened men had stormed into the defeated Germans' homes, demanding 'Frau, Frau' and many, very many women, including family friends of Alexander's, had only just survived multiple rapes and abuse. However, this soldier stood silently in front of my dressing room door with a case full of costumes which he solemnly handed to me.

Visiting Dresden, we found the medieval city centre still flattened after its almost total destruction, weeds growing out of the rubble where palaces, museums and an opera house once stood. We performed in Weimar, Erfurt and Magdeburg where, as everywhere on the tour, performances were sold out and aroused considerable interest as so very little else had been seen from the West. Although we had a free day following the performance in Magdeburg, the organisers had arranged for us to leave the town immediately after the performance. As they knew most things about Alexander, they also knew that his father and grandmother still lived in the city, and a meeting would not be approved of. Unexpectedly, it only took a few words of protest to have the decision reversed, resulting in a moving reunion as, at that time, it seemed unlikely that they would ever meet again.

The theatres in East Germany had been well looked after in general as theatre-going remained an important part of most people's lives, doubtlessly encouraged because it could also be used as a propaganda instrument, but standards were good and sometimes excellent. It made touring a pleasure for us with good-sized stages, as many technicians as we could wish for, as well as good technical facilities. It was then with mixed feelings that we came to the end of the tour to set off for a series of performances in France. We had taken the foolhardy decision to risk taking some money out of the country with us and hid this discretely among the costumes and props. Back at the border crossing, surrounded by border police, VoPo and Alsatian dogs, being photographed from underneath, and probably from all around, the car crept through the barriers, our hearts beating, palms sweating. However, we were not even stopped and carried on along the motorway through the GDR, and finally out and into West Germany. We could have smuggled out a whole family, and also a lot more money, which we immediately regretted for now we were left to our own resources.

The first town on the French tour was Annecy, not far from the Swiss border, where the snow-capped Alps border a cobalt-blue lake. The medieval city centre is built around meandering canals, picturesque castles and towers, picture-postcard squares and fountains. The theatre is situated in the modern part of the town, which seemed to be bursting with life and light. The shop windows sparkled with the goods on offer, clothes and furniture, jewellery and cosmetics, all elaborately lit up and decorated. We wondered if it was already Christmas, until it dawned on us that after six weeks behind the Iron Curtain we had become used to the sparseness, the dullness, even the general ugliness. However, we were also back to the real world of the 'Wild West', bringing us to check at the box office for the ticket sales, making mental calculations of how much we could hope to earn that evening. Changing some marks into francs proved almost impossible, although we were advised to find an Algerian bank as they were trading partners with East Germany and might have some use for the currency. Finally, we could do this in Paris, but only a limited amount; fortunately, by that time, some of the German banks had helped us out, more out of pity than anything else, giving us enough cash to continue our way across Europe. Happily, the tour of France went well, in fact better than all expectations, leaving us with a healthy financial profit and with the assurance that the performance had become a viable success.

We had decided to return to Berlin – West Berlin this time. Alexander had many friends and ex-colleagues there and the city seemed to have a lot to offer. He also had a guest contract for the Christmas period and, above all, we still had a lot of money in East Berlin, with a permit to cross the border and to shop there – impractical as that may have been. For future seasons we had decided it wiser to plan for a spring and an autumn tour for the recital programme, to try to arrange performances or short tours for a small group of dancers in Berlin, as well as guesting and possibly teaching. The cultural department at Berlin's city council was generous in its support of new ventures, already having given their provisional agreement to a series of performances with six dancers in the new year. As always, we appeared to be irrepressibly optimistic and full of new ideas; while Alexander was busy with rehearsals and performances, I gave a short series of classes in Audrey de Vos's method of teaching for dancers from the Mary Wigman school and from the Gsovsky studio. We visited the studio where Mary Wigman still ran a school, and were excited to meet the small, elderly woman with an interestingly wrinkly face; nearly eighty, Mary Wigman was still bursting with energy and obviously a popular and much-loved teacher.

I made regular trips to East Berlin, and much to the surprise and the amusement of the border guards at Checkpoint Charlie would return with a shopping basket full of the meagre choice of goods available – potatoes, sausages, apples, bread, and once even with a bucket and a broom. At the same time I considered the ever increasing pile of letters which had awaited our arrival in Berlin. Performances for the following season needed to be confirmed, more letters needed to be written, appointments with agents and promoters needed to be arranged, but somehow the pile remained unattended. First of all Christmas was upon us, and we were able to spend this with Gertrud Steinweg and Georg Groke in East Berlin. Alexander was delighted when his former mentors came to see one of our performances during the tour of East Germany, as he had no idea what had happened to them after Steinweg lost her position as dance director at the Komische Oper. Not long after Alexander's departure from the East, politics and intrigues had taken hold of the dance world and Steinweg, always a rebel, was sidelined, considered not politically correct enough, and indeed was not successful in working again. However, she and Georg Groke lived simply but quite happily in East Berlin. Georg Groke, besides being a successful solo recitalist, had been Steinweg's principal character dancer both in Leipzig and Berlin, creating with particular success the role of the Devil in *The Devil in the Village* at the Komische Oper, and had been instrumental in assisting Alexander to the success he won in the same ballet. In a way, Alexander had now come full circle and we were happy to spend a truly magical Christmas Eve with them; although none of us were 'believers' we opened the window at midnight to let in the 'Christ Child' as is the German tradition, and downed a couple of bottles of Crimean champagne. Most touchingly, Steinweg gave us a huge bundle of her old costumes which we used for many seasons ahead.

chapter four

London Interlude

As with many events during our careers, the offer to join the recently formed London Dance Theatre came out of the blue, in the form of a telegram delivered to us in Berlin on New Year's Day 1965. Despite the many plans for the coming year something had stopped us finalising any of these. Although we had undoubtedly achieved a certain success with our venture of a recital programme, it was possible that we had exhausted the possibilities of this intense but introverted form of performance. Equally, we were not sure that the time was right to form our own company with the enormous amount of time, money and energy this would demand, so the offer to move to London was considered as a chance to reconsider things, and was accepted immediately.

London Dance Theatre was directed by Norman McDowell, a former dancer turned stage designer, who was perhaps best known through his collaboration with the choreographer Jack Carter. He was joined by former Royal Ballet ballerina Anne Heaton as associate director. Some London critics had hailed McDowell as a new Diaghilev and he had certainly, ambitiously, commissioned a brand new repertoire for the company involving a number of well-known choreographers, designers and composers. The company was unsubsidised, relying, as had Diaghilev, on private patrons and sponsorship. They had completed a successful first season before we joined them, and had a busy schedule ahead, albeit only for a few months. Alexander was asked to contribute a new ballet to the repertoire, and he chose to rework one of the duets from our recital programme, enlarging the cast to five dancers. *In War With Time*, retitled *Circuit*, was the sort of contemporary ballet, using both ballet and modern dance techniques, which the company was interested in including in its repertoire.

Robin Howard, the extraordinary English restaurateur turned patron of dance who had been responsible for bringing the Martha Graham Dance Company to London, and who was shortly to form the London Contemporary Dance School and the affiliated company, watched a rehearsal of *Circuit*. Generously, he offered his sponsorship to stage the work for the forthcoming season in central London. Philip Prowse, later to become an internationally acclaimed designer and theatre director, was commissioned to design the ballet, producing a striking black and white marbled set and attractive costumes. *Circuit* was well received by most of the London press: 'rewarding and highly promising' (*The Times*), 'a worthwhile, well danced effort' (*The Sunday Times*), while Peter Noble writing in *What's On in London* found it 'well danced and presented, this augurs well for Mr Roy. He is a choreographer to watch.' Clive Barnes wrote of me 'giving a beautifully warm and tender performance', while Clement Crisp remained 'uneasy' about dancing to Bach. Following the premiere Robin Howard made his way backstage into the cramped dressing rooms of the Vaudeville Theatre in London's West End. This was no mean feat for a man with two prostheses (he had lost both legs on one of the last days of the Second World War) and he was clutching a bag of eggs, which he presented to Alexander. These he claimed to have rescued from a would-be egg thrower in the audience, ready to protest at the first performance of modern dance by a British ballet company. It was a good joke, and possibly history was made on that day.

However, this first experience of choreographing for a company brought home the hazards a choreographer has to face when working for a company which is not his own. Firstly, the title of the work was changed as 'it needed to be more modern'; secondly, the work was shortened by about ten minutes, which meant eliminating the most innovative sections where we danced to spoken text rather than to music. We had discovered that Shakespeare's

Alexander's ballet *Circuit* with London Dance Theatre in 1965.

sonnets had a natural rhythm and were easy to dance to. But worst of all, our programme notes, which quoted a few lines from one of the sonnets that effectively described the theme of the ballet, were replaced by a couple of quotations from the Bible which had no relation to the work. Alexander only discovered this when he saw the printed programme on the opening night.

Besides dancing in *Circuit*, I took over the title role, from Belinda Wright, in Janine Charrat's *La Répétition de Phèdre*, while we both appeared in Rudi van Dantzig's *Jungle* as well as in ballets by Andrée Howard, Jack Carter and Terry Gilbert. It was enjoyable working with the Dutch choreographer Rudi van Dantzig, whose style was a happy mixture of classical and contemporary dance. *Jungle* was once of his earliest ballets, and had been very successful with the Dutch National Ballet in Holland. A tough and demanding choreographer, he had some problems with the company, but we worked well together, Alexander and I feeling much more at home with his style than with some of the British choreographers. One of these, stumped for ideas, would demand of us 'Come along, boys and girls, show me what tricks you can do', while another sought to reassure us with 'Darlings, you'll be covered with feathers and glitter.' Van Dantzig created his most famous work, *Monument for a Dead Boy*, in the same year (to become one of Nureyev's favourite ballets) and shortly after he worked with us in London he took over the position of director of the Dutch National Ballet.

After six months London Dance Theatre had run out of both funding and bookings. A tide had turned in Europe, while in the UK both Ballet Rambert and London Contemporary Dance Theatre assumed major roles in the development of contemporary dance in Britain. Funding was unlikely to become available for a medium-scale ballet company requiring a full orchestra and all the accoutrements of a touring ballet company. It is also questionable as to whether London Dance Theatre's repertoire and artistic policy were still realistic at this time of change within the dance world. Works such as Andrée Howard's inconsequential *Barricade*, which involved a reverse striptease, a drunken Irish maid and a live Chihuahua, and Jack Carter's orgiastic melodrama *Agrionia*, although much praised, could hardly be taken seriously by any but the most diehard of balletomanes. The company disbanded, leaving us to set off for Paris, where we hoped work on a short-term, freelance basis might be more readily available than in London. Once again, fate played an unexpected role as a few days after arriving in the French capital we were stopped in the street by a Spanish choreographer who had recently seen us performing in London. Juan Corelli was in need of two more dancers for a ballet film he was making for French national television and 'would we be available?'

With Terence Etheridge in Rudi van Dantzig's ballet *Jungle*.

chapter
five

Paris – A Turning Point

Coming to Paris and working with Juan Corelli for French national television proved to be a turning point. Firstly, it was an unexpectedly interesting opportunity to meet and work with two celebrated former collaborators of the Diaghilev Ballet; the composer Henri Sauget and the librettist Boris Kochno. Responsible for so many libretti both for the Diaghilev Ballet and Les Ballets des Champs-Elysées, Kochno had created the TV scenario for *The Prince and the Pauper*, the reconstruction of a traditional story, and Corelli had engaged a very international cast of dancers, with Royal Ballet principal Gary Sherwood taking the dual leading roles. It was a thrilling experience to see Boris Kochno's familiar dome-like head – famous from so many drawings, notably by Picasso and Jean Cocteau, while present at rehearsals with the Ballets Russes – as he now watched our rehearsals. It was also thrilling when he suggested to Sauget to write a small extra piece of music for me to have a solo as a bird. This was done by the next day, and Corelli choreographed a charming short piece which, unfortunately, ended up on the cutting room floor. Corelli was fortunate in finding in the French national television an eager collaborator, and he had already made a series of ballet films by the time we worked with him. In fact, we were able to make three consecutive films, Alexander also working with him as his assistant, leading us to decide to base ourselves in Paris, settling close to Place Clichy and Montmartre with easy access to the all-important ballet studios.

Paris meant one thing for us at this time – ballet classes. There is probably no other profession where training with a teacher is necessary for the duration of one's career. Singers and musicians do continue to work with a teacher or a coach, but this is usually done as private, individual instruction, usually for a specific role or concert. Dancers prefer to work in a classroom setting, together with a group of dancers, under the instruction of a teacher, although, for those who can afford it, private tuition remains irreplaceable. However, the proximity of other dancers lends a camaraderie, be it the challenge of competition or the presence of mutual support, or even allowing the numbers to provide a protective hiding place within which one can work quietly to coax a tired or sore body. We have been extremely fortunate in being active as dancers at a period when there was a remarkable choice of teachers. There were still those who formed a direct link through their own careers to the traditions of the Ballets Russes, to the Diaghilev Ballet, and even to the nineteenth-century ballet in Paris and in Russia. These were followed by the next generation, teachers of the Paris Opera Ballet and the Royal Ballet, who had formed the best dancers of our time. There were also the innovators, those individuals who were discovering new ways of moving, evolving a new ballet technique recognising the developments in contemporary dance, with new methods of teaching prioritising the care of a dancer's body. We owed much to teachers in London, above all Audrey de Vos, Stanislas Idzikowski and Anna Northcote, as well as in later years Eileen Ward and Brian Shaw, who gave open professional classes besides their commitments to the Royal Ballet. However, it was Paris we would choose to come to, between tours, after holidays or simply whenever there was the time.

France and Russia have preserved their long tradition of dance with care; in those countries there has always been the normal transition from performing dancer to teacher, handing down teaching methods and the performing repertoire from one generation to the next. There has also always been an interchange of these between the two; Marius Petipa leaving France to settle in Russia to create the golden era of classical ballet and the migration of a new Russian dance, through Serge Diaghilev's Ballets Russes, to France. As a result of the Russian revolution, western European dance was greatly enriched with the arrival of a generation of Russian dancers in Paris, becoming outstanding teachers. If in the 1960s the state of the Paris Opera Ballet was at an all time low, the standard of the teaching was unbeatable. It was perhaps due to the fact that the Paris Opera Ballet dancers performed only once a week, with obligations to rehearse for just two hours daily, that the open professional classes were packed with some of the best dancers in Europe. Dancers need to dance and if they can't perform enough, they want to do a class.

A few years earlier we had spent our honeymoon in Paris, attending morning classes before setting off on day-long marches discovering the city and its many treasures. Paris was, at this time, a noisy, backward, smelly city despite all its beauty and its interest. The smell of the Metro pervaded every footpath with the pungent, warm air from the underground tunnels and caverns seeping through the grates. The new *'Les Misérables'*, the many *clochards* eking out an existence on the streets of Paris, used these sources of warmth to spend the day, half reclining, half-heartedly begging, most likely drinking, while at night they stretched out covered in layers of grubby, oily clothing to drop into unconsciousness. Descending into the Metro the smells increased with more human ones – mixtures of garlic, red wine, body odour – making one nearly choke while studying the almost incomprehensible maps of the train routes, or squeezing into a packed rush-hour train. The cafes were another good source of odours; the cigarettes, the Gauloises, the Gitanes, burning, weedy smells with exotic overtones of herbs, the rough, sickly smell of the pastis, drunk at bars and bistros across France from about eleven in the morning, while propping up a bar and arguing about the state of the world, the government, or the day's horse races. Then there were the *'pissoirs'* – small areas encircled by a metal shield, covering the man inside from the shoulder to the knee while he urinated publicly – on many street corners and public squares. However, large, graphic notices were painted on the walls of public buildings, stating that urinating and spitting were forbidden on those spots.

In the mid nineteenth century the tall, honey-coloured stone apartment houses which covered Paris from the Bois de Boulogne to the Bois de Vincennes, and from Pigalle to Montparnasse, were elegant, modern buildings housing the newly prosperous city dwellers. By the mid twentieth century the buildings were black with grime, with families packed into three-room apartments, two and three generations, with some sleeping in spaces as small as a broom cupboard, in niches under a staircase, or on a folding bed in the kitchen. Students and single people occupied the attics – tiny, cramped rooms under the sloping eaves, where they might share a washbasin or an electric cooker on the landing. Many apartments had no bathrooms, and many shared a lavatory with their neighbours on a stairwell, or even with the entire block in the dingy courtyard at the rear of the building. The noise was constant; cars hooting and revving while waiting at a traffic light, mopeds screeching to a halt and roaring away along the long, straight boulevards which cross the city in all directions. The noise continued all day and all night, when the traffic noises would be joined by police and ambulance sirens, by trucks collecting rubbish, lorries delivering goods and late home-comers, shouting and laughing along the canyons of the long, narrow streets.

Dancers traditionally stayed in the small hotels in the Montmartre-Place Clichy area because of the proximity to the dance studios. Many of these hotels housed people on a permanent basis, as accommodation in Paris was difficult to come by and expensive. There were still elderly Russians, refugees from the revolution, living in the hotel we frequented in Rue Lecluse, just off the Place Clichy, and there were writers and artists and musicians from all over the world. The rooms were small, washing facilities limited to a washbasin, and although cooking in the rooms was formally prohibited, everyone did so. The proprietor took the precaution of fixing very low amp fuses in the fuse box next to his office, so he could check who was daring to use an electric cooker, or even a hairdryer, as this would plunge several parts of the hotel into darkness. However, many used small cookers, fuelled with methylated spirits which, despite the obvious dangers, must have been tolerated. After a full day of classes and filming, or rehearsals in studios scattered across Paris, we had little patience for fiddling with a spirit cooker, and so were happy to find a choice of restaurants in the area where we could eat for as little as three or four Francs for a three-course meal, a sum just within our budget.

We were fortunate in coming to Paris while we were working, or perhaps between seasons, but there were many would-be professional dancers whose life in Paris was very hard. Work was always sporadic, mostly short term, and not always well paid. Most of the French dancers lived at home, but there were many foreign dancers, Americans, Germans, Dutch, who in order to finance their daily ballet classes had to find work. The men often worked in the Pigalle nightclubs, not finishing until three o'clock in the morning, or even all night at Les Halles, unloading and heaving huge crates of fruit and vegetables through the markets. It was more difficult for the girls and many lived in very difficult conditions, in tiny sixth-floor attic rooms, becoming noticeably thinner by the week. However, they would all be at class at eleven o'clock each morning, and probably do two or three classes daily, especially when the teachers were considerate, perhaps letting them clean the studio in return for tuition.

The dance studios of the Salle Wacker were at 69 Rue de Douai just off the Place Clichy. The street level was occupied by a piano showroom packed with rather dusty grand pianos. On the first floor there were more pianos scattered messily on the large landing and facing one was the restaurant and the noticeboard – the Parisian 'market place' for dancers. Many of the best teachers in Paris had taught here since the 1920s, and until 1960 the Russian ex-ballerina of the Maryinsky Ballet Olga Preobrajenska was the 'star' teacher, having trained generations of dancers, creating many of the most famous. Retiring finally when she was nearly ninety years old, 'Preo' was loyally supported both personally and financially by those dancers and ex-dancers until her death a couple of years later. Her former colleagues from the imperial Maryinsky Ballet in Saint Petersburg, who also settled in Paris to teach, were Lubov Egorova and Mathilde Kschessinkaya, both of whom married Russian princes, and who presumably managed to bring at least some of their wealth from revolutionary Russia with them. Kschessinskaya, a former mistress of Tsar Nicholas II, was the undoubted star dancer of the trio, both beautiful and talented, leaving Russia even earlier to perform both at the Paris Opera Ballet and with Diaghilev's Ballets Russes. Among those teaching at Salle Wacker when we arrived in Paris was Nora Kiss, her aunt Madame Roussanne, and Victor Gsovsky.

The restaurant with its long bar was a traditional meeting place for dancers, in and out of work, as it was for ballet masters, company directors and agents. If you were looking for a job, you could be lucky by the end of the day; you would have found one, either by attending a class, searching the noticeboard or listening in to the latest news over a coffee at the bar. Ballet classes took place all day long, with Madame Nora giving three classes daily as well as pas de deux classes and private lessons. Before continuing further upstairs one was interrogated by a severe looking woman behind a polished wooden counter who needed to be convinced that one was attending a class, and not attempting to use an empty studio without paying. The building was a warren of studios, tiny ones for singers and musicians, the dance studios of varying shapes and sizes. The staircase wound up the centre of the building with lavatories built into the walls between floors. Without any space inside, and lacking a landing outside, it was a battle to flush the traditional 'hole in the ground' and exit before soaking one's feet and losing one's belongings tumbling back down the stairs.

The main professional class at midday was packed with *'étoiles'* from the Paris Opera Ballet, the many freelance dancers in Paris, as well as visitors from abroad. As I already knew Madame Nora from my first visit to Paris, before joining the American Festival Ballet, I was eager to go back to her classes and to introduce Alexander to her. Madame Nora must have left her native Georgia at an early age as she had studied in Paris, notably with Volonine (Pavlova's favourite partner). She had danced with various Ballets Russes companies, including that directed by George Balanchine, after Diaghilev's death. Madame Nora appeared to speak faultless Russian, French,

Italian, German and English, to know everyone in the dance world, and was always au fait with all the latest developments. She was also an indefatigable learner, studying Rudolf Nureyev in performance, the details of his *tours en l'air*, the speed of his arms in a pirouette or his landing after a jump. She would watch gymnasts, skaters or even horses on TV for new insights into the technical problems of jumping or landing or balancing, enticing us to try them out in class the following day. In today's ballet classes, many teachers have abandoned giving corrections; dancers prefer to cover themselves in layers of bulky practice clothing, disguising weak feet, or a bad posture, unwilling to surrender to the scrutiny of a teacher. In Paris, we had little choice: Madame Nora would make fun of a Paris Opera Ballet star, like Attilio Labis, thumping the colossus of a man firmly on the back until he did as she wished, or chase an unwilling Milorad Miskovitch out of the changing room following a heated argument.

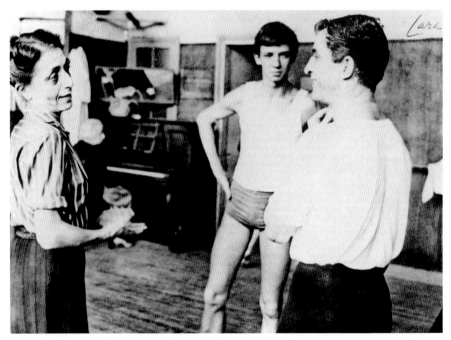

Madame Nora in the studio at Salle Wacker with Maurice Béjart and Patrick Belda, c.1960.

Her classes were long, a good two hours, but basically very simple. Rather than give choreographically interesting enchaînements, she taught how to turn better, how to jump higher and how to improve all of one's skills. Her method was unconventional, and she would surprise one by coming up to one at the barre, while attempting a complicated exercise such as a series of double frappés, interspersed with pliés and relevés, as well as changes of arms and head positions, demanding to know where one was living or if one had seen a certain film or performance. It was a ploy, of course, to stop tension, to make one work without straining the head and shoulders, while using all the necessary strength in the feet and legs. Another 'trick' was to make one sing along with the music while exercising, which, of course, is highly effective at making one relax. At lunchtime she would take up her position at a small table in the first-floor restaurant immediately in front of the main studio entrance. From there she could keep an eye on everyone coming or going, and would challenge any unfortunate who attempted to creep past on their way to another class or audition. She often demanded to know where one had been the previous day, what time one had gone to bed, even what one had eaten the previous evening, and she had suggestions for improvements on all matters. She did also often have serious rows with many of her pupils, and the Paris studios were full of one-time followers of Madame Nora who either did not dare go back to her class or who had sworn never to do so again. It is said that the only time Madame Nora missed a day of classes was when she joined the huge funeral cortege for Edith Piaf which filled the streets of Paris, and whom she did physically resemble.

Another of our favourite teachers was Serge Peretti who taught at the Studio Constant next to the Place Pigalle. Although Italian born, Peretti trained at the Paris Opera Ballet School and at twenty years of age became the first dancer to win the title of *danseur étoile*. He was a real 'star' of the Paris Opera Ballet, creating innumerable roles for director and choreographer Serge Lifar, later becoming *professeur de danse* for the *étoile* dancers of the company. Besides working for the Paris Opera Ballet, he opened his own studio in 1948, with a long list of famous pupils including Yvette Chauviré, Roland Petit, Jean Babilée and Zizi Jeanmaire. The studio owner was Roger Constant, a former cabaret artiste, and adorning the front of the studio building were photos of him in bejewelled briefs, balancing scantily clad girls on his up-stretched hand or on his shoulders, sometimes even with a python wrapped around him, presumably for extra effect. In later years he had become somewhat rotund, toothless and totally bald. However, he still ruled Studio Constant, dressed in tights, with a black jockstrap over the tights, and black leather ankle and wrist bands. He continued to give instruction to would-be acrobats and contortionists, enticed, no doubt, by the studio's proximity to the many cabarets and music halls in the Pigalle district.

Besides Roger Constant, there were a number of colourful characters in the studio; one of Peretti's pianists would arrive red-faced and panting having bicycled across Paris to reach the studio a minute or so before class. She was always accompanied by a large cat which sat in a basket attached to the handlebars, remaining there with the bike in the hallway. Accompanying class she sipped beer from a bottle left on top of the piano, and was able to play with her feet propped up on the end of the keyboard. Among the regulars in Peretti's class was an older dancer who would unpack raw steak from her bag, carefully wrapping this around her toes before stuffing her feet into her pointe shoes. This may have been a trick she learnt from the nearby Pigalle boxing ring.

Several well-known teachers used the Studio Constant but Peretti was the most celebrated. Following his day's work at the Paris Opera he gave two classes at five and at six o'clock – just sixty minutes, but those short classes covered everything, including pointe work for the women, and tour de force with all the most difficult jumps and turns for the men. The dancers were a mixed lot; there were older dancers who had worked with Peretti throughout their careers, professionals doing a second class of the day, as we would, or those using the class as a warm-up before a performance at the Paris Opera or one of the music hall theatres. There were similarities with Idzikowski's class; the barre exercises were always simple, hardly varying from day to day and, most importantly, were done at speed and without pauses. Peretti remained seated throughout most of the class, elegant and even dapper, often with a scarf at the neck and his whitening hair carefully coiffed. He would keep time with a stick, tapping the floor, and when at odds with the pianist, which at times was quite frequently, he would jab the floor noisily to insist on a tempo and in exasperation would lean across to the piano to thump his fists on the keys. In the best tradition of the Paris Opera, he believed the pianist should follow the dancers, especially if the dancer was an *étoile*. He did stand briefly to show some exercises, but would do this only once and was most impatient if a dancer didn't follow immediately. The enchaînements were simple, but with unusual accents, musical dynamics to underline the take off for a jump or the finish of a pirouette. He would pretend to be angry or frustrated at our failure to keep a balance, or finish a pirouette, but he gave a lot of encouragement and many corrections, although one had to be alert to take advantage of those.

I worked with Maître Peretti over a period of about fifteen years, obviously at irregular intervals, and although he never knew my name, he was always welcoming, addressing me as 'Mees English', encouraging me to stay on to do the second class on pointe, and without charge. As with Idzikowski's class, one left the studio hot and sweaty, but with an extraordinary feeling of floating above the ground. We would make our way back along the Boulevard Pigalle and on a summer's evening sit on one of the park benches devouring an ice cream to watch the bustle of the evening rush hour, the multicoloured garish neon lights of the cafes and nightclubs, the parade of people coming and going and think that there was nowhere else in the world we would rather be.

There were also younger teachers making a name for themselves and winning popularity, notably Raymond Franchetti, who while still actively dancing at the Paris Opera was giving classes in the studios of Françoise and Dominique Dupuy, well-known, independent dancers of the time, on Boulevard Pigalle. He taught those very long, slow classes with attention to detail which were to become his trademark when he moved to his own studios in a vast building behind the Moulin Rouge. Franchetti was to become 'the' teacher for professionals from the 1970s, with dancers including Nureyev, Baryshnikov and Makarova in his morning class. He also became director of the Paris Opera Ballet at this time, and he carried all the traditions of the Paris Opera into his studios, including the raked floor – at exactly the same slope as the stage of the Paris Opera – the dressing rooms for *étoiles* and a strict hierarchy as to who stood where, in which line and in which group. If we sometimes felt out of place in Franchetti's class, and he had little interest in foreigners who came and went, we learned an enormous amount and assimilated much of his teaching into our own classes. It was a fascinating insight into the strengths of the Paris Opera Ballet training, simpler and purer than the Russian school, while being stronger and more demanding technically than the English training. The French teachers seemed to produce generation after generation of dancers with perfect physiques and great technical facility; on the other hand, French dancers often lack musicality and genuine expressivity.

A teacher we did have a rapport with was the Russian-born Misha Reznikoff, who had been a dancer with the Marquis de Cuevas company. He gave a daily morning class at Studio Constant, packing the small studio to bursting point. Reznikoff was physically a huge man, which proved useful when space at the barre was at a premium and it became necessary for three or four of us to hang on to him for support while doing the exercises. I have no idea what his background was or how his 'method' came about, but it was interesting and unusual that he commenced with a series of warm-up exercises, using almost modern dance technique, and while being very strengthening the class was also very choreographic. Regular visitors at that time included Zizi Jeanmaire and Roland Petit as well as their protégé, Félix Blaska, who had just started his own small company. It was difficult not to just stand glued to the barre watching the utter perfection of Zizi's legs and feet, but she worked hard and honestly and was at that time starring in a revue at the Casino de Paris. Reznikoff was a very 'hands on' sort of teacher who would prod and push one to bend more, to lift the legs more easily, to jump higher, and much to my amazement, even had me turning four pirouettes on pointe.

At the Paris Opera, ballet performances were given only on a Wednesday, and the repertoire offered little of interest. The star dancers, although prodigious technicians, had little of the quality of the past generation, dancers who included Yvette Chauviré, Nina Vyroubova and Alexandre Kalioujny. The opera house, always known as the Palais Garnier, seemed more like the Sleeping Beauty's palace, stifled in a web of outdated tradition and inactivity. Performances scheduled for 9 p.m. rarely began with less than a twenty-minute delay as it was taken for granted that theatregoers must have a good dinner before the performance, and the advertised starting time seemed more of a guideline than a reality. The first half hour of the performance would then be interrupted by latecomers being shown to their seats with the accompanying hoarse whispers of the usherettes, the jangle of coins for the obligatory 'pourboire' and the shuffle along the rows of seats of fur coats enveloped in a cloud of red wine, garlic and Chanel No. 5.

It was not until Rolf Liebermann came from Hamburg to take over the direction of the Paris Opera in 1973 that changes were made. Among the first things he did was to change the 'Turkish WCs' (the dreaded hole in the ground) both backstage and in the foyers, to modern toilets, and the starting times of the performances to a punctual 7.30 p.m. Naturally, this brought about vehement protest from the Parisians, but earlier performances did catch on, filling the opera with office workers and students besides the traditional theatregoers. Respected and liked as Franchetti was, it is more than probable that Liebermann was responsible for bringing in outside choreographers such as George Balanchine, Jerome Robbins, Merce Cunningham and Carolyn Carlson. He also changed the dancers' working hours from the traditional couple of hours in the afternoon to a full working day, essential if new and demanding works were to be mounted. Even then, there were principal dancers in the company who would tell an international guest choreographer that he, or she, didn't, and wouldn't, do this or that step. With a new generation of highly talented, eager young dancers ready to take their places, the Paris Opera Ballet was finally woken from its long slumber by the mid 1970s.

Even if there was little in the way of dance performances to excite one at the Paris Opera house in the 1960s, there was much else to discover. There were visiting companies such as Jerome Robbins' Ballets USA and the Alvin Ailey American Dance Theatre, from New York, both energetic, exciting and inspiring dance companies. The old Théâtre Sarah Bernhardt had been renovated, the layers of boxes, circles and galleries ripped out and replaced with a broad, open auditorium giving one a perfect view of the wide, clear stage from every seat, and it was renamed Théâtre de la Ville. A programme of modern dance and drama, a foyer with a welcoming cafe and restaurant, a sense of accessibility and openness attracted huge young audiences, we among them. André Malraux, the minister of culture, was the visionary who revived France's ailing cultural life, declaring the historical centre of Paris a historical monument to save it from developers on the one hand, and creating new theatres and a new cultural climate on the other hand. In 1961 he instigated the chain of Maisons de la Culture across France with the aim of attracting interest in art and culture among those who avoided the rather stuffy old municipal theatres and opera houses which were often privately run. However, in Paris there were still many tiny, often rundown, studio theatres giving one the opportunity to experience outlandish productions of works by Samuel Beckett and Alfred Jarry, Ionesco and Sartre.

If we only understood half of what was going on, it was all incomparably exciting, as was the plethora of new films opening every week by Fellini, Antonioni, Pasolini, Godard, Warhol and others. Our favourite cinemas were all on the left bank, tucked away in the tiny, winding streets off the Boulevard Saint Michel. We would walk there, from Montmartre, down the steep hill to the Paris Opera, along the smart streets with the luxury boutiques and jewellery shops to the Palais Royal. Then there was a choice of routes but we favoured a walk along the river to the Place du Châtelet in the shadow of the huge facade of the Louvre and besides the many stands along the riverbank packed with second-hand books, antique books as well as new books, their pages still uncut. We'd cross the bridge to the Ile de la Cité, between Notre Dame and the Palais de Justice, to arrive at the Boulevard Saint Michel in time for a *'menthe à l'eau'* (a dash of a violently green mint *syrop* in a glass of water) before the cinema. After the cinema, on a summer's evening, it was hard to leave the left bank, with the bustle of the cafes, the street performers, the choice of cheap, student restaurants and the general air of well-being. The Metro trip back to Place Clichy would be a stark contrast with the dirty, draughty platforms, the rattling, smelly compartments and an alarming assortment of fellow passengers as well as those hanging around the platforms and the stations, whom we tried best to avoid.

In the summer of 1965 we spent three months rehearsing and filming with Juan Corelli, mostly at the television studios, but also at Théâtre de l'Odéon, and finally at the Château de Sceaux where we danced in the magnificent gardens. On one notable occasion, which is actually very typical of film work, we waited to dance, and to be filmed, from ten o'clock in the morning to eleven o'clock at night when we were finally called to perform our three-minute pas de deux, freezing cold and on the damp, slippery grass. The French unions could not have been very efficient in those days, as I noted in my diary that we had just one coffee break during that marathon day. However, we did not complain as this work was fulfilling a very useful purpose in financing those rehearsals which had already begun for our own company, and for which the first performances were already planned.

A couple of days after the final day of filming at Sceaux, Alexander and I wandered into Salle Wacker to find a row of desolate looking dancers at the long coffee bar. There was only one other occasion when we had seen a similar scene, and this was after the news of the disbandment of the Grand Ballet du Marquis de Cuevas in 1962. Much as dancers had complained at the low wages, the excess work, the over-long tours (don't they always?), this company had provided work for dancers in France for nearly twenty years and it would not be easy to replace. On this August morning in 1965, the news had already got around that Juan Corelli had left Paris overnight after 'complications' with the tax authorities, and that there would be no more television films in the near future. This left the way clear for us to make the final break, to complete plans for an autumn tour with our new company and, most urgently, to continue rehearsals in earnest.

chapter
six

A Company is Born
1965-1968

Paris in August – the city was empty as everyone deserted the stifling town centre for the country, the mountains and the seaside. Butchers and bakers closed their shops, cafes and restaurants struggled with inept students replacing the usual waiters, while the ballet teachers followed their students away from Paris unless they opted to benefit from the influx of foreign dancers who, incomprehensibly for the French dancers, thought that the summer holiday period was a perfect time for some serious study. For us it meant that the rehearsal studios were empty and in the cavernous interior of the Salle Pleyel, above the famous concert hall, were rows of studios on several floors with only a sleepy concierge far below in the marble-columned lobby in charge of bookings. Either he didn't realise, or he simply couldn't be bothered to check on us, but it was possible to book one studio for two hours, and stay for the entire afternoon, even using two or three studios as we needed them. There were five ballets to mount for the new company, and now the filming was completed, we finally had our dancers together. Rehearsals had already taken place during the days between filming, leaving us to rush across Paris from a morning class in Pigalle to the television studios in Boulogne-Billancourt, back again into the city centre to Salle Pleyel, finally finishing rehearsals around seven o'clock, when we would all gather in a local cafe on a warm summer evening, exhausted, dehydrated, aching, but totally elated.

First we had to find a name for the company. It was not to be too serious a name, nothing pompous or pretentious, and the theme of travelling players appealed to us – a company which belonged in any country, in any culture, in any language, free of the pressure of belonging to an institution or an organisation, be it a national one or a commercial enterprise. So International Ballet Caravan was born. There was considerable interest among the Parisian dancers in the new company but it was not easy to find those with whom we could work successfully. Dancers in Paris were used to working on a freelance basis; rehearsals would be unpaid, and arranged according to everyone's availability, with an inclusive fee paid for the performances as and when they occurred.

This meant building up huge bills while they awaited payment, especially with their teachers for daily classes, but these were traditionally helpful, waiting patiently for payment. There was work available elsewhere in France with secured contracts and regular salaries in the many opera-ballet companies scattered throughout the provinces, but Parisian dancers would only leave Paris if there was really no alternative. It was also usual in the smaller companies for dancers to perform their own choice of a classical pas de deux or a short contemporary work, which would, with a couple of rehearsals, be incorporated into a mixed programme. These 'pick-up' companies would be easy and inexpensive to put together and with real stars could still be viable for special occasions, but we knew that to create a new ballet company, we had to work in the manner we were used to from our previous experience in companies across Europe. It was also necessary to find dancers who were prepared to work on the only conditions we could offer, now known as 'profit-sharing', whereby the income from the performances would be shared after deduction of the costs. Naturally, we paid for the rehearsal costs, the scenery and costumes, the publicity material, from our earnings, thanks to the television films, funds which were diminishing all too rapidly.

Among the dancers was Jacotte Bordier, a highly experienced dancer who had worked with the Grand Ballet du Marquis de Cuevas and with other companies in France such as that of Janine Charrat; from Roland Petit's company came Francis Héranger, who also contributed a ballet to the first programme, and Miguel Navarro from the ballet company in Barcelona, both strong technicians and experienced soloists. But best of all, teacher Solange Golovine (of the famous Golovine family of dancers) recommended a young eighteen-year-old who had just graduated from the Paris Opera Ballet School. Muriel Belmondo was the daughter of a famous sculptor and sister of an even more famous film star, and she was eager to work in a company with a new and different approach. With two or three extra dancers on call, we had a company, a tour of twenty-seven performances in Germany, Switzerland and France booked to the end of the year, so we were able to get to work.

Alexander created an opening abstract ballet to a piano and violin sonata by Beethoven which already posed challenges for the dancers, who were unused to unconventional arm or body movements in an otherwise classical work. They tried their best, but when we attempted to remount *Circuit*, a purely contemporary work, this was pushing them too far, and above all, there was not the time available. Alexander therefore set the work for three dancers with Muriel, the most adept at exploring new ways of moving, joining us in a trio. We used another ballet from our recital programme, rearranging *Le Manège* for the full company as a closing ballet. Francis choreographed his ballet, *Nathalie et le Taxi-Bird*, for himself with Muriel, and as we were including a classical pas de deux, this left Alexander with just the major dramatic ballet of the programme to choreograph.

We had planned *The Gentleman Caller* for some time, and had been able to see several versions of Tennessee Williams's play *The Glass Menagerie*, which tells the story of a shy and introverted young woman, a domineering mother reliving a world of memories from her time as a belle in a southern household, and the frustrated brother who is persuaded to bring a visitor into the household, the long-awaited 'gentleman caller'. This visit, instead of providing a hoped-for suitor for the daughter, wrecks the delicate harmony of the family with dramatic results. The work had a meaty, dramatic plot and offered a number of challenging roles. Finding the right music proved difficult, but when, by chance, we heard César Franck's *Piano Quintet* on France Musique, the French classical music radio station, we knew this was the perfect solution. Franck had written the work while he was engaged as a church organist and had fallen passionately, and hopelessly, in love with a married woman. The music, full of drama and yearning, is also superbly danceable. Alexander had just four days of rehearsals left to create the ballet so the tension of the rehearsals was heightened by the effort of keeping up with his choreographic outpouring on one hand, along with the excitement we all felt that we were creating an important work. I have rarely known a ballet to take shape so effortlessly and it was all the more unusual in view of the fact we were a new ensemble working together for the first time.

Our first performances with International Ballet Caravan in 1965, performing *Le Manège*.
We are together here with Muriel Belmondo and Martine Vuillermoz.

It was generally known that the *The Glass Menagerie* was inspired by Tennessee Williams's own family; his sister was considered mentally ill, even undergoing a lobotomy with disastrous results, while he himself escaped the claustrophobic confines of the family home to become a soldier. Many years later new biographers suggested that brother and sister may have had an incestuous relationship, and while working on the ballet, Alexander decided that the failure of the gentleman caller's visit (in the play he is already engaged to be married) would have destroyed the family, leaving them blaming each other and seeking solace in each other. In Alexander's ballet, created before these biographical details were revealed, I, as the daughter, Rose, did lose my mind, bringing the ballet to an end with brother and sister in a violent and intimate pas de deux.

With the programme completed, we set off with the company from Paris in early September in a bright-blue Volkswagen van, squeezed in along with trunks of costumes and props. Francis caused a scare when he ordered us to collect him as well as the scenery for his ballet, a detail which hadn't been expected, and in fact he had a number of small scenery flats which ended up on top of a pile on the roof rack. The first performance was in Bad Wiessee in southern Germany, a Henry James style watering place where those 'taking the waters' promenaded through the immaculate parks and gardens, having drunk several glasses of the foul sulphuric mineral water, and spent the afternoons drinking coffee and eating cream cakes while the local palm court orchestra played in a glassed-in pavilion. As with almost every German spa town, the theatre had a fairly busy programme of concerts, plays, dance performances and entertainments. It was a perfect venue for our beginning; a medium-sized stage, simply but adequately equipped, where we could work undisturbed all day with the first and only dress rehearsal. We suspected the evening performance would also be a relaxed occasion as it was well known that a good number of the audience were likely to nod off, either through age, ill health, or possibly just as a result of a surfeit of fresh air and early morning treatments in the hot waters and mud baths.

Performances in other spa resorts followed, allowing us to enjoy a balmy late summer in southern Germany, as well as venturing into Switzerland; after a week we were ready to tackle the theatres scheduled in the larger cities such as Saint Gallen and Zurich in Switzerland, with their own opera and ballet companies and more discerning audiences. There were very few touring dance companies in Europe at that time. After the demise of the Grand Ballet du Marquis de Cuevas in 1962, and the early tours of companies from France such as Béjart's or Miskovtich's, the American Festival Ballet dominated the market; it had been taken under the wing of a German impresario and, as we had experienced, had toured relentlessly throughout Europe. However, by the mid sixties, touring companies had become a rarity. This offered us a niche to fill, but on the other hand we feared a battle to be taken seriously besides the more established national or regional companies. As far as the press was concerned, we need not have worried, as the company received some marvellous reviews on those early tours – lengthy and detailed criticism, with each ballet and each dancer receiving attention. The German and Swiss audiences were as warm and welcoming as they had been for the *Soirée de Ballet*, when we revisited several venues from our former itineraries.

There was an unexpected and welcome visitor to our performance in Zurich; Nicolas Beriosoff was then director of the resident ballet company and knew us both from London and Paris. 'Papa' Beriosoff, as he was universally known (he was father to the Royal Ballet ballerina Svetlana Beriosova), was one of the busiest dance directors and ballet masters in Europe at that time; he had held positions with numerous companies, including the Stuttgart Ballet, where I had first met him, as well as with London Festival Ballet and the de Cuevas company. During those years before we founded the company, we would inevitably bump into him in the studios in London and Paris, when he would regularly offer us a contract with the company he was directing at the time. It became almost a joke to await our annual offer, knowing that for one reason or another it would come to nothing. On one occasion, he telephoned us at our hotel in Paris asking if we would dance a pas de deux for him the following morning before he left Paris to return to Zurich. His early departure meant 'auditioning' at eight o'clock in the morning in one of the studios at Salle Wacker. This must be the only occasion we have had to dance at that time of the day, and it is definitely not to be recommended. Somehow, we got through the *Don Quixote* pas de deux, despite numb feet and dazed heads, being grateful that only one of the smaller studios was available. 'Papa' offered us a contract for the following season in Zurich; however, on his return there he discovered that the intendant had just engaged a Hungarian tenor and his ballerina wife, exhausting the ballet budget for that year! When we met him after our performance with the company in Zurich, he was enthusiastic about the performance and in his usual solemn and serious way said to Alexander, 'You must just keep going, keep going and you will succeed.' It was simple advice, but something which helped to sustain us during the many struggles which lay ahead.

———

At the end of September we headed back to Paris with a tour of sixteen cities throughout France ahead of us. The first of these was in Toulouse, 700 kilometres from Paris, a very long, sixteen-hour drive on roads which crossed the Massif Central, the Dordogne, finally reaching Toulouse, nestling in the foothills of the Pyrenees. The theatre was a cinema–theatre with a wide if very shallow stage, but a regular venue for touring companies. The first thing I noticed was that the stage floor was scattered with glitter, which could only indicate a recent visit by the Tournées Tichadel, a Parisian music hall company made up of near naked show girls, comedians, a conjuror and probably a group of acrobats. They were extremely popular, especially in southern France, and toured incessantly and repeatedly to the same towns. On the morning of the performance, the theatre looked dark and gloomy, the director dour and incommunicative and the box office seating plan ominously blank. However, our French dancers were happy to be back in France, so optimistically we set up the stage and were ready to start at nine o'clock.

We were used to the erratic system of actually starting a performance in France, especially in the south, where the scheduled time was never taken too seriously. We waited backstage, warmed up again and piled on the woolly tights, pleading with the director to let us start – perhaps she was waiting for a bus-load to arrive or simply hoping that a few more customers might turn up after dinner – until finally we had the go-ahead with the stage manager giving the traditional *trois coups*, pounding the stage floor with a special stick announcing the beginning of the performance. I have no recollection of that first performance, but I do remember the director coming on stage at the end and declaring that the programme as it was would never be successful, that something had to been done about the costumes. We needed feathers, she shouted, and above all, glitter and sequins on all the costumes – without which we would never be a success. Tichadel-on-pointe, no doubt, but we tried to look compliant, hoping that the deficit would not be too much. In the end there were 220 francs to pay to cover the publicity costs and the next day we fled from Toulouse swearing never to return.

A performance in nearby Auch was scheduled for the next day, which we had booked despite knowing it was a very small town, but in the hope that an extra performance might make the long trip more viable. Auch is typically southern; at that time it was a sleepy, dusty, rundown small town boasting a very small *théâtre municipal*. Before even looking for the stage door, we checked the state of the bookings at the box office. Not a single ticket had been sold. There was also no evidence of any of our posters having been distributed, not even one in front of the theatre, no photos, no sign that anything had been done to prepare the residents of Auch for our arrival. The box office manager, who was also the theatre caretaker and cleaner, produced a bill for a newspaper advertisement, which apparently had appeared in the local paper, suggesting we pay this and cancel any plans to give the performance. This seemed the wisest decision so we headed back to Paris, a trip which took us all that night and the following day, with the dancers taking it in turns to stay awake and to sing in canon 'Frère Jacques' and 'Sur le Pont d'Avignon' to keep Alexander, who was at the wheel, awake and alert.

Things could only get better, and fortunately they did, with visits to towns we already knew from our recital programme, and others which became regular venues during the years ahead. Perhaps the highlight of the tour was a performance in Marseille, where Joseph Lazzini, having cancelled his evening rehearsal, came to our performance accompanied by all the dancers of the Marseille ballet company, giving us a wonderfully encouraging reception.

The tour finished in December, a week before Christmas when we left Paris for London. There must have been some time during that hectic period when a decision was made; a decision to return to London where, in fact, we still had an apartment from our time with the London Dance Theatre. To base the company there in a climate which could be easier, kinder and more familiar than that of Paris and France of the 1960s seemed appealing. Most of our French dancers had other plans for the New Year, and it was obvious that they could not continue to exist on the meagre earnings from those early tours. They had been wonderfully cooperative and enjoyable to work with, but Alexander felt the need to find dancers with whom he could work on a more permanent basis and more creatively. (Of our 'French' dancers, Muriel Belmondo went on to make the most successful career, as principal dancer with the Ballet Théâtre Contemporain and other contemporary groups which were emerging in France at that time, and later became director of classical dance at the Paris Conservatoire.)

Besides all the performances and the thousands of kilometres we travelled, we had managed to keep up correspondence with theatres and agents making some plans for the following year. Christmas was not the best time to find new dancers for the company in London but we had already found our first English dancer, a girl from Anna Northcote's studio, Lissa Kidson, who had once been Anna's prize pupil and had since worked professionally in Germany and in France. Domy Reiter, the Israeli-born dancer with whom we had worked in London Dance Theatre, joined us, as well as a young German, Alexander Hoffmann, who had turned up in Berlin to take my classes there in 1964. This period was also the beginning of our association with the British Ballet Organisation, whose studios in West London we were able to use.

Edward Kelland-Espinosa, always known as Eddie, was one of the unsung heroes of England's independent ballet companies, as he put his studio at the disposal of Western Theatre Ballet in its very beginnings and then London Dance Theatre, in which he took a personal interest. Eddie came from a famous family of dancers and dance teachers; his Spanish-born grandfather, having been trained at the Paris Opera Ballet, became a dancer with the Bolshoi Ballet before settling in London to open a ballet school. His son Edward continued the tradition; Ninette de Valois was one of his pupils, and he was also one of the founders of the Royal Academy of Dancing, and later in 1930, of the British Ballet Organisation. Eddie, his son, became chairman of the BBO, settling in the elegant mansion in Barnes which is still the headquarters of the organisation, while spending his professional life in musicals and variety, specialising in choreographing and producing Christmas pantomimes.

The studio was in a former conservatory with a glass roof and huge glass windows looking into the garden, baking hot in summer and freezing in winter, with a rough, slippery, wooden floor. The walls of the studio were covered from the floor to the ceiling with photos of generations of the Espinosa family as well as the stars they had worked with, all generously autographed; there were cards and letters from celebrities in the theatre world and, in prize positions, letters and telegrams from the royal family congratulating the Espinosas on their birthdays and other important occasions. If it was not perfect – the irresistible distraction of the wall coverings being the most difficult to cope with – it was, in its way, 'home' and it was free. All Eddie asked for in return was for us to perform at the annual BBO congress when the studio would be packed with teachers gathering in London from the provinces and even from the Commonwealth; these would spend a week in meetings, conferences and demonstrations, culminating in a final afternoon with a mini performance. This would include a couple from the Royal Ballet dancing a pas deux, possibly Brenda Last to perform the 'doll' dances from *Coppélia*, while some of our dancers would perform an excerpt from the company's repertoire.

After a month of rehearsals our new company set off for a two-month tour, in a new, more comfortable minibus, to perform in France, Germany and Austria. Alexander choreographed *Capriccio* to Hugo Wolf's *Italian Serenade*, a slight and zany play with movement built around the talents of the four new dancers. It was now possible to guarantee salaries, albeit modest ones, as earnings from the performances were consistently improving. We had also won the interest of a Parisian impresario who offered us a month-long tour in France during the summer, the German agent who had toured the American Festival Ballet had proposed an autumn tour of Germany, and a London agent was showing signs of interest in bringing us to the UK.

However, there was a long gap with no performances ahead, and Alexander and I were glad to be offered the possibility of appearing with the Harlequin Ballet, a London-based company, for a tour of the UK. We were to replace former London Festival Ballet principals Belinda Wright and Jelko Yuresha as guest artists, performing with the company in *Swan Lake* and *Chopiniana* as well as dancing the pas de deux from *Don Quixote* and *The Nutcracker*. The opening performances were at the Theatre Royal in Bath, a lovely Georgian theatre in a pleasant city, and if this was our first daunting experience of dancing eight performances a week, as is usual in the UK, it augured well for the tour. This continued to Cheltenham, with another attractive theatre, then Bognor Regis and other coastal cities from where one could still return to London each night.

A tour of Scotland, and performances in Rotherham, Barnsley, and Bridlington followed, where we had our first taste of real British touring life. In the early spring, these theatres appeared to be unheated; gaps in the dock doors at the rear of the stage would allow gales from the North Sea or the Yorkshire moors to whip through onto the stage; the 'digs', the famous theatrical bed-and-breakfast lodgings, were grimy, smelly and very cold. In Rotherham, our landlady, who like most dictated that breakfast would be served only from 7.30 a.m. to 8.10 a.m., was worn and weary; she looked out with us on to the rows of workers' houses – 'two up and two down' – stretching in long, narrow roads weaving their way towards the belching chimneys and steaming cooling towers of the iron or steel works. 'Ay, we're lucky to have the works,' she sighed, probably having lost a father and a husband to bronchitis, or worse, and now eking out a living in the smoke and the dust and the dirt of the industrial north of the 1960s.

The Harlequin Ballet was run by John Gregory and his wife, Barbara

Vernon, former dancers and teachers eager to carry on the tradition of Russian ballet master Nicolai Legat. The company was made up of a number of student dancers with about six or seven professionals, performing a mixed repertoire of small-scale versions of the classics, some contemporary ballets and Russian folk dance. At that time, with some support from the Arts Council of Great Britain, they were obtaining more and better engagements. Eager to add more contemporary works to their repertoire, as indeed was expected of them by the Arts Council, Alexander was asked to contribute a ballet, so he mounted *Capriccio* (retitled *A Little Nothing*), and created a new ballet, *Passing Encounter* (which the company called *Jump Over The Moon*) to the *Serenade for Strings* by Lennox Berkeley. Both were first performed when the company appeared in London at the end of the tour, when we also appeared in a new duet to music by Carl Maria von Weber. Harlequin Ballet continued to perform both ballets for several years, but we were glad when, in June 1966, we could resume our own rehearsals for the summer tours which lay ahead.

Performing in the holiday resorts of France and Switzerland was always an agreeable way to spend the summer, but as these were often located either by the sea or in the mountains, the logistics of criss-crossing Europe on secondary roads was both complicated and exhausting. The Parisian impresario Raymond Duchemin had booked us a month of performances in the French casino theatres; towns such as Vittel, in the centre of France, Chamonix in the French-Swiss Alps and Cauterets in the Pyrenees were lively, elegant resorts, attracting both people wanting to take a 'cure' as well as those more interested in gambling. All had theatres; some beautiful, ornate mini opera houses, while others were in dire need of restoration and modernisation. The directors, no doubt seasoned by dealing with awkward situations arising at the gambling tables, as well as the notoriously badly behaved variety stars of the time, were mostly very tough and very autocratic. Performances started on the dot, we were allowed no longer than a two-minute pause between ballets, and an hour-long interval was obligatory so the members of the audience could use the gambling rooms. In return, free accommodation in the luxury hotels which adjoined the casinos, and often free meals, were offered, so we did not complain and got used to the very long evenings.

An extra performance was added to the schedule when we took part in an open-air festival in Geneva. As was mostly the case, due to the lengthy drive, we did not arrive at the theatre, in a park in central Geneva, before mid afternoon. The open-air stage meant we needed no scenery, but, as was usual, the rest of the day was spent setting up, doing class and rehearsal then finally getting ready for the performance. Storms clouds had been threatening through the afternoon, but no one had taken these too seriously and the audience started to arrive about half an hour before starting time. The rains started unexpectedly and in torrents, leaving us amazed to see the impresario bundling the costumes and the dancers into a coach while shouting to us, the only people remaining, that we should make for the *patinoire* – the skating rink! Not knowing Geneva at that time, we had no idea how or where we should find the *patinoire*. Leaning out of the window of our minibus in costume and full stage make-up, pleading for instructions, we left most people in the street speechless, but somehow, and quite by chance, we pulled up right in front of the *patinoire* to see hundreds of people pouring into the huge building. Apparently, it was a common event in lakeside Geneva to have open-air performances washed out, so without warning us the *patinoire* had been made ready, the lighting rig adapted, and not only the audience but a full crew of technicians were ready in what was a huge auditorium with a wonderfully big stage. Alexander and I had just fifteen minutes to get ready but we were all greeted by a huge shower of applause when the performance got underway.

Monsieur Verleye was an elderly and very senior Swiss impresario, responsible for bringing the greatest artists to Geneva. He knew how 'green' we were, and must have sensed it all the more when his offer of one hundred pounds for the performance was accepted without hesitation. A guaranteed fee to perform in Geneva seemed to us at the time a dream come true, and we were more than happy with the deal. In the interval Monsieur Verleye came rushing into the dressing room. *'Un succès, Monsieur Roy, un succès, formidable!'* he declared and embraced Alexander warmly. It was a success too, we got some good reviews, and a hundred pounds, while Monsieur Verleye got not only the income from the thousand tickets sold but also a subsidy from the city for the festival. However, he did invite us back to Geneva on several occasions so I think we might have got 'even' with him by the time he ceased working.

The new season, 1966–67, started with a lengthy tour of France, Switzerland and Germany, while in December we gave our very first performance in Britain, in the tiny but exclusive Rosehill Theatre just outside Whitehaven in Cumbria. This bijou theatre was designed for the owner, Sir Nicholas Sekers, the millionaire Hungarian-born owner of Sekers Fabrics Ltd, by the theatre designer Oliver Messel. Arriving at the theatre in the early evening, after a marathon drive from London, we found the auditorium glowing in gold paint, with tiny rose red silk chandeliers lighting the theatre manager, Anthony Phillips (later director of the Brighton Festival), seated at the piano, playing Bach. It was a unique and unexpected sight, one, we were soon to find out, not typical of English provincial theatres.

By now we were under contract to a London-based agent who had recently come to prominence introducing Nederlands Dans Theater and the Joffrey Ballet from New York to London. This seemed to be the answer to all our prayers; to be free of the work of finding bookings and organising tours, and be able to concentrate on the artistic side of performing and running the company. The agent booked a short season in London, in order to introduce the company to the British press, at the Questors Theatre in Ealing. The theatre had been used by other smaller dance companies, but it was amateur run, which meant that the technical 'crew' were only available at the end of their normal working day. This left us working through the entire night before our Tuesday opening and without technical staff of our own, Alexander and I spent the night with the initially keen, but inevitably weary, crew. It did not help that nothing was prepared; every lamp had to be hung into position, the bulbs needed replacing, every cable and its matching plug seemed to be missing, and each piece of colour filter had to be cut to size.

Ominously, it was a situation to be experienced over and over again in British theatres, professional theatres too, and one which made touring so much more difficult than on the Continent. In France and Germany the theatres were mostly council or city run, properly funded, with permanent technical staff on regular salaries. These theatres were almost always clean and well looked after, while backstage all the stage and the lighting equipment was well maintained and ready for use. Crews wanted to work quickly and efficiently, whereas so often in the UK they were paid by the hour, making it in their interest to spin out the day's work, which they so often did, finally being ready just half an hour before the performance. In a busy touring theatre this left little time for cleaning or maintenance, and an overwhelming sense of struggling to manage at all seemed to dominate their lives.

For the performances in London we now had a company we could feel confident with. Among the leading dancers was Leo Guerard, an American dancer from the School of American Ballet, a member of American Ballet Theatre, and later of the de Cuevas company in Europe. Highly competent and experienced, he was an asset to the company, becoming a long-term member. Susan Weldon was an attractive dancer who had been a member of Gore's London Ballet, Joanna Banks came from Ballet Rambert, and Sylvia Kim was another American who had worked with Antony Tudor. The press

In *The Gentleman Caller*, taken in performance at the Questors Theatre, London, in 1967.

On Tour in the 1960s.

came out to Ealing in their numbers. If Alexander was still so groggy from our all-night activities coping with the lighting, the sound, and everything else, to dance the choreography of the coda instead of that of his solo in the *Don Quixote* pas de deux, everything went well enough to win praise from the 'heavyweights' including the critics Alexander Bland, Clive Barnes and A.V Coton. It was particularly rewarding that *The Gentleman Caller* won some serious praise with comparisons with choreographers Gore and Jooss.

Following a two-month tour in France, British touring started in earnest with a week in each of Plymouth, Salford, Stoke-on-Trent and a short visit to Rotherham. It was a gruelling and depressing month, and the conditions in the northern cities where the dirt, the filthy air, the overriding gloom caused by the poverty, and general dilapidation of the cities, made us feel physically ill. Dancing four and five ballets each performance, the strain of eight performances weekly in difficult conditions on such a small company was heavy.

It was then with a sense of relief that we set off for a two-week season in Dublin to play at the famous Gate Theatre. The Gate had been founded by the actors Micheál MacLiammór and Hilton Edwards in the 1920s, and at its peak was considered as important as the Moscow Art Theatre. Both actors were English born but Micheál, in particular, who spoke fluent Gaelic, for many years denying his English background, had become Irish by choice, and they considered themselves to belong to Dublin and to Ireland. Micheál was then enjoying huge international success with his one-man show *The Importance of Being Oscar*, a character well suited to his own flamboyant, Wildean personality, but fortunately he was in Dublin during our season there. We immediately liked Dublin; it seemed lively and almost Continental, at least in the city centre around the theatre where there were restaurants still open after the performance. Despite the rather lackadaisical management, we also felt comfortable with The Gate; it felt like a 'real' theatre, although it had never been used for dance before. Whether it was for this reason or because of the relentless rain which fell in torrents day and night, there was great difficulty in attracting decent audiences. Perhaps it was just that laid-back Irish temperament which meant audiences waited until the reviews were out, until word of mouth had got around, before coming, and in fact by the end of the second week the theatre did fill up, alas too late to make the visit financially viable.

On the second day of our stay, the theatre manager rushed into the dressing rooms to warn us that Micheál was on his way to see us. 'Don't be alarmed by the make-up,' he gasped but Micheál was already behind him, pancake and blue eyeshadow all too visible. However, he was a charming and lovable person, and during our stay 'The Boys', as they were generally known, were

127

generous with their hospitality. After the final performance they invited us all to dinner at their home, and we were seated at a huge table with Micheál in a prop throne borrowed from *Hamlet* or *King Lear* at the head of the table. We were entertained with their reminiscences and stories; it was said that Micheál 'spoke with wit and fluency in every European language', which may have been an exaggeration, but the stories rolled sonorously and entertainingly off his tongue while Hilton busied himself with the housekeeper and our dinner. At the end of the meal, as we all made our way to the sitting room, Micheál and Hilton managed to ensnare Alexander in the dining room, where he needed all his skills as a dancer to escape the clutches of those two wily old queens, trying to trap him between them like a sandwich!

That summer, besides the now usual Continental tour, we spent four weeks performing in the London parks under the auspices of the Greater London Council. It seemed a risky prospect to trust the London weather for a whole month, but that summer of 1967 must have been an exceptional one as it stayed fine and dry, just when we would have welcomed a respite from the relentless eight performances weekly. For the week in Holland Park, the most prestigious of the venues, the company was augmented with guest artists Marilyn Burr and Jean Paul Comelin, from London Festival Ballet. It seemed by now that the relationship with our British agent was working well, shown by the fact that the annual number of performances had increased from the initial sixty to one hundred and sixty in 1966–67. However, the fees from the British performances were so low, and the loss made in Dublin serious enough, to have brought us into financial difficulties, difficulties which we, and the agent, believed we would resolve during the following season.

Of all the theatres we visited during those early tours of Britain, possibly the most inspiring for us was the Victoria Theatre in Stoke-on-Trent. The theatre was created in a former cinema in 1961 by the visionary theatre director, Stephen Joseph, and the manager and director, Peter Cheeseman. Their aim was to form a true community theatre with a permanent company of actors, playwrights and directors working and performing in what was then a revolutionary concept, a theatre-in-the-round. Stephen Joseph was to move to Scarborough where a successful theatre bearing his name still exists, while Peter Cheeseman, a former actor turned director, built up the theatre in Stoke, always underfunded, constantly run on a shoestring, but with a faithful following of local people, producing seasons of successful plays, often written by local writers. Cheeseman was of the era of theatre directors who spent their lives in the theatre, working as actors and directors before taking over the running of a theatre, so different from today's 'chief executives' who have university degrees in business management, or possibly arts administration, and to whom the sole objective is 'bums on seats', at any cost.

When our London agent suggested our visiting the theatre, he queried anxiously if we may be 'compromising our integrity' in playing in such unconventional surroundings. There had never been any dance in the Victoria Theatre, while we had never performed in-the-round, but the idea was appealing as it was very much in line with recent events we had been witnessing in the theatre – the opening of The Roundhouse and the Open Space in London as well as the Théâtre du Soleil in Paris. We played for a week of eight performances at the 'Vic', dancing the classical *Don Quixote* pas de deux to all four sides, with some difficulty. Alexander managed to jump the twelve entrechat six in his solo while revolving in a circle and I did the same with the fouettées in the coda which upset all the usual tricks of 'spotting', or fixing one's gaze on one particular spot with each of the continuous turns, to help overcome dizziness. But we enjoyed the immediacy of the contact with the audience in works such as *Circuit* and *Le Manège*, and noticed with amazement that members of the audience returned two and three times to see us, an event which was, apparently, quite common at the 'Vic'. Although we had to admit that dance could only be performed really successfully in such a setting with works choreographed specifically to be looked at from four different angles, it was an interesting lesson in control, when a spectator is just a leg's length away, and in understatement, when every emotion is as close as across a table.

Everyone employed in the theatre had multiple jobs; it was the custom at that time that actors starting out on their careers in the theatre would also work as assistant stage managers, ASMs, leaving them busy backstage, helping with scene changes when not on stage, and spending long weekends working through the night with the 'get-out' of one production and the 'fit-up' of the following week's play. In Stoke the office staff also helped out backstage so we soon made friends with a young man from the publicity office; Chris Meredith had never acted but was drawn to the policy and aspirations of the theatre, enjoying his work there. He came to visit us again when we played in Manchester when we sensed that he was eager for some adventure and to see more of the world.

It was therefore agreed that Chris should join us for the following season as a general assistant, administrative and technical. We were living in Holland Park at that time in one of the magnificent white stucco four-storey houses which back on to the park but which at that time had deteriorated into a warren of bedsits. An extra room had been rented to serve as an office, an attic room where Chris soon settled in. A skylight gave him access to the roof, and during the summer days he could be found perched outside on the rooftop, brewing Turkish coffee in a small copper pot while listening to Haydn string quartets and clattering away on his portable Olivetti. The main drawback was the lack of a telephone. It was extremely difficult to get a telephone line at that time, with a waiting list at least a year long, leaving us with no alternative but to share the payphone on the second-floor landing with the rest of the house. Fortunately, there were very few other residents at home during the day so the jangle of the telephone would bring Chris leaping two and three steps at a time to arrive panting on the second floor to receive a long-awaited call from a theatre director. An even greater problem was to have enough coins on hand and to try to disguise the inevitable clang of them falling into the box when making calls.

About this time it became apparent that things were not working out with our London agent. The huge increase in bookings for that first year were, to a great extent, due to the number of Continental bookings we had handed over to him on signing up the exclusive contract. As time went on, these dwindled while the increasing number of British bookings brought us into ever smaller venues and with unacceptably small fees. We were perform-ing in civic centres, school halls and town halls, touring for regional arts associations in the south-west and the Pennines, with the occasional treat of a visit to repertory theatres such as those in Derby or Manchester. While the major British companies, Sadler's Wells Royal Ballet, London Festival Ballet and Ballet Rambert, toured annually to the 'Number 1' theatres in the bigger cities, it appeared that the only openings for a company of our size were in very small venues or in towns without a 'real' theatre. The middle ground did not exist; even theatres which could have been suitable were occupied by the very busy repertory companies which offered just one week a year for visiting companies. We were to wait until the 1980s and 1990s for a chain of modern, well-equipped theatres, seating 600 to 900 spectators which were our 'natural' venues. Touring in those small and ill-equipped halls it was difficult to attract good, experienced dancers, and impossible to create interesting and challenging new works to add to the repertoire.

The terms of our contract did not allow us to approach theatre directors ourselves, but matters came to a crisis, and it became clear that we could not carry on as we were. It took a couple of weeks of haggling for our agent to finally agree to hand back to us the responsibility of the foreign bookings. The crisis came to a boiling point in the spring of 1968, on a Friday – a payday. We had simply run out of money, leaving us with no means of raising enough for the week's salaries. While the company rehearsed at the BBO studios, I paced up and down at Holland Park considering all the options. I found my-self facing the mantelpiece looking at the beautiful porcelain statuettes bought in Dresden during our tour of East Germany when we had a surplus of East German marks, and were thrilled to find these charming figurines in an antique shop. I considered if it should be the blue and white troubadour playing a mandolin, or the delightfully entwined salmon pink and white Columbine and Pierrot. Deciding I could get more for the latter, I carefully wrapped it in tissue paper and set off for the antique shops in nearby Portobello Road. The 'crisis' was solved for that week but it was clear that we would have to lay off the company during the summer when there were no bookings at all, while the following autumn season was far from satisfactory.

Our agent was a 'gentleman agent', not one of those chain-smoking, deal-clinching, multi-tasking West End impresarios, but the owner of a bijou house in a quiet Chelsea street where his ground floor office looked over a well-kept garden. He negotiated our fees in guineas rather than pounds and his large polished desk was empty apart from the photos of his wife and daughter and a diary. There was no sign of any papers, books or files but we were amazed to see that these were all kept under the seat of a leather sofa in considerable disarray. Several afternoons were spent in Chelsea arguing our case, and attempting to free ourselves from the three-year contract to which we were committed; Chris was also involved, typing out our notes scribbled in the bus, backstage, anywhere we had a free moment, and three-page letters full of accusations and incriminations went flying back and forth, to and from Chelsea on a daily basis. It was no one's fault, and once again, we were impatient, and had been as unaware of conditions in Britain at the time as the agent was inexperienced in foreign business. His solution of disbanding the company between tours and performances, as was the usual procedure, was also totally unacceptable for us. Finally, we came to an agreement to terminate the contract at the end of 1968, following a couple of gruelling tours through the islands and highlands of Scotland where we existed on tea and sandwiches for a full month, and in the Mid-Pennines where our lighting effects caused the almost derelict lighting board of the town hall to crash, plunging with it large areas of Oswaldtwistle into total blackness.

Unexpectedly, an offer came for Alexander to appear, as a dancer, at the Glyndebourne Festival Opera in a new production of *Eugene Onegin* choreographed by Pauline Grant, and he was able to bring with him two or three of our dancers. Working at Glyndebourne is always a prestigious engagement; it gathers together the best conductors and directors with the cream of young, talented, international singers. The opera company, founded in 1934 at the manor house of John Christie in the Sussex countryside, was initially a refuge for musicians, singers and conductors fleeing Nazi persecution. The annual festival soon became not only an important musical event but also a major occasion of the London season, bringing patrons in evening dress and attracting enough financial patronage to assure its continuing existence.

Working conditions, although pleasant, were disciplined to the point of being military; rehearsals started without a minute's delay, lunch breaks were kept to a minimum and should a rehearsal room not be available, Pauline Grant would continue, unperturbed, rehearsing the dancers on the immaculately kept lawns. Performances always start mid afternoon at Glyndebourne, with a two-hour interval, to allow the audience to enjoy champagne picnics in the grounds, a practice which must pose problems for the singers, as it does for the dancers, necessitating continual warm-ups. However, this filled a summer season successfully while Chris and I worked on booking performances for the new 1969 season, when we would be back where we felt happiest – on our own, and independent.

chapter seven

Exploring and Expanding
1969-1973

Asked where he came from, it is said that Socrates replied, not that he came from Athens, but that he came 'from the world'. We could also say, in a more diffident way, that we felt we belonged to the world, even that the world belonged to us. Crossing the Channel and setting off along the endless grey ribbon of a road stretching across Europe always released a great sense of freedom; problems and worries disappeared, anxiety about the forthcoming tour were non-existent, reservations as to the strength of the company seemed unnecessary. Driving through France, almost elated with confidence that everything was possible, or achievable, we were also engrossed in observing the changing landscapes; the wide, fertile fields of northern and central France, where one could watch the seasons changing, through times of ploughing and sowing, crops swelling and ripening until the harvest time, mostly under a baking summer sun. Without a motorway, the road wound through towns and villages, where we saw the cafes crowded with early morning workers, the market traders setting up their stalls and goods.

We drove through medieval gateways, passed chateaux and fortresses and watched housewives polishing their front door steps or scrubbing their washing in the communal wash houses.

Sometimes, we fought our way through the larger towns and cities, where traffic rushed and screeched, the drivers hooted their horns while shouting with impatience; at night when the shutters were firmly closed, the houses were silent and dark, the cobblestones glistening in the glow of the street lights. The Route Nationale 7, the longest, busiest road in France at that time, stretched from Paris to Marseille, and it was halfway, in Lyon, that the countryside changed dramatically, and one knew that one had reached 'the south'. South of Lyon today, the motorway is packed with trucks battling past oil refineries, chemical plants and gas works; the sky seems heavy with the foul air, and grey with misty cloud. In the 1960s and 1970s, the south opened out after crossing Lyon with a rocky, dry landscape, but the sky was a brilliant cobalt blue and the air seemed soft and sweet. Spring came early in February with mimosa and almond blossom, while the summer seemed to go on and on well into the northern European autumn.

The French tours were also the dancers' favourites; they enjoyed performing in the nineteenth-century opera houses which offered good-sized stages, some beautifully restored, although at that time others were in dire need of renovation. Alexander and I were grateful for the generous number of stage crew always available, and if the two-hour obligatory lunch break extended an already long day (performances never began before nine o'clock), they usually worked fast and efficiently.

The greatest problem was with the still almost archaic technical facilities, especially the lighting systems. Theatres were by now acquiring modern stage lamps to complement the older rows of battens of coloured globes, but the lighting boards were technically half a century behind the British ones. These boards often had a hundred or so dimmers, or levers, a foot long to operate the individual lamps. Resembling nothing less than a Heath Robinson contraption, they could stand two metres high, stretching over an entire wall, often three metres long. There were ways of locking these levers onto wheels at the end of the row, even ways of bringing some lamps up while other would roll down or off. But it needed a team of trained electricians to operate, so the preferred method seemed to be to use a broom stick to push multiple levers up or down. Obviously, our ever increasing use of stage lighting effects meant long, tedious lighting rehearsals, but the ever present possibility that the *chef éclairagiste*, along with the *chef machiniste*, the chief electrician and the stage manager, would arrive for the performance that evening with a bottle of wine tucked under each arm left one unsure of the ultimate outcome.

Another problem was the lack of communication between the stage manager, the electricians and the stagehands during a performance. In the UK, as in Germany, these were mostly linked by earphones and an intercom system, or at least with a system of buttons and lights – 'red' for 'stand by' and 'green' for 'go' – to give orders for lighting changes, scene changes or to open or close the curtain. In France, at that time, we often relied on hoarse whispers to the electricians, who were usually perched on a gallery above the stage manager's desk, a system of semaphore-like signals to the stagehands to warn of a scene change and, worst of all, a loud buzzer to the stagehand, squashed into a corner in the flies high above the stage, who was delegated to open and close the house curtain. As he could see little of the stage from that bird's-eye-view, he would probably have dropped off during the perform-ance, but the ringing tone would bring him to literally leap a couple of feet into the air, grab the thick rope in front of him and use his body weight as a counterweight to lower or lift the huge red velvet curtain. It also warned the audience that applause would shortly be expected. Amazingly, things usually did run smoothly, probably just because the technicians were used to working that way, but also because they had retained an interest in their work. For the dancers the long trips and the long days were, of course, helped along by the excellent food; in fact, the French tours were usually referred to as the *tournées gastronomiques*', and in many ways the company felt most at home during those early tours of France.

We started the new year of 1969 with a mammoth three-month tour of France and Switzerland, followed by a month in Germany where we visited a number of major theatres and opera houses – Bamberg, Baden-Baden, Nuremberg and Saarbrücken among them. It seemed advisable to include live music in these performances, and we were lucky in finding an excellent trio which included a brilliant young American cellist, Gayle Smith, who had been replacing renowned British cellist Jacqueline du Pré in the concerts she was forced to cancel due to her ill health. Performing in these major German theatres and opera houses was certainly the biggest challenge the company had experienced to date. The opera house in Saarbrücken is an enormous theatre, built by Goebbels, Hitler's minister of culture, in a typically bombastic style. That in Nuremberg is similar, while theatres in cities such as Bamberg and Baden-Baden, with a rich musical background, were packed with expectant audiences.

Our modest van would be unloaded in ten minutes by a crew of twenty technicians, huge men in dungarees sporting leather belts hung with tools of every description, and our meagre belongings were certainly the object of much suspicion. We were just seven dancers and three musicians to fill the vast open spaces of those stages, and to cause even more wariness, we insisted on keeping the full width and depth of the stages, creating a stage within in a stage with varying lighting effects. The performance opened with Gayle, seated alone, centre stage, cradling her cello and playing movements from Bach's suites for unaccompanied cello. The dancers entered one by one, gathering around her, one seated, another kneeling, someone warming up discretely, leading us into the opening ballet, *Suite for Dancers*, danced to a trio by Carl Maria von Weber. Perhaps it was the simplicity, almost purity, of the presentation which appealed to the German audiences, but in any case the performances won a string of exemplary reviews, long and detailed ones, while there was always rewardingly warm applause from the ever-generous German audiences.

Suite for Dancers, performed on tour in Germany in 1969.

It was also during this tour that Alexander managed to complete a new ballet, *Nepentha*, using music by the British pop group Procol Harum. Living in London in the late 1960s, it was inevitable that we would be influenced by the tumultuous events that were taking place all around us. 'Swinging

London' brought innovation in film, fashion, literature and also in music, dance and the theatre. It was youth orientated, dynamic in its optimism and ruthless in breaking down barriers of conventionalism. *Nepentha* was a lively ballet, almost athletic in its movement, but it was also a social comment, involving a bowler-hatted city gentleman surrounded by the youth of 'new' London, intoxicated by their music and the readily available drugs, hedonistic and sexually carefree. However, instead of creating a new world based on love and peace, *Nepentha* warned that the City gent and all he stood for would ultimately survive, leaving the youngsters little alternative but to return to a more conventional way of life, which would continue despite all the uproar. The bowler hats did disappear but the importance of the City gentlemen has not! Alexander danced the role of the bowler-hatted gentleman and the principal female lead was danced by a newcomer Alexander had discovered in Anna Northcote's studio a year earlier. Prue Sheridan was just eighteen, having recently left the Arts Educational School in London. She was still carrying some puppy fat, was decidedly rough and unfinished but had attracted his attention with her intensity and very individual style of move-ment. By the time she danced *Nepentha* she had slimmed down and was proving to show real 'star' quality. Prue stayed with the company for sixteen years, always a reliable and often exciting performer, as well as developing as an original choreographer.

Nepentha was soon followed by an even more ambitious work, which we teasingly called *The (Immoral) Story of a Small Town and the Visit of an Old Lady*, claimed by the critics to be the longest title in ballet. Alexander had always been fascinated by Friedrich Dürrenmatt's play *The Visit*, called in German *The Visit of an Old Lady*. It is a story of the corruption of power and riches, and how these can be used to destroy. Heavy stuff for a ballet! How-ever, it offered me a meaty role as the young girl who is banished from her home village after being seduced by a local man, and who returns many years later having become the richest woman in the world to claim her revenge. Alexander put together a sound collage in place of a musical score, while we included some verse by an American poet, Walt Christopher Stickney, who had attached himself to the company; Walt Christopher had followed us around from venue to venue, even finishing up sleeping as a watchman in the rehearsal premises. His poetry, which I bravely declaimed from stage while dancing, was reminiscent of Gertrude Stein's, and with the poet himself racing down the aisle to throw flowers onto the stage, it all seemed extremely daring and exciting.

By this time, I had assumed another role in the company; that of a light-ing designer, and in line with the psychedelic taste of the day, boisterously flooded the stage with cyclamens, golds, aquamarines and midnight blue. We lit from the wings, from the back, from the floor, even bringing back foot-lights. The costumes were mostly all-over tights, tie-dyed in contrasting colours, while the dancers were kept busy performing multiple roles. We had bolstered the numbers for the season by engaging Bob Smith from Ballet Rambert, Irene Dilks from London Contemporary Dance Theatre and William Farrell, recently arrived from New York. All were very individual and experienced dancers and filled important roles in the repertoire.

The Visit was premiered at our first central London season, in October 1969, at the Jeanetta Cochrane Theatre. Finding a suitable theatre for a mid-sized ballet company in London is always a problem, and at that time even the newly reformed Ballet Rambert used the Cochrane for their seasons. The theatre had a reasonably sized stage, but run by the Greater London Council it was dogged by rules and regulations, with the staff working strictly accordingly to the rules of the London theatre stage unions. The season, when we presented two different programmes, started modestly, attracting mainly friends and colleagues, but after the 'rave' review of a kind one can normally only dream of by the doyen of the London critics, Richard Buckle, audiences built up for the second week. In *The Sunday Times* Buckle wrote, 'Alexander Roy (from Berlin) is the choreographer, and he is a very able one too. He is eclectic and apart from a basic classical tradition, one can discern the influence of Jooss, Graham and Tudor. *The Glass Menagerie* theme of Tennessee Williams *(The Gentleman Caller)* is most skilfully arranged to César Franck's Quintet, in his building up of drama, in his moments of torment and ecstasy, Roy is not only true to the music but weaves a choreography which would be a pleasure to look at even without music. It is a very rare experience to see so accomplished a work by an unfamiliar choreographer.' *The Gentleman Caller* and *Circuit* received generally excellent reviews, while amazingly, many of the critics took *Nepentha* and *The Visit* in their stride, finding them inter-esting and atmospheric. But at the end of the two-week season the bills came piling in; theatre rental, endless hours of overtime for the stage crew, salaries for usherettes, firemen, the printing of tickets, posters, leaflets, newspaper advertising and so on. It proved just possible to pay the salaries to the dancers, the musicians and to our general helpers, but we were left with no alternative but to sell our only important asset, the minibus.

Besides all the preparations for the London season, Alexander had mounted *Passing Encounter*, originally created for the Harlequin Ballet, for the Scapino Ballet in the Netherlands, having already given them *Capriccio* a couple of years earlier. He had also been involved in discussions to take part in the 'Movement Group' to be formed at the London Coliseum, together with the move of the Sadler's Wells Opera to the theatre and the creation of the English National Opera. However, there was little temptation to give up our own company and the hard-won independence which was now being threatened by bankruptcy. This was saved once again by an unexpected offer to collaborate in a new production at the Théâtre Royal de la Monnaie in Brussels. The Monnaie, also inspired by the new cultural climate, was to mount a 'pop opera' and after one of their directors had seen *Nepentha* during the London season, the offer was made to Alexander to bring the company to Brussels, for two months, following a month of rehearsals in London.

Publicity photo for the London season at the Jeanetta Cochrane Theatre – I am with Bob Smith in the middle of Tottenham Court Road.

Before leaving for Brussels and emboldened by the favourable critical reception the London season had afforded us, as well as in a desperate attempt to win some financial assistance, a meeting was arranged with the Arts Council. John Cruft was then director of music and dance and we met at the Arts Council's headquarters in an impressive building in Piccadilly. He listened to us politely; how the company was going from strength to strength, how we were becoming part of the British dance scene, how many projects were planned for the future – and how badly we needed some financial assistance. He suggested making a formal application which would be considered at the next Council meeting. Chatting about our Continental tours, he jovially questioned, 'Well, I suppose you prefer touring the south of France and travelling around the Swiss Alps to spending all your time in south-west England, for instance?' It seemed like a joke, and we laughingly agreed, neatly falling into his trap. The Arts Council together with several regional organisations had recently set up ballet companies in the regions; Northern Ballet Theatre in Manchester as well as the Scottish Ballet in Glasgow. Possibly they were then considering the creation of more regional companies, and ours may have appeared to be a suitable candidate. This would have meant settling in the south-west, or the north-east, far from London and everything it meant, spending most of our time giving lecture demonstrations and workshops to local dancers, instead of creating and performing. It is worthwhile work, and there are now companies scattered throughout Britain doing exactly this, but despite the comparative financial security, it was never a possibility we could have considered, and no doubt that response went down in the records. The Arts Council did consider our application and regretted not being able to help us.

Le Voyage sur la Lune, or A Trip to the Moon, was an ambitious work for what was otherwise the rather staid, old-fashioned opera house in Brussels. The very famous Belgian *chansonnier* Jacques Brel was to be involved, as well as his long-time collaborator, the composer François Rauber. The production included an international cast of singers, the chorus and orchestra of the Monnaie, and our company, enlarged to form a group of twenty multi-racial dancers. The libretto, a science-fiction story of a group of humans from earth arriving on the moon (it was the year of the first manned visit to the moon), gave scope to all kinds of adventures, but best of all it assured us of three months' work, both in London and in Brussels.

It was easy enough to find African, West Indian and Asian dancers in London for what was to be a series of dance scenes in a very contemporary style. We hired a large church hall in West Kensington and set to choreographing and rehearsing. Alexander was called to Brussels for weekly production meetings, returning each time more and more perplexed as to how the production could work. We translated the French text into English, and even into German, to see if it could make more sense, but it was undeniable that the operetta style of the scenario, along with a definitely dated musical score,

Alexander rehearsing for *Le Voyage sur la Lune* in London,
ahead of our engagement at the Théatre Royal de la
Monnaie in Brussels in 1970.

was totally at odds with their plan to mount a contemporary 'pop' opera.

Once the company had moved to Brussels, Alexander was called upon to rehearse with the chorus in an attempt to create a group of singing, dancing performers, in the fashion of an American musical comedy. Richard Wagner's description of the opera chorus in the nineteenth century, as 'scenery that has learnt to march and sing' was apt in this case, and the Monnaie chorus were not prepared to do much more. Jacques Brel, who had not made an appearance at all during rehearsals, did turn up for the final dress rehearsal, sitting silently in an auditorium box. While the dancers gave every ounce of energy to the dance scenes, it was painfully obvious there was a serious lack of direction in the rest of the production; in fact, nothing much was happening on stage at all. After the dress rehearsal we were all asked to remain in the theatre while the singers were called, one by one, into the director's office. The word soon got around; the production was to be cancelled, the singers were no longer needed, and in fact would leave that evening. The possibility of having twenty dancers under contract for another month, but without work and income, seemed very real.

Maurice Huismann was a very typical opera house director of the day; a cultivated, cultured man, one who had helped to make Maurice Béjart's Ballet of the 20th Century, based at the Monnaie, the phenomenal success it had become. Obviously, he was a balletomane, and although he retained a certain remoteness, Alexander had learned to like and respect him. In his office, he confirmed that the production would be cancelled, but he would also have to replace it as a matter of urgency. To do this, he was planning performances of *Die Fledermaus*, which could be mounted with a minimum of rehearsals, and asked if we could provide a fifteen-minute ballet divertissement which could be inserted into the ballroom scene. I gasped, albeit silently, when Alexander agreed immediately that this would be possible, and that we had a suitable short ballet to the divertissement music from Donizetti's *La Favorita*. It appeared that this proposal was acceptable, saving the situation for the company, but as we had less than a week to the premiere, I wondered how some of our present dancers, African and West Indian contemporary dancers who had never stretched a foot, let alone turned a pirouette, would fit into their new roles in what was a straightforward classical divertissement. The only solution was to replace some of those dancers, so sadly we paid them out, sending them back to London while, in the meantime, we managed to get Leo Guerard to rejoin us in Brussels as well as the Venezuelan dancer Vicente Abad, who had been with us for the 1969 tours.

Alexander then surprised me further by announcing he would choreograph a new version of *La Favorita*; it would be a parody of a classical divertissement in which I would 'star' as an ageing ballerina, with Leo as an 'unhelpful' partner. With the amount of work involved in giving daily classes to the company as well as assisting with the all-day and all-night rehearsals for *Le Voyage sur la Lune*, I had not danced for two months, and so it seemed one crisis was leading to another. There were just three days to the first stage rehearsals when we discovered that the decision to perform *La Favorita* as a parody was a wise one. As it happens so often in opera productions, we found ourselves fighting for space on stage, while surrounded by tables and chairs, as well as the full company of singers. The extremely sloped 'rake' of the Monnaie stage was an added obstacle, threatening, as it did, to bring one sliding downstage into the conductor's arms. By the first stage rehearsal the ensemble scenes had been finished, but my solos and choreography had been left to last. This left me either improvising or standing around on stage, leading Monsieur Huismann to query if I was going to be able to cope with the role. Alexander managed to reassure him, and with the added bonus of some perfect costumes from the Monnaie storerooms we were ready for the premiere.

If the theatre itself was old-fashioned, the Brussels opera audience of that time was made up of the most solid, conservative bourgeoisie. The ballet and the opera audience did not mix, and by this time Béjart's company no longer performed at the Monnaie, but in a huge circus tent in the centre of town. It was not immediately obvious that *La Favorita* was a parody and for the first few minutes the audience was inevitably uncertain, and then taken aback, on that opening night in Brussels. I think we all feared that it could fall very flat, but I continued through the opening section, nearly falling off pointe, nearly missing Leo's hand, and so on, as the choreography dictated. A small giggle came from the stalls, and then another, a good laugh from the gallery, and soon it seemed as if the whole theatre was rocking with laughter. The relief was enormous, and after the performance Monsieur Huismann came by to my dressing room with a bouquet of flowers, and to congratulate us all. No doubt he would still have to answer for the catastrophe of the cancelled production, but the immediate crisis was solved, and *La Favorita* entered into our repertoire to be performed for the next ten years. Belgian theatre in general remained resolutely conservative for some more years, and when Alexander mounted *Nepentha* for the Royal Ballet of Flanders in 1971, some of the reviewers wrote of the shocking incident of 'pop' music being played in Antwerp's opera house.

With Alexander in *La Favorita*.

At the end of our stay in Brussels we set off, in a new minibus and with a new van, for a tour of France, performing both *Nepentha* and *The (Immoral) Story of a Small Town and the Visit of an Old Lady*. These works must have come as a shock to the provincial French audiences, but the programme was 'balanced' with some lighter works, including *La Favorita*, and performed well with a strong company of dancers. Only in Nice, at the Palais de la Mediterranée, did we experience a really good French *'scandale'* when at the end of *The Lady* the audience was split in two, one half booing loudly while the other half shouted 'bravos'. It reminded us of performances in Paris, when during one of their first visits to France the Merce Cunningham Dance Company was received at the Théâtre des Champs-Elysées in a similarly volatile manner, something one rarely experiences today. However, in Nice, we still received a standing ovation at the end, and could feel rewarded that the performance had stimulated some strong reactions!

We returned to the Palais de la Mediterranée just one more time, in 1973, this proving to be another memorable occasion; we were to perform Alexander's 1972 production, *Fanfares*, and were amazed to see, on entering the director's office, an original painting by James Ensor, one of several which had inspired the ballet, on the wall behind him. More surprises were to come: before the matinee performance the following day, Alexander returned to the theatre and was crossing the stage in the half dark of the working lights when a huge block of iron fell from the flies above the stage to land a couple of feet from him. This was followed by a second crash, another block also just missing him. He could only surmise that iron counterweights from the stage pulleys had, for some reason, been attached to a lighting bar, and that these had come loose.

Obviously, the stage director was summoned and a thorough investigation, with a check of all the stage equipment, took place. Nothing was discovered, and we had no choice but to go ahead with the performance – which went off uneventfully. It was not long after this that news got into the press of a battle between an Italian organisation, planning to turn Nice into the 'Las Vegas of the Riviera', and the Palais de la Mediterranée, whose directors were unwilling to part with the building. This came to a head when the director's daughter was kidnapped, her whereabouts still remaining a mystery, and the Palais did, in fact, close its doors, only to reopen in French hands and following a huge revamp thirty years later. Maybe someone just wanted to give Alexander, and the theatre's directors, a fright – we shall never know.

In the spring of 1970 we gave our first performance in Paris, at the Théâtre de l'Ouest Parisien, one of the chain of new Maisons de la Culture across France set up by culture minister André Malraux. With a wide thrust stage, it suited our new repertoire well and we were fortunate in having one of France's leading solo violinists, Patrice Fontanarosa, to play the Bach partita for *Circuit*. The performance was well received, with the critics suggesting that for our next visit, the Théâtre de la Ville, in central Paris, would be a more suitable venue.

The company returned to Britain, where most of the dancers, with Alexander, were again contracted to appear at the Glyndebourne Festival Opera season. Unfortunately, working permits were not forthcoming for our male dancers, all of whom were foreign nationals. Finding good male dancers was, at that time, a constant problem. The main British companies gobbled up all the best graduate students, and experienced dancers had a choice of companies eager to offer contracts. Although Commonwealth dancers could still work in Britain at that time, few male dancers seemed to make their way abroad, although we did engage a good number of Australian and Canadian female dancers over the years. Continental and American dancers could only be employed with working permits, which took months to be issued and were often refused. This left us only able to offer short-term contracts to these dancers for the duration of our foreign tours, and with the necessity of finding replacements in Britain.

In the autumn of that year, Pauline Grant also offered me and Alexander the opportunity to perform at the Wexford Opera Festival in Ireland, dancing a short 'gypsy' pas de deux in Bizet's opera, *La Jolie Fille de Perth*, which she was to choreograph. It was just possible to squeeze in these performances, although it meant leaving the company for a few days during a tour for the South West Arts Association. The opera festival in this tiny town is a unique happening, made possible partly by the association with Glyndebourne, with several of their best singers, directors, designers and conductors regularly making their way to Ireland. Originally an ancient sea port town, Wexford was rebuilt by the Georgians as a prosperous eighteenth-century spa town, much in the style of Bath or Cheltenham. It has just two main streets, and two hotels with restaurants, leaving festival goers promenading from one end of the town to the other, waiting for lunch or dinner.

The food was very good, but the group of French singers with whom we spent any free time – and they were very good company – felt it essential to train the cooks in the French art of cooking steaks. Every day they would order a rump steak, or an entrecote, ask for it to be 'rare', and day after day they would send it back to the kitchen, claiming it was overcooked and inedible. They would even do this twice during the same meal, but each time the cooks would dutifully try again, until, by the end of the second week, they could claim success. The theatre, with 400 seats, was tiny, the stage narrow and raked, but the productions were of the highest calibre and the singing magnificent. Our very brief appearance still won us private dressing rooms and a dresser; she was a small, excitable woman who would hook up my costume with a non-stop babble of local news. After our pas de deux and once I was back in the dressing room, she would come puffing up the stairs and burst into the dressing room, shouting, 'Gorgeous, gorgeous, you've never been so gorgeous. I couldn't take me eyes off you!' We all like praise, but I knew perfectly well that she had spent the time I was on stage in the little bar at the stage door.

The early 1970s was an interesting period in the theatre, with barriers being broken down in every way. We had already been bowled over by the excitement of events in the theatre in Paris, especially by the Théâtre du Soleil, the theatre company run as a commune and based in the old Cartoucherie, the armaments factory attached to the Château de Vincennes in eastern Paris. The cultural department of the city of Paris had offered a home and subsidy to this company, and a carte blanche to create a whole new kind of theatre. Led by the remarkable visionary theatre director Ariane Mnouchkine, the company worked collaboratively over a long period preparing their first works, which exploded on the Parisian theatre scene. In line with Peter Brook's ideals, the 'fourth wall' of the stage, the imaginary wall to the auditorium, was broken down. Actors mixed with the audience, even served them at the bar or in the theatre restaurant; the audience walked past their dressing rooms on the way to the auditorium and could watch them making up and preparing for the performance. Performances were given in the round, in a traverse, or with the audience and performers intermingling. No one present at the opening of Mnouchkine's production, *1789*, the story of the French Revolution, where the audience became part of the crowd, the sans-culottes, ripping down the facades of the Palace of Versailles, will ever forget the experience.

In London, similar companies emerged, performing at The Roundhouse or at the Open Space Theatre, and dance companies, although mostly keeping to their conventional venues, reached a peak of popularity with newer companies like the reformed Ballet Rambert and London Contemporary Dance Theatre playing in London to capacity audiences for long seasons. In the spirit of the times, we started to open up the stage, having the dancers warming up as the audience entered the auditorium, sometimes playing in a completely empty stage with the walls, entrances and exits all visible. We decided to do away with the formality of bowing and curtain calls, inviting the audience to stay at the end of the performance to put forward their questions and to chat with us generally. We performed for the regional arts associations, building up a chain of theatres, mainly university theatres and arts centres, throughout Britain with young, adventurous directors who took a personal interest in the company, and with whom we could discuss programme plans for future visits. Performing conditions were often far from ideal, but we built up a repertoire which was adaptable, collecting a group of dancers ideally suited for the work.

There were also promoters in France looking for ways to move dance performances out of what were now considered elitist, opera house surroundings, bringing us to perform in a circus tent for several thousand people in Poitiers, and to spend some weeks mounting workshops for local dancers in Limoges, while in Saint Quentin we performed three and four times a day in kindergartens, tough technical high schools and retirement homes. The Arts Council of Great Britain made us their first grant in 1972, a production grant for Prue Sheridan's first ballet, *Quintette* which proved to be a popular addition to the repertoire. In the same year, Alexander created *Playground*, in response to the huge demand for mid-week school matinees, and, with a generous grant from the Gulbenkian Foundation, as well as a production grant from the Arts Council, *Fanfares*, which we premiered during the 1972 Summer Festivals of London.

It was becoming more and more a requisite in obtaining a booking, especially in the better theatres and larger towns, to offer a suitable programme for young audiences. In those days, before Mrs Thatcher's slashing of public funding to the regions, it was usual for the schools to bus in hundreds of children to the local theatre for a mid-week matinee. Today, not only has the funding for this disappeared, but the emphasis has moved to demanding the theatre companies and orchestras create 'outreach' programmes, sending companies into the schools. In fact, it appears to be an essential element of any funding from national or regional organisations that companies provide this service. I remain unconvinced that a group of dancers, untrained as educators, and possibly unwilling as teachers, can make a serious contribution in developing a taste for 'culture' among schoolchildren in this way. It is a serious drain on a company's budget, its resources and its manpower; these funds and those hours of work could surely be better spent in creating, rehearsing and performing. Can children be won over by an afternoon spent in the school gym with a group of strangers in jogging pants and sweatshirts running in circles or rolling on the floor? In bringing children, and adults, into a theatre they can be introduced to the ritual of a performance and shown that a performance is a kind of illusion, is about imagination and creation, pretending and dressing up to become someone else. Also, watching dance professionals challenging their bodies to perform the near impossible, to display what discipline and physical effort can achieve, is surely more likely to win over future performers, be it professional or amateur, as well as future spectators. In our production of *Playground* the dancers were required to speak and to act as well as dancing everything from a typical ballet class to excerpts from the classical repertoire, as well as the company repertoire. It provided an appropriate introduction to dance and we attempted to make it also a lively and entertaining theatrical performance.

One of the rewards of being part of the creative process is the discovery and study of other art forms; the works of painters, writers, composers. Alexander has often based his ballets on other artists' works and my contribution, working as a dramaturg researching and collecting material for this, has always been enjoyable. *Fanfares* was inspired by the paintings, and the life, of the Belgian surrealist artist James Ensor. Ignored and derided for much of his life, Ensor descended into an absurd, almost nightmare fantasy world, made up of the masks and carnival figures which had filled his parents' novelty shop in Ostend. His paintings made fun of the bourgeois Belgian life – the ministers, the ambassadors, the generals and the magistrates – culminating in his greatest work, the *Entry of Christ into Brussels*, a huge carnival procession complete with fanfares and tolling bells, of which his own funeral became a replica, and by which time he had become Belgium's 'Prince of Painters' and a knight of the Legion of Honour.

After the premiere at London's Cockpit Theatre, several of the critics described the work so well that I think it is worth quoting some of them: 'At the Cockpit Theatre, where the stage is surrounded on three sides by wide mounting steps, as in a Greek theatre, the informal atmosphere suits Ballet Caravan. Their new work, *Fanfares*, is a masque of grotesque, semi-human creatures who, on entering, parade round in order to inspect the audience. They make horrible mocking noises. This is an excellent start, for we are unused to enduring such criticism and sit up in alarm.' *(London Evening Standard)*. Philip Hope-Wallace, *The Guardian*'s senior critic, wrote: 'The soundtrack then played, then crowd noises, fairground marches, effects of fireworks and storms at sea. Mostly in white tights with trimmings of bedraggled hats and umbrellas, the dancers grovelled, pranced or formed strange clusters, looking perhaps to the dismissive eye like end-of-term charades at an art school, but achieving striking images of bum-to-bum or crawling togetherness of louche masked characters which got close to catching the spirit of this strange painter in some of his moods. The dancers were waves in a rough sea

The (Immoral) Story of a Small Town and The Visit of an Old Lady, inspired by Dürrenmatt's play *The Visit*, was first performed at the Jeanetta Cochrane Theatre in London in 1969. In the spirit of the times, it was a controversial work, using contemporary choreography, the spoken word and electronic music. I am seen here as The Old Lady, returning to the village of her birth to wreak vengeance, and Bob Smith as The Man sentenced to die.

Bob Smith as The Man during The Trial and, below, the opening scene, The Wedding Procession.

After the excesses of the 60s and early 1970s, the company, encouraged with production grants from the Arts Council of Great Britain, produced more conventional works including an abridged version of *Coppelia* (above) with Christine Lassauvageux as Swanilda and Francis Pedros as Franz, and Terry Gilbert's *The Last Day of Summer* – 'all chiffon and Brahms waltzes'.

On tour in Europe and South East Asia:

Keith Rosson, Prue Sheridan, Christine Lassavageux and Francis Pedros whiling away the time on the bus. Alexander rehearsing with Christine on the open-air stage in Nice and posters competing for space in France. *A Midsummer Night's Dream* on the huge stage of the International Congress Centre in Berlin.

Time off in Aix-en Provence, and on the wharf in Macau, awaiting a Jet-Foil back to Hong Kong. Nigel Clark, our lighting designer, and technician, at work backstage in Hong Kong, and with me and Prue outside the theatre in Bombay (left).

All through the 1970s
Alexander choreographed
profusely - ballets in varying
styles and moods:
(top) *Housewarming* to
music by Francis Poulenc
and (middle) a trio to
Albinoni's *Adagio*. Clair
Symonds is here in
the foreground.

The company in 1976 – seven dancers, the magic number.

In 1980 an enlarged company started to produce longer narrative ballets, the first of which was *A Smile at the Bottom of the Ladder*, inspired by the life and times of the painter, Henri de Toulouse Lautrec.

Pictured here are (above) Alexander's set for the ballet, and (middle) Natalie Mai as the clown, Cha-U-Kao, and Prue Sheridan as La Goulue, both stars of the Moulin Rouge. Below are Harmen Tromp (lying) and Alexander as The Artist.

Beauty and the Beast was a full-length ballet based on the famous fairy story. Above is John Broome as The Jester, Alexander as The Father with Donna Stevens and Rachel Smith as The Sisters; Alexander with Sheila Styles (centre) and (below) Sheila as Beauty with Paul Payne as The Beast.

A Midsummer Night's Dream, created in 1980, remained the popular work in the company's repertoire until the very last tour in 1999. Pictured above are Clair Symonds as Titania, lifted by Alpo Pakarinen as Oberon, Alexander as Bottom, 'seated' on Prue Sheridan as Puck and Natalie Mai, Tania Fairbairn and Jonathan Rant as The Lovers. Below left, Clair Symonds as Titania and Alexander/Bottom 'transformed' into an ass. The drawings by Heath Robinson inspired the costumes for the 'rude mechanicals'.

In the 1988 production of *The Magic Flute*, Alexander followed the scenario of Mozart's opera, but was also inspired by science-fiction images and Julie Read based her costumes on these. Above, Caroline Heming is on the right as The Queen of the Night and Mark Longthorn on the left as Tamino. Below, Graham Woodward as Monostatos and Caroline Heming as the Queen of the Night.

Nicole Wamsley as
Pamina and (below) Mark
Longthorn as Tamino
with
John Broome
as Papageno.

On tour in North and South America:

John Broome gasping for oxygen 3,000 metres up in the Andes in Quito, Ecuador. Alexander in carnival mood on the Caribbean island of Aruba. (below) 'Proclaimed' in Miami (for services to the theatre) but 'impounded' by immigration in San Juan.

'Going places' with our driver. Checking in and (middle) one of the elaborately decorated theatres we visited on the American tours. (below) Sight-seeing in the New Mexico desert.

The company's last
production was *Alice -
Dreams and Wonderland*,
a theme which had intrigued
and interested Alexander for
a long time. Pictured above
are Emma Brunton as Alice,
David Shipp (seated right) as
The Mad Hatter, Emma
Payne second from left, and
Stephen Brennan (on the
floor) as The Doormouse.
(middle) Alex Rose as
The White Rabbit/Lewis
Carroll and David Shipp as
The Mad Hatter. (below)
Masha Roddy's model for
the stage set.

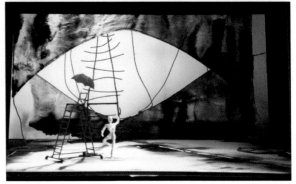

Marsha Roddy's designs for Tweedledee and Tweedledum and (right) the Red Queen. (below) Alex Rose as The White Rabbit/Lewis Carroll with a group of 'Alices'.

Basilio, one of my designs for the 1992 production of *Figaro, Figaro* – with a costume budget of £100. Anthony Crickmay's photo of Stephen Brennan as Figaro and Gina Long as Susanna. Below, the offending scene from *La Ronde* with Paul Payne as the Young Gentleman and Antoinette Goodfellow as the Chambermaid.

Fanfares performed at the Cockpit Theatre in London in 1972.

Fanfares performed at the Cockpit Theatre in London in 1972.

or survivors on a raft: they were afflicted beggars and drunks. The tolling of bells sent them to their knees. Fireworks set them off standing on their heads with amazement. The gymnastic prowess was admirable, quite like the Military Tournament. Taut muscles, sharp pointes, ingenious pantomime-horse assemblies took the eye briefly and the masks leered at us in a surprising fashion.'

Alexander put together a sound and music collage and we found the costumes in a second-hand shop in Portobello Road – a cream satin wedding dress, a gold matador suit, a scarlet taffeta overcoat, feathery hats and a whole range of interesting accessories. As we were to perform in so many unconventional venues there was no need for scenery, but the Belgian Embassy made us a present of a collection of colour slides of Ensor's works which we projected before the performance. Not all the audience were so taken by the dancers' entrance as the critic of the *Evening Standard*, and I can remember Peter Brinson, then director of the Gulbenkian Foundation, seated in the front row and doubtlessly unsure of just what their grant was to bring to life, watching in horror as some of the dancers, unaware of who he was, approached him as they entered the auditorium and circled his seat, inspecting his clothes and chortling disapprovingly. However, it was also a good

150

venue for *The Lady* which, over the years, had become both stronger as a dramatic work and more enjoyable to perform as a provocative piece. *Nepentha* completed the programme, which formed a good illustration of this new stage in our development as a company – an individual style of ballet-theatre – and despite continuing penury we still aspired to fulfil the description made in Richard Buckle's review of the Cochrane season that 'the company has an air of distinction'.

Of course, not everyone was so enthusiastic about our new contemporary and experimental style. As part of the Festivals of London we were to perform in Hackney, at the Stoke Newington Town Hall. Half an hour before the opening of the performance, the entertainments manager, soberly dressed in a dark suit but sporting a bright-red carnation in his lapel and awaiting the arrival of the lady mayoress to the performance, came racing down the aisle of the auditorium, demanding that the house curtain should be closed immediately. It was explained to him that the performance would commence with the dancers warming up on stage as the audience entered, which brought forth an explosive protestation: 'You might be able to do things like that on the Continent, but not here!' However, it was all too late and the audience were already taking their places, leaving him no alternative but to accept these 'foreign' goings-on. We returned to Hackney for several years, having won over the entertainments manager, and he must have been good at his job as the very large town hall would be filled to capacity each time, both for the schools' matinée and the evening performance. I doubt if this would be possible today.

After a short season at the Commonwealth Institute in Kensington, we also appeared at the most unusual of the venues in London, an open-air stage under the Westway motorway. This was constructed by the local Notting Hill community organisation with the aim of creating a permanent theatre for the local residents, but survived only for a couple of summer seasons. Entrance was free, and the atmosphere very informal and relaxed in the hope of capturing as many people as possible who would otherwise not come to the theatre, and certainly not to a ballet performance. We used a nearby office as dressing rooms, performed in front of a mixed audience of families, many from the local Afro-Caribbean community, giving a short performance and, despite the noise from the motorway and the comings and goings of passers-by, were successful enough to be asked back for several more visits.

That summer of 1972 proved to be an especially hot, summery one and following our performances all over London we set off for Nottingham and the Nottingham Festival, at the start of what promised to be an exceptionally exciting summer tour. The organisers in Nottingham had tentatively queried if we would consider performing in the town centre market square at midday, and toughened by our experiences at London's Westway we jumped at the idea. Fortunately, there was a good-sized stage, but it was surrounded by passers-by, shoppers, unemployed miners glad of an unusual diversion and children on holiday looking for trouble. We were assured that if things got too rough or too loud, and Nottingham had the reputation for both, we could simply stop and we would be escorted to safety. In the event, after the initial whistles and catcalls which greeted the dancers' appearance on stage in costume, a few curious bystanders were joined by more, and more, and soon hundreds of people gathered around, attentively and relatively quietly, while we performed *Nepentha*, pushing the volume of the Procol Harum's music up to maximum. This led to an invitation to repeat the performance the following day.

We also performed at the Nottingham Playhouse giving two performances, a matinee and a late-night performance, sandwiched around Marcel Marceau's first British appearance for some years, before a new season at Sadler's Wells Theatre in London. Accompanied by his partner, Pierre, who introduced each of his mime scenes dressed exquisitely in *commedia dell'arte* costume, while carrying a board announcing the title of the scene, Marceau rehearsed endlessly before his first performance. On stage he seemed morose, scowling on his exits and throwing his props angrily in the wings, while Pierre sat desolately backstage between his appearances, rocking to and fro like a distraught monkey. Even after the fifteen curtain calls, a huge ovation, Marceau remained displeased and apparently nervous about his forthcoming London premiere, a fact which we, who had seen his brilliant performances many times in London and in Paris, found fascinating, if inexplicable.

From Nottingham, the company left for the Continent, commencing the tour in Locarno on the Swiss–Italian lakes. The performances were given outdoors, surrounded by palm trees, wisteria and bougainvillea, but we were left dodging in and out of showers, just managing to perform. We found time to visit nearby Ascona, our favourite town in Switzerland, wandering through the tiny winding alleyways now filled with boutiques packed with French designer clothes, and antique shops full of golden altar pieces, crucifixes and angels, all doubtlessly salvaged from derelict Italian churches. Out of the maze of cobbled pathways one burst upon the Lago Maggiore stretching across to Italy, its quayside decked with cafes and restaurants and these, on a Sunday afternoon, were filled to capacity with prosperous Germans and Italians. Our itinerary took us further up into the Alps to Davos, at that time still a charming mountain resort, where we performed in a small theatre attached to one of the hotels. By chance we stayed in a typical chalet-type pension run by a Russian woman who told us that Anna Pavlova had performed in Davos, in the same theatre, and had stayed at her pension. Apparently, Pavlova had just forty spectators for her performance; in those days the rest of the population may have been too busy looking after their cows. From Davos we drove for two days across France to the gentle green hills of Normandy and the casino theatres of Bagnoles-de-l'Orne and Granville, where we jealously noted that the following day the two most popular young pop stars of the day, Johnny Halliday and Sylvie Vartan, were to fill the theatre to capacity while we entertained a modest two hundred or so.

The one question I always dreaded on being interviewed, be it on radio, TV or by the press, was, 'What was the worst thing that ever happened to you when touring with the ballet company?' Apparently, the public, or the media, has an insatiable appetite for stories of how ballerinas battle through a performance with a broken foot, how a choreographer, while directing a rehearsal on stage, can fall off the edge into the orchestra pit, or how a theatre company can lose most of their premises and belongings in a house fire. In fact, we did experience and survive all of the above, but when the interviewer's inevitable question arrives, my mind is always completely blank, leaving me to fluff a vague generality about the hardships of touring life, or the occasion when I forgot all my pointe shoes in a Paris hotel. However, there was an incident, or rather more of a series of disasters, stretching over two or three days, when there appeared to be a jinx on us determined to thwart every move we made. The fact that we did manage to survive, and to continue the tour, was no doubt due to our youth and adventurousness as well as to the group of dancers with us, who showed amazing resourcefulness and resilience.

Things started to go wrong on the long, long drive from Granville, on the Normandy coast, to Bandol, on the Mediterranean. By midday on the second day, we had reached Lyon and were battling down the motorway which would bring us to Bandol for the performance that evening. It was mid August, the sun blazed down, and we pushed our third-hand Transit bus to its limits. The ominous signs of overheating were all too obvious and the bus just limped on, while we desperately calculated and recalculated the possible arrival time at the theatre. Before the days of mobile phones, there was no possibility of finding a telephone without leaving the motorway, and not wanting to lose more valuable time we hoped that our technicians would have arrived well ahead of us and have everything ready, so we could literally jump out of the bus and onto the stage.

With enforced stops to allow the engine to cool down every few kilometres, we finally arrived in front of the Bandol theatre at ten minutes past nine – ten minutes after the scheduled starting time. The director had taken the initiative and cancelled the performance and my recurrent nightmare, that one day we would arrive at a theatre for a performance to find it dark and closed down, became reality. We attempted to find a hotel for the night, but at that late hour, at the peak of the summer holiday time, this proved to be impossible. The beach lay temptingly before us, a full moon glistening down onto the water and the night was warm and balmy. A few couples had already decided to spend the night outdoors and so we joined them, stepping gingerly around the shadowy forms stretched out on the sand to find a vacant spot for a dozen weary dancers. However, before collapsing into sleep we were entertained by an extraordinary display; it is known in France as '*La Nuit des Etoiles Filantes*', or the night of the shooting stars, which happens regularly in southern France in midsummer, when the sky is almost ablaze with comets flashing across the heavens and exploding again into darkness.

There was now a day off between performances, when we had planned to travel on to Nice to have a full day to prepare for what was probably the most important performance of the tour. In the event, a garage was found where we could leave the bus for repair, but as this was to take several days, Alexander and I took the first train to Toulon in an attempt to find a minibus or other suitable vehicle for hire, leaving the dancers to have a day on the beach and to scour the town for hotel rooms. The only vehicle available in Toulon at this busy holiday time was a '*deux chevaux*' van, the favourite vehicle of every plumber or handyman in France; a tiny two-seater, made, so it appeared, out of corrugated iron. We had no choice, and made our way back to Bandol by evening. The following morning, by piling most of the costumes into the back of the *deux chevaux*, the technicians bundled two more dancers on-board their van, and we ferried the rest to the station to make their way by train. Our Canadian dancer, Brian Pruden, insisted on hitchhiking, but we were soon to pick him up, sitting desolately by the side of the road, and pack him into the back of the *deux chevaux*, where, sitting on piles of costumes, he was able to put his head through an opening in the roof. Halfway through the trip, as the roads became more hilly, it became obvious that the *deux chevaux* was seriously overloaded, and once again we slowed down to creep past St Raphael, Cannes and finally to arrive in Nice, at the open-air theatre, the Théâtre de Verdure, several hours late for the get-in. As the afternoon dragged on, we became anxious about the fate of the rest of the dancers, if they had been able to cope with the rail network, and if they would find their way from the train station to the theatre, right across the sprawling city of Nice. In fact, a couple of them only just made it in time, leaving us glad, for once, that the performance started, as usual, well after the advertised time; it was also fortunate that the programme included *Fanfares* and other contemporary works which, although physically demanding, didn't challenge the dancers technically as would purely classical ballets.

After the performance, we spent a welcome hour or so with friends who had unexpectedly turned up, but the problem of accommodation for the night remained, as there was apparently not a single hotel room available in Nice. There was only one alternative – to unpack the camping gear several of us had brought with us for the holiday which was to follow the tour. We set off from Nice, squeezed into our two unsuitable vehicles, looking for a camp-site to discover, once again, that everything was full up. Beyond caring at this stage, we built up the tents in a field at the side of the road and everyone settled down in the tents or around them, oblivious to the traffic which continued to roar by all night.

The next day we were to perform in Cannes, just 30 kilometres away, and another high spot on the itinerary, where a balletomane audience could be expected, both from the city itself and from Rosella Hightower's International Dance Centre. When the Grand Ballet de Marquis de Cuevas folded in 1962, Rosella Hightower founded the dance centre in a new property development in the centre of Cannes. It was a vocational school for dance students, as well as a meeting place for professional dancers, gathering in their hundreds every summer to take classes with some of the best teachers in Europe, while also taking advantage of the nearby beaches. It was a stimulating and exciting place, presided over by the gentle but commanding presence of Rosella Hightower, who gave regular classes, private coaching and special pointe classes for the girls, sharing some of the secrets of her own formidable technique. In 1981 Rosella retired, pleased that the school was then made a national institution, but over which she still kept a careful eye.

On our arrival in Cannes, everyone was badly in need of a shower, a good meal and above all, a bed. We were amazed, and in awe, of the dancers who, continuing to cope with this series of disasters, suggested that we should make straight for the camping place just outside Cannes, where they could spend the afternoon setting up the tents and resting before the performance. The camping place was a good one and, having found a suitable site, we left them as Alexander and I had to rush off to Toulon by train to return the hire car and then to travel on to Bandol where we could pick up our minibus. It was an inconvenient detour as we knew the theatre in Cannes was a difficult, if typical, casino theatre, with a stage more suited to variety, but it was well situated in the centre of town. By the time we finally arrived back in Cannes, the stage was, miraculously, ready and the dancers already turning up in taxis. As expected, there was a good audience, and a 'ballet' audience as well, which added more tension to the evening. In the still warm evening air, in a nearby cafe on the Croisette, we finally celebrated with a group of friends from the ballet world what we believed must be the end of the saga with a couple of bottles of champagne.

Thunderstorms arrive on the Côte d'Azur with the power of the apocalypse; mostly unexpected, with lighting slashing through the sky, followed

155

by thunderclaps shattering the air and echoing as the sound bounces back from the mountains, rumbling back out to sea. The rain is never far behind and can fall in torrents, so fast and so heavy that even the parched soil cannot absorb it, leaving the water to form rivulets and streams, even cascades of water tumbling down the roads, the gutters and the pavements. That night we were woken by the first thunderclap and despite the pitch blackness, were soon aware that our campsite was seriously under water; our sleeping bags were sodden and one dancer, remaining resolutely asleep, was literally floating on his air mattress. We desperately tried to wake everyone, pushing the mattresses together to lift them from the water, which only caused more confusion and protests, with Prue, who had managed to find a dry spot on a higher level, shouting at us to keep quiet as she couldn't sleep with the rumpus going on. Alexander braved going outside, managing to dig an improvised ditch around the tent, which at least left us in safety, and there was little more to do but to wait for daylight. As this arrived, some emergency vehicles from the town turned up, and fortunately also the sun, into which we struggled, wet and dirty, to take stock of our situation. There had been some fatalities that night; people were trapped in their cars, some caught in an underpass, so although we were actually fortunate it seemed that we were caught up in a chain of disasters which was just getting worse. On the other hand, perhaps the thunderstorm had broken the spell, as once we had spent the day, fortunately a scheduled 'day off', getting dry and clean, we were able to continue on our travels, completing the tour without any further problems.

The tour took us into the Pyrenees and to the Atlantic coast, where we gave the final performance in Dax, a small thermal resort in the Basque country, founded originally by the Romans in their constant search for healing thermal waters, and still a popular holiday town and rehabilitation centre. One of those truly unexpected events which do happen on tours came about at that performance in Dax. Among the audience was a countess, the Comtesse de Rochefort, accompanied by a gentleman who introduced himself as the director of the Museum of Modern Art in Paris, still housed at that time at the Palais de Chaillot. He was a dance lover and a mutual friend of people in the dance world. Apparently the performance pleased them sufficiently to invite us all to a magnificent dinner, accompanied by several bottles of champagne, in the theatre bar after the performance – which seemed a deserved reward after the trials we had just survived.

There was just one problem with the theatre in Dax. After hanging up the costumes in the basement dressing room, we spent a couple of hours soaking up some sun in a pavement restaurant, to return to a curious sight in the dressing room. The costumes hanging in a row from a bar in the centre of the room were moving, jiggling and wiggling, as well as being covered in small brown spots. They were infested with fleas – sand fleas, not as serious as some of their cousins, and after the initial shock we gave the costumes a good shake, which did send them scattering. During our meal with the countess, most of us noticed an uncomfortable itching creeping up our legs under the table; it seemed bad manners to leave the table in order to have a good shake, so we tried to ignore it, while grateful that the beasts didn't attempt to crawl further than our knees.

Half of the company returned to London by train, air travel not being an option in those days, while the rest of the dancers stayed with us for two weeks, camping in a pine forest directly behind the dunes which led to one of the greatest beaches in Europe. At that time, in the 1970s, the southern Atlantic coast of France stretched for hundreds of unspoiled kilometres of wide, sandy beaches and rolling breakers. Unfortunately, much of this has gone with the development of marinas and holiday resorts, apartment blocks and mini villages of bungalows and chalets. Large chunks of the magnificent pine forests have disappeared and even the beaches and tidal currents have been radically and dangerously changed. However, during that holiday in 1972, Alexander slept virtually non-stop for two weeks, while the rest of us swam and sunbathed, drank far too much wine around the evening camp fire, finally catching up on our sleep as well. However, it was the only time we attempted to combine camping with performing.

The company was, by now, giving well over one hundred performances annually, building up a circuit of regular theatres and tours, both in the UK and on the Continent. But we were still nomads, without a fixed home, apart from our rented apartments which also served as the company office, and, what was becoming more and more difficult, without a permanent base for rehearsals. The British Ballet Organisation's studio was proving to be too small, but we had found, thanks to the Greater London Council, a property where we had not just a rehearsal studio but space enough to store scenery and costumes. The GLC had a scheme by which they allowed theatre companies to use properties awaiting demolition and redevelopment, offering us the opportunity to occupy one in West Kensington, a former small factory, which, after a good clean, served us as a base. However, by the summer of 1973, they had given us notice to leave and we were desperately searching for new premises, assisted by friends and family.

And so it came about that we found North House, a five-storey mansion on Eton Avenue, a tree-lined avenue which stretched from Swiss Cottage to Belsize Park in north-west London. It was not an ordinary sort of house – more a late-Victorian folly. Passers-by often thought it a church because of the high, stained glass windows but it was originally built as a family house, in 1890, for a well-known artist of the day, the Honourable John Collier. Collier married, successively, two daughters of the eminent scientist and philosopher T.H. Huxley, becoming uncle to the scientist Julian Huxley, and his brother, the writer Aldous Huxley, who spent many holidays as children at North House. In fact, in the early twentieth century the house became a lively meeting place and centre for artistic and scientific life in London.

Listed as being in the 'Flemish Renaissance' style, it was also graciously Victorian, with overtones of mock-Gothic; the interior impressively grand with some curlicue embellishments which could only have been inspired by the Orient; it boasted a 40-foot long drawing room where a whole wall was taken up with an ornately carved fireplace and mantelpiece; there was a morning room, a dining room, a smoking room, numerous bedrooms, but only two bathrooms, children's rooms and servants' quarters under the roof, while down below in the basement was a huge kitchen, a scullery, a wine cellar, a coal cellar, a pantry, a housekeeper's room, a linen room; there were servants' entrances, servants' staircases and bells and strange talking pipes with which to summon them; there were storerooms, cupboards under the stairs, behind the stairs and nooks and crannies on every floor. As the former home of an artist, there was also a glass-roofed artist's studio, with the remnants of a lift shaft which had served the whole house. At the rear of the house a large garden, with overgrown sycamore and poplar trees, sheltered the house from the encroaching noise and pollution from an ever-growing city. The house had remained in the Collier family until the 1940s, when during the war, the large ground-floor rooms had served as a theatre for several Jewish theatre groups, and then, in 1948, it became a music school.

By the time we acquired it, North House had become, like many in Eton Avenue and the surrounding streets, a warren of bedsits, housing twenty or thirty people. The residents included Maltese waiters, a Bulgarian tenor, an Australian pianist with a grand piano, an out-of-work Jamaican, Japanese students and a mysterious African. The drawing room and adjoining 'morning room' were perfect as rehearsal rooms, while in the basement we removed the huge cast-iron cooking range, the sinks and kitchen cupboards, to provide offices and changing rooms. Alexander and I lived in the artist's studio – fulfilling a dream held since we wandered around Montmartre fascinated by the many glass-roofed studios there – under a leaking roof, and with a coal stove as our only source of heat. The cavernous space below became

North House – our new home in London – 1973.

Rehearsing in North House.

storerooms and workshops for scenery and costumes. It was perfect, and when our original eighteen-month lease expired we managed to acquire another lease and eventually, very much later, became the freeholders. Gradually renovations and conversions were made, allowing ourselves more living space with the luxury of central heating. Several of the bedsits were taken over by company members, but the remaining tenants claimed to enjoy the strains of Rossini and Chopin wafting through the house and amazingly, the neighbours did not complain about the trucks and buses loading and unloading, arriving and departing, at all hours of the day and night.

The move to North House was just in time to prepare for a lengthy tour arranged by the Jeunesses Musicales de France (JMF), a national organisation which worked indefatigably bringing music and lyric theatre to young people in France. The JMF had run its own ballet company for many years, notably with the French choreographer Pierre Lacotte as director, but by this time were engaging companies on a seasonal basis. They offered us a tour of thirty-five performances in twenty-three days across the north and north-eastern regions of France, often performing two one-hour school matinees of *Playground* as well as an evening performance. The JMF provided a forty-seater coach with driver, and a tour manager, guaranteeing a well-organised tour, with the hours of travel to twenty different cities squeezed in besides the packed performing schedule. However, before committing themselves, the JMF had laid down one condition: a change of name for the company – International Ballet Caravan was simply not 'serious' enough. It couldn't have come at a better time. Although we had never lived nor performed in a caravan, the title had been right for us during those early years of independence, but now settled permanently in London it was inevitable that we would become a different company, needing a different image. So the company became Alexander Roy London Ballet Theatre.

The 1973–74 season continued with tours throughout Britain, Germany, Switzerland and France, including a return visit to Paris, where we performed for a week at the Théâtre de la Cité Internationale. Here we premiered a new ballet, *Visages d'une Femme*, based loosely on the Japanese film *The Woman in the Dunes*, in which I danced the role of an insect-like woman, destroying any man she could entice into her lair. It was a good, strong piece and the performance proved successful enough to bring the audience to clap non-stop throughout a ten-minute interval; an extraordinary and unusual happening. As often in Paris, it was a time of unrest on the streets, with strikes and protests building through the week. The theatre technicians had been holding meetings, with the threat and danger that they would decide to go on strike. This happened during our last performance, and without warning we were left on stage for the final ballet, *Nepentha*, with the tape recorder already running, and no technicians to be found to open the stage curtain. With the opening bars of music Alexander rushed across the blackened stage, bringing him to collide with Prue already in place centre stage, resulting in him cracking his nose. Fortunately, he was able to continue crossing the stage, in the dark, and landed with his finger on the appropriate button to open the curtain. As the lighting operator belonged to a different union and had remained on duty, we were lucky in being able to continue the performance. Travelling back to London the next day, we shared the Channel ferry with a team of British rugby players who eyed Alexander's bruised and swollen nose suspiciously, but fortunately didn't demand any explanations from him. The Paris season was a good ending to an eventful year, with what was now a 'new' company, and we felt ready to move on and set off on new paths.

chapter eight

Stretching Our Wings
1974

The company now had a home and a new name, both of which established the fact that we were a British company and, although uninvited, had come to stay. Despite remaining in contact with the Arts Council, and relations had improved with the appointment of former dancer Jane Nicholas to the newly independent dance department (formerly shared with the music department), a regular subsidy was as unlikely as ever. Government finance had become so limited at that time, that subsidies were restricted only to those companies already receiving regular funding. We did continue to receive modest production grants for new works, but only for those by outside choreographers, as the Arts Council now insisted on more criteria – and in particular, there was to be no funding for choreographers who were also company directors, or for companies directed by the principal choreographer.

At one meeting with Jane Nicholas I could not resist asking if this would apply if Martha Graham, or Maurice Béjart, were directing British companies, and the answer was in the affirmative. She suggested that our applications for funding would be more sympathetically received if we were to use choreographers from the Arts Council list of 'approved choreographers'. We protested that this nullified the whole point of our existence; to establish an individual company, different from any other, with a unique repertoire, rather than replicating choreographers' works which could be seen in numerable other companies. Obviously, this policy has now changed with the result of a proliferation of companies directed by active choreographers. However, for us to retain our ideals of a company with a unique identity, we were left with no alternative but to support ourselves from the income we received from performances. This continued to pose huge problems in attempting to cover not only salaries and running costs, but in mounting new productions, and the constant need to invest in new equipment, publicity material, costumes and scenery.

The company had remained at seven dancers for most tours, increasing only for seasons in London or in major venues, but it is a useful size. One can even fill a large stage with seven dancers, while the numbers guarantee a homogeneity which becomes difficult to retain with a larger group. It is also a practical number. When the famous American choreographer Merce Cunningham was asked in the 1960s why his ballets were almost always choreographed for seven dancers, Cunningham replied that with John Cage, the composer and his long-term collaborator, at the wheel, it was just the right number to fit into a Volkswagen minibus. And indeed the VW proved to be an essential vehicle for so many small groups of dancers, musicians and actors in those early days.

Touring in the UK in the 1970s was becoming more and more difficult with strikes and shortages, as well as surging oil prices, leading to a three-day working week. There were power cuts which left theatres without heat, forcing the audience to remain with their coats on while everyone froze backstage and in the dressing rooms. Theatres, pubs and restaurants closed by 10.30 p.m., leaving the company racing from the theatre after a performance to find a drink and something to eat before going back to an unheated bed and breakfast. Inflation reached double figures, sending expenses soaring, requiring us to constantly revise our budgets and seek more income. It also meant that a different repertoire was needed in order to attract more bookings while we had to look farther afield for new 'markets'. It was, therefore, providential that we received an offer from the Singapore-based impresario Donald Moore to make a lengthy tour of South East Asia in November and December 1974. We put together two programmes, balancing the more modern works with lighter pieces while also including some excerpts from the classics.

⁓

The tour was a year in the making but up to the very last it looked as if it might never happen. The British Council, an organisation somewhere between the Arts Council and the Diplomatic Service, and responsible for most of the national theatre and dance companies' performances abroad, had recommended the travel agent. The tour required us to take ten people from London to Bangkok, and then on to Penang, Kuala Lumpur, Singapore, Hong Kong, Manila and back to London, while the flights needed to fit into an already existing schedule of performances. It was also essential to find an airline with a 'flexible' policy towards a group travelling with a number of large trunks, containing all our costumes, props and belongings.

The travel agent did not appear to have an office, so we had only been able to speak to him by phone, but the fares he offered were highly discounted, and much better than anything we had been able to find ourselves. Finally arrangements were made; he would hand over the tickets on the eve of our departure, in a pub in a backstreet behind Tottenham Court Road – and we should bring cash. The auspices were not good, but we had little choice. Sharing the thousands of pounds between us, Alexander and I arrived at 5.30 p.m. just when office workers poured out of the surrounding buildings, rushing into the Underground station and the neighbouring pubs. In the crush of the appointed pub, a seriously obese young man with a highly flushed face and sweat-stained shirt introduced himself and we exchanged packages. There was little point in attempting to check the huge bundle of tickets in the overcrowded, noisy pub and in any case, there was no time now to rectify any mistakes.

The next morning, we all gathered at the British Airways terminal at Cromwell Road at 5 a.m., bleary-eyed and already confused on a dark and wet November day. It was light by the time we changed planes in Paris, and travelling on a bright, clear day we could follow the flight path across Europe to the Mediterranean, and on through the Middle East, helped by the generosity of Air France, which in those days offered excellent food at all too frequent intervals. The plane paused on the tip of Arabia, at Abu Dhabi, where I rushed to the open door to breathe in the exotically 'foreign' air of

Arabia, marvelling at the star-filled sky. Then we were off to Delhi, where we stopped again, still imprisoned in the jumbo, while it was brushed and cleaned, loaded and unloaded, while one became aware of the warmth outside and the inevitability of it really staying warm. Following a night of fitful sleep, we arrived at Bangkok's Don Muang Airport, after swooping low over the first sight of the lush jungle growth of Thailand and the tiny box-like houses on stilts skirting the ribbons of the many rivers.

At the airport we were met by the local promoters, expat British, and were escorted into Bangkok in a rather large, shaky bus. The first thing one notices in Thailand are the trucks; there are trucks everywhere, bearing down on our bus, overtaking intrepidly, swerving and diving around us like flights of playful swallows; shining silver-plated monsters, studded and almost jewelled, painted and gaudily decorated, daubed with fairy lights and showing glimpses of pin-up girls next to religious icons. The trucks are loaded, even overloaded, with sacks and baskets almost tumbling over the sides: fruits and coconuts as well as passengers hanging over the back or perched, precariously, on top of it all. Then one notices the water; in the country there are endless fields and streams of water, while in the city, all around us, filthy, muddy water, which splashed us as we rushed by in our rumbling 1940s-model bus, and also splashed those crouching or sitting on the pavements, cooking, eating, selling and watching.

Arriving at a pleasant hotel, we were offered a wonderful Thai buffet lunch of enticing salads and tropical fruits, a kaleidoscope of extraordinary new colours and smells and tastes. After lunch some of us ventured out of the air conditioning into the heaviness of the heat outside where the eating was still going on. Everyone, it seemed, was cooking or eating or selling food. Women crouched over their charcoal burners on the pavements, concocting delicious looking dishes of meats and vegetables, salads and desserts; little stands served sizzling meat dishes and fresh fruit juices; the shops were jammed full of salted fish, fresh meat, most of it unidentifiable, fruit and vegetables, puddings and pastries. A great living feast was taking place among the exhaust fumes, the flooded gutters, the noise, the smells and the heat. For most of us it was the first experience of an Asian country, and the first encounter with poverty on a scale we had never imagined, although by Asian standards, Bangkok was, even then, an almost westernised city.

The National Theatre is part of a large university complex, and the first surprise was to find not just one very large stage, but two, one directly behind the other. This is obviously an advantage for Thai drama performances, where elaborate scene changes can be carried out on the rear stage while action continues on the forestage. In order to use the full lighting rig we needed to perform on the rear stage, but this left us much further away from the audience than we would have wished. It also seemed necessary to curtain off a huge papier mâché Buddha who brooded over us voluptuously, and who would have been rather out of place during *The Gentleman Caller* or *La Favorita*. We had been warned that the stage crew could be uncooperative, and often were with foreigners, but perhaps due to our delight with everything they proved to be efficient and helpful. Some of those less occupied had a tendency to 'drop off' between jobs, falling fast asleep still clutching a piece of scenery, but the heavy, humid heat was certainly an inducement to take things easy. Most of the crew appeared to live in the theatre, or even on the side of the stage, as wives and children filled the wings and the small rooms surrounding the stage. Cooking smells pervaded everything, beds were rolled up against the walls and washing was draped around to dry.

Despite having a good lighting rig, with literally hundreds of lamps, there was no way to focus these from a ladder or the usual scaffolding tower we were used to in Europe. Instead, the bars were lowered to head height and adjusted, with considerable expertise, judging where the light would fall once they were winched up to full height. This hit or miss method worked quite well for general 'washes' of colour, but obviously caused problems for tight 'specials' where a lamp was needed to focus on a small area, or even just on one person. It was decided that anything too demanding would have to be abandoned, until I noticed a technician above us in the flies, running along the lighting bar, and crouching to focus the lamps. Taking the precaution to do this with bare feet in order to have some grip on the narrow bamboo pole, he was, all the same, at least 30 feet above the stage floor and had nothing to hang on to.

No doubt the excitement kept us on an adrenalin high, unaware of jet lag, tiredness or the heat. The performance began punctually, and with great relief, everything backstage went off perfectly. We had been daunted by the thought of entertaining a thousand Thais with European classical dance, even more so knowing that their own dance was very highly developed technically and artistically, but they concentrated, reacted and even laughed as the best of European audiences. During the numerous curtain calls the dancers were garlanded with huge leis of sweet-smelling frangipanis, before fleeing back to our air-conditioned hotel and to sleep. Due to a last-minute change of dates, the company had three free days to fill in Bangkok before going on to Malaysia. Fortunately, the theatre could be used for a daily early morning class and the days were then packed with sightseeing. The performances were promoted by the local music society whose chairman was a languid Englishman of the old school. Six foot tall and gangling, in a crumpled linen suit, he thought nothing of letting his chauffeur wait for him for one or two hours in the baking heat. The music society's secretary was also an Englishman, fortyish, a bachelor, with possibly more reasons for wanting to remain in Bangkok than attending to the music society's correspondence. He was a good companion, leading us to a different restaurant every night, from a bustling workers' diner to beautiful and fragrant garden restaurants. He was able to down a bottle of Thai whisky in an evening while we were preoccupied with the multitude of new taste experiences, and in trying to avoid the deadliest of the red hot chillies.

The tourist guides make a tour of the floating market an essential part of any visit to Bangkok, so dutifully we set off at seven o'clock one morning. Sadly, the original floating market of peddlers selling their goods from boats on the river, or the *'klongs'* (canals), has been driven off by the tourist traffic, but some colourful boats remain, hawking fruit and vegetables. There were young boys leaping and diving from the houses on the riverbank into the water, women washing their clothing and scrubbing their cooking pots; some brushed their teeth and washed their hair, and paddled in the river with their babies, collecting water for cooking and possibly for drinking. One could not help noticing that the water was the colour of black coffee, thick and soupy and filthy, doubtlessly full of waste and sewage. Perhaps to take our minds off this, the boat pulled up at a floating shop full of gaudy shirts and cheap brass ornaments, which kept most of the tourists happy. The numerous *wats*, or temples, also on our tourist itinerary and which are the highlight of the city, were magnificent – huge buildings, ornately and richly decorated – and there were many unexpected treats such as happening upon a street theatre, where we watched the beautiful actress-dancers making up behind a flimsy curtain right on the pavement, and adjusting their huge golden headdresses.

There were terrifying taxi drives, hurtling from our hotel to downtown Bangkok; the dilapidated cars often caused problems, even on occasion forcing us to abandon the car while the driver fought a threatening blaze. We chanced upon Chinatown late one afternoon and were overwhelmed in the maze of narrow alleyways by the abundance of tiny shops and stalls where fish and vegetables tumbled out of baskets, clothes and bales of silks were stacked on the pavements, with underwear and shoes, brassware, silverware and jewellery, and above all, the pungent smell of salted, dried fish, coriander and spices which pervaded everything. We also visited the weekend market, a huge field of open-air stalls, near the temple of the Emerald Buddha, which comes to life every Saturday morning. Here we discovered, besides the usual mix of exotic foods and cloths, live cockerels and rabbits, cobras and scorpions, fish of every imaginable colour, nestling besides huge cauldrons of bubbling lemon grass soup and sizzling barbecuing chickens. Despite all the warnings and good resolutions, we tried many of the local dishes, burning our palates over and over again with the powerfully spiced food.

Wandering through the packed weekend market as well as through the streets of Bangkok, through the terrible squalor and real poverty, one couldn't help wondering who was doing all the buying, as most of the population seemed to live by selling. Also on sale, with the Vietnam War still at its height, and with Bangkok a popular R & R destination for American GIs, were the young Thai women we had seen hanging around the gaudy bars and massage parlours in downtown Bangkok. However, we were next off to Malaysia on a superbly comfortable Thai Airways International flight, laden with presents of fresh orchids, scented towels and innumerable free cocktails, which made the East seem very civilised.

After the initial shock of Bangkok, we had no idea what to expect in Malaysia. Could things get worse – that is Bangkok, but more so – or would we find something entirely different? Arriving in Penang, the second city of Malaysia, at midday, we immediately noticed that we must be much closer to the equator: 'Good you've come in the cool season,' someone said to us as we felt the first onslaught of the 35°C heat on leaving the plane. We were greeted enthusiastically by the very exuberant Indian promoter, who was awaiting us in the immigration hall. 'Let me have the working permits,' he ordered. Obediently I searched my handbag, then the briefcase and the overnight bag. No working permits. My mind was a complete blank, I hadn't the slightest recollection of where I had, so carefully, packed away the document.

The working permits for Malaysia had caused some trouble. For some reason these could only be issued in Bangkok and as our stay had progressed, my telephone calls to the Malaysian Embassy became more and more anxious. Friday came and went, when the embassy closed until Monday morning. However, our flight for Penang left on Sunday, leaving me filled with terror at the thought of us all being detained on arrival in Malaysia as undesirable aliens, and possibly incarcerated in an Asian prison. The Malaysian promoter had finally telephoned to assure me that the permits had been issued and sent, by telegram, to the Malaysian Embassy. He added that we could neither enter nor perform in Malaysia without them. He had left things a bit late! Commandeering the first of the many taxis lying in wait outside the hotel, and without the usual bargaining procedure, I gasped to the driver to get me to the Malaysian Embassy. On the way we passed the British Embassy, which was throwing their annual 'Olde British Fayre'. I remembered hearing that this was the social event of the year, with invitations to everyone from the different embassies – no doubt also the Malaysian staff. Entering the long drive up to the embassy, I noticed that everything was ominously quiet. A large peacock pranced across the lawn while a lone gardener was stretched out, asleep, under a hibiscus bush. The main front door was wide open and, asking the driver to wait, I timidly made my way inside, expecting to be confronted by the usual guard with a machine gun at the ready. However, the hallway was completely deserted and in front of me in the centre of the hall was a large polished wooden table. A telegram lay on the table, the envelope opened, so I could see clearly that this was the authorisation of our performances in Malaysia. Knowing I had to be reckless, I stuffed the telegram into my handbag, was out of the door and back in the taxi. For once, I was grateful for the utterly daredevil speed of the Bangkok taxi drivers.

Before leaving Bangkok, this vital document was packed away with great care. There was only one possibility, and that it was in my suitcase which was now arriving on the luggage carrousel – on the other side of the immigration hall. Taking the proverbial 'bit between my teeth', I breezed up to the passport control. 'On holiday, madam?' 'Just a few days,' I replied. 'Have a pleasant stay,' he wished me. The passport was stamped and I was through. It didn't take long for me to locate the missing telegram and hand it on to the impresario, who was visibly shaken, at my side.

If Bangkok is the real 'East', then Penang, at that time, still resembled a British colony from another age. Elegant white weatherboard houses set well back in neatly kept English-style lawns, surrounded by tall, graceful palm trees, bougainvillea and frangipanis, exuded a leisurely, comfortable lifestyle. At the slightly rundown colonial style hotel, there was no air conditioning, but huge revolving ceiling fans and a light musty smell pervading everything. The restaurant menu was limited to traditionally English dishes, all served with chips. The waiters were elderly Chinese gentlemen who shuffled along in baggy trousers, unsmiling and apparently somewhat unwilling. Out on the streets, there were no beggars, no street stalls, no women crouching over their pavement kitchens and not even any diesel fumes. But there were a good number of extremely scrawny elderly men pedalling trishaws which appeared to be almost as much hard work as the older rickshaws.

The performance was to take place in a large auditorium in the centre of Georgetown, which was reached by ferry from the mainland. There was only one drawback to the excellently sized stage – a total lack of stage lighting. There was just one row of what looked like coloured car headlights, probably disco lights, leaving us performing in red scenes, blue scenes, yellow scenes and even green scenes. More problems with the electrical system caused havoc with the theatre's tape recorder: towards the end of the final ballet, I noticed with horror that the music tape had broken loose from the spool and although it continued playing, albeit increasingly slowly, the loose end was snaking out on to the stage. The ballet finished just in time, with a curious droning noise and puffs of smoke billowing from the machine.

The following day we travelled on to Kuala Lumpur and again were struck by the orderly, business-like appearance of the town, which, at that time, was a fascinating mixture of Victorian stateliness and Islamic exotica among newer gleaming glass and steel high-rise architecture. We stayed at the Majestic Hotel, whose royal claims were somewhat faded, but we found real live rubber planters in baggy white slacks with Whisky-pinked cheeks and hearty British accents lounging in the lobby. We performed at the huge university theatre, which proved to have first-class facilities and a professional crew, and where both London Festival Ballet and the Australian Ballet had recently preceded us. It was a good stimulus to face a more discerning and experienced audience, reminding us that the more challenging part of the tour now lay ahead of us.

It was just a short flight to Singapore where our arrival was uneventful but well organised; we were escorted to the Goodwood Park Hotel where we were to stay, as well as giving two performances. The Goodwood, like the more famous Raffles Hotel, is a reminder of the old colonial days in Singapore, a beautiful and ornate white stucco building set in an immaculate green tropical park. Originally a restaurant and entertainment centre, the Goodwood once boasted Singapore's best theatre, hosting Anna Pavlova's company during her tour of the region in 1922. In 1929 it became a hotel patronised notably by the Duke of Windsor, Noël Coward and countless celebrities. Whether it was for old time's sake, or whether our expat British promoter was not welcome at the now fiercely nationalistic 'National Theatre', I am not sure, but the Goodwood was chosen as the venue for our performances, with a specially constructed wooden stage mounted on top of the swimming pool in the middle of an open-air restaurant, surrounded by tropical plants. It was very glamorous, but not really very practical. However, everyone obviously enjoyed staying in the first-class hotel with air conditioning, room service and all the luxuries.

171

The obligatory press conference was held after lunch, when the already rather weary dancers posed gallantly around the pool and in the gardens for a battery of cameras. The journalists, as in the other venues already visited on the tour, were young and fairly inexperienced as far as theatre was concerned. Soon latching on to the news that Alexander and I were married, the interviews inevitably centred on this. The first question would always be: 'What work do you do when you are not dancing?' The concept of a professional artist who earns a living from art was totally foreign to them, and indeed even today in Asia most dancers, actors and musicians usually keep their 'day jobs'. The next question would then be a blunt demand to know how old one was; again, they would find it extraordinary than anyone older than twenty could be a dancer. And then the main point of interest: 'How many children do you have?' At first, we laughed this off, but soon realised that it was considered a serious failing, if not a major tragedy, for a married couple to remain childless. Apart from the prestige for Asians in having a large family, they would find it difficult to imagine that in London we did not have a staff of housekeepers and amahs (or nursemaids) to do all the work.

November is the rainy season in Singapore, leaving us to dodge in and out of the showers all afternoon until about an hour before the performance when the sky magically cleared, and with the almost instant tropical change from daylight to night, showed up a dazzling ceiling of stars. The warm, humid air proved marvellously conducive to dance. Legs flew up in arching arabesques, jumps took off and landings were cushioned by soft, elastic muscles. Only the pointe shoes suffered when the glue literally melted and turned the blocked toes to pulp while the short tutus drooped, heavy with moisture, to become knee-length skirts. The second performance, on the following evening, coincided with a rare total eclipse of the moon. This memorable experience, with a jewelled sky displaying stage effects of light and shadows, happened during the *Les Sylphides* pas de deux, where Alexander and I danced to Chopin's magical waltz, surrounded by tropical flowers and plants, as well as the towering skyscrapers which make up today's huge city.

There was just one free day to see Singapore, when we tried to avoid the shopping malls, the huge modern hotels, the snack bars and the duty-free shops to find the 'real' Singapore. It appeared that much had been built during the past twenty years, with the city government intent on 'sanitising' the city by razing Chinatown to the ground and fining people on the spot for dropping a sweet wrapper or smoking in forbidden areas. The 'Welcome' brochure at the airport warned that people with long hair would be served last in any government shop or office and in fact, men with hair falling below their collars were in danger of being detained at the airport to be given a quick trim. Obviously, an interest in promoting Singapore as a tourist destination has led to a change in all these regulations. We did discover the Thieves' Market, full of antique curios and jewellery, mostly run by Indians, and the notorious Bugis Street with its street stalls, night-time restaurants and more daring types of entertainment.

We spent the evening eating satay and drinking fresh pineapple juice on Singapore harbour, and making our way back to the hotel on foot we stumbled across a Chinese street opera performance (or wayang). The custom is for residents to hire the performers, who bring with them an ingenious transportable stage. As fellow performers, we were fascinated by the casualness of the performance, how in full view of the audience the musicians, when not playing, would join in games with their children, or an actress waiting for a cue would thoughtfully file her nails – all the more incongruous in their highly elaborate costumes and make-up.

We left Singapore the next day on our way to Hong Kong and flew over Vietnam. One could clearly see a Riviera-like coastline, sandy beaches and wooded mountains, even the curving ribbons of the Mekong Delta. In 1974, it was difficult to associate this idyllic landscape with the reality of what was taking place right beneath us.

We arrived in Hong Kong with a typhoon named Irma, feeling the first bumps of the squally wind as we made for Hong Kong's old airport which stretched out into the South China Sea. In many ways Hong Kong was to be the highlight of this first tour and we had a marvellous welcome at the bustling, noisy airport with a fleet of buses, a truck as well as a Cadillac for Alexander and me. The rains started in earnest as we set off for our hotel, giving us our first view of Hong Kong as we peered up at the canyons of high-rise buildings covered with garish multicoloured neon lights, now shimmering through a curtain of wetness. Apart from the downpour of water, the streets were empty and eerily quiet. Hong Kong was holding its breath, waiting for Irma to pass. Once settled into our hotel in Kowloon, the rains did stop, and apparently Hong Kong was saved from serious damage while Irma swept out to sea. Wandering out into the darkened, still empty streets, we followed an intriguing sound – loud clicking and clattering noises we couldn't identify. This led us into the smaller backstreets where we discovered groups of men sitting around tables at the opened windows of the now steamy and dripping apartment blocks, playing mah-jong. They played the game without speaking, but with great concentration and a certain aggressiveness, slamming down the small pieces of ivory, which echoed down the narrow streets.

The following day was a busy one. Arriving at the Lee Theatre in downtown Hong Kong, we found a get-out for the Cantonese Opera in full swing. An army of coolie-like stagehands carried out crate upon crate of costumes and props, balancing them on their heads and shoulders. The quantity of it all made us uneasy at the simplicity of our own touring equipment while we also regretted not having made the effort to see their performance the previous evening. However, we were happy to discover the very good-sized stage, which was excellently equipped, and an expert crew. Lunch was a rushed one during a break in the lighting rehearsal and an introduction to dim sum, with tiny baskets of steaming dumplings, others with deep-fried seafood, sautéed vegetables and a score of different dishes, all carried around a packed restaurant by an army of women squawking out the contents of their trays as they circled around us. That evening over a thousand people were in the audience and all the ingredients were right to give the best performance so far and, perhaps for the first time, to be aware of a real contact with an Asian audience. We had come to recognise the nature of the Hong Kong Chinese, warming to their charm and liveliness, and above all, their humour. We had worried how they would take to the parody of *La Favorita* and if the rather subtle take-off of Western classical ballet could possibly mean anything to them. But they took to the humour immediately, in fact, quicker than many a Western audience. More recent visits to Hong Kong leave me wondering if those attractive characteristics of the people have been lost. Hong Kong is set on joining the rat race in becoming faster, noisier and richer, and in so doing has become a much tougher, colder sort of city.

After a second performance we were fortunate in having two days free before flying on to Taiwan. There were the usual interviews for the local press, visits to the Taiwanese and Philippine consulates to pick up visas for the company, a courtesy visit to the British Council, after which we managed to pack in a full schedule of sightseeing. Hong Kong was already much more westernised than any country we had visited so far, but there was still evidence of a more traditional China to be found in the backstreets of Central District, especially Ladder Street, a steep incline of steps packed with shops and stalls, and the Cat Street Market bulging with antiques and jewellery. One could still come across a Buddhist temple, like a little oasis in the midst of a street of huge multi-storeyed buildings, all squashed into the limited space available. From our hotel window we could observe one possibly typical Hong Kong family in an apartment opposite. There appeared to be a shift system of sharing beds and space between those working during the daytime and those who worked at night. In what should have been a scenario of complete chaos, about a dozen people lived and slept in a tiny two-roomed apartment, even finding time and space to do their t'ai chi exercises in what appeared to be a harmonious household.

Ignoring the usual tourist routes, we travelled in a rattling public transport red double-decker bus right around the island, stopping off at small fishing ports and market towns. It was interesting to see how quickly one could leave all the hustle and bustle to enter an older and simpler world. One of the greatest treats during our stay in Hong Kong was the daily trip by Star Ferry from Kowloon to Hong Kong Island. This remarkable ferry service has survived the creation of tunnels and train services and still exists, ferrying people across the harbour every few minutes for a fare of about twelve pence. It is still the greatest way to see the city, the massive skyscrapers as well as the bustle of the water traffic, the ferries, the junks and sampans criss-crossing the harbour, and to see, in the distance, the huge container ships making for the South China Sea.

We had no idea what to expect on Taiwan. The island seemed to be shrouded in secrecy. With it having no embassy or consulate in the UK, we were not able to obtain much advance information about the country or any details of the theatre in the capital city, Taipei. We knew something of the history of Taiwan and how General Chiang Kai-Shek, after a bitter war with Mao Tse Tung, who had been an earlier comrade in the Chinese revolution, then broke away from the communist movement, moving with two million followers to occupy the island of Formosa, close to the Chinese mainland. He ruled the island, now rechristened Taiwan, with a heavy military presence, and with considerable help and encouragement from the USA, as a hard-line anti-communist state. At the time of our visit, in 1974, Chang Kai-Shek was soon to be succeeded by his son. Taiwan had not been admitted to the United Nations and the regime was generally disapproved of, especially once moves had been made, with President Nixon's famous visit to meet Mao, to accommodate China into the international community.

There were surprises in store when we landed a little warily at Taipei International Airport; an army of about twenty photographers was waiting for us, managing to get right up to the plane as we disembarked. As we walked onwards towards the arrivals hall, they advanced, backwards, towards the terminal and then further along the many corridors. Teasingly, we walked a bit faster, sending them crouching and scrabbling before us through the various control points, flashing and snapping with a score of cameras. This was the first visit by a British theatre company and we were to make front page news. There were rushed interviews and more photographs, once our hosts had met us, and we were then whisked away to the hotel. Once there, we had a full-scale press conference with more interviews and photos. Apparently, Taipei boasted at least a dozen daily newspapers and innumerable radio and TV stations. Finally, it was finished, and we gratefully settled into our super-comfortable hotel rooms at the huge and grandiose Grand Hotel, an imitation Chinese palace on the northern perimeter of Taipei.

No one had prepared us for the scale of the Asian theatres, the size of their stages, the warmth of the Asian hospitality, as well as the importance of our visit to the local media. And nothing had prepared us for Taiwan. Curiously, our visits to the Republic of China, as the Taiwanese refer to their island state, became of the greatest importance to the company, leading us to return visits, giving an ever increasing number of performances, in 1975, 1977, 1979 and 1981. These visits were thanks to a remarkable man, a true lover of the arts and a generous patron and impresario. Adam Chang was born in Taiwan, but attended university in Germany, following his passion for Western, classical music. He was almost alone in importing Western music and dance to Taiwan where a huge following had been nurtured. He also exported Taiwanese culture, being responsible for introducing the Cloud Gate Dance Theatre company to Europe and to the US where it continues to enjoy great success. The Taiwanese government built the theatres, such as the Dr Sun Yat-Sen Memorial Hall, where we performed in Taipei, mainly for prestige purposes, but was content to put on daily performances of Chinese opera. These gorgeously colourful shows, a mixture of acrobatics, music and folk dramas, filled the auditorium with schoolchildren every midday, but it was left to private promoters to organise all other events. Adam Chang was known as 'Mr Electronics', as he apparently owned, and ran, a good part of Taiwan's burgeoning electronics industry. No doubt this success allowed him to be generous, and we were most fortunate to have been able to benefit from this.

The Memorial Hall holds three thousand people and all three of our performances were sold out before our arrival. The stage was immense and well equipped, but on meeting the stage manager shortly after our arrival we came across one of those typically Asian differences of understanding to which we had to adapt. An early start for the technical fit-up the next morning had been requested, as we were anxious to leave enough time for the company to

The company with our promoter, Adam Chang, outside the Grand Hotel in Taipei, during the tour of South-East Asia in 1974.

rehearse on stage and to get used to the huge space they had to fill. We confirmed we would be at the theatre the next morning at nine o'clock. 'One o'clock better,' came the reply. 'No,' we answered, 'we must keep the prearranged nine o'clock schedule.' Once again: 'One o'clock better,' was the reply. The stage manager kept smiling and nodding, leaving us to believe we had won the day.

The next morning we were at the theatre early, when the vast foyer and marble staircases were eerily empty. Cleaning women went about their business, leaving our little pile of costumes and scenery boxes unattended. Ten o'clock came and went, but soon afterwards the theatre came to life. A crew of technicians arrived, not for our performance, but to set up the daily Chinese opera performance scheduled at midday. Duly the auditorium filled up with hundreds of schoolchildren, dressed identically with military precision, and all sporting those curiously doll-like haircuts with the 'pudding basin' finish. They chanted and sang the praise of their president and founding father, whose huge portraits dominated the walls on each side of the stage, after which the performance began. There was little we could do, but by now we were too nervous to join them in the auditorium and continued to pace the corridors waiting for the performance to finish. Sure enough, and promptly at one o'clock, the theatre was emptied, our stage crew arrived, and we could start work. 'One o'clock better,' the stage manager repeated yet again and we understood that he had little choice in the matter, but it would have been much too impolite to refuse our request, leading him to lose face towards a visitor, a disaster for any Asian.

Fortunately, the stage crew were good and efficient, even experienced in working with dance companies, due to the regular visits of companies from the US. But again, in spite of being excellently well equipped, there was no tallescope, or scaffolding tower, from which to focus the hundreds of stage lights. We could only watch and admire their skill and the speed with which they worked; this time, even the smallest of our 'special' light spots was adjusted from shoulder height and once the lighting bar had been hoisted to its position six or seven metres above the stage, we marvelled at the precision by which the light would hit exactly the right spot. That night, and the following ones, we played to theatres packed not just to capacity as far as the seating would allow, but filled with people sitting on every step on the huge staircase reaching back through the steeply sloped auditorium. They also stood around the walls of the auditorium, filled the orchestra pit and overwhelmed us with the warmth of the reception they gave us.

Adam Chang showed his appreciation in many ways, being eager to introduce us to as many Chinese customs as possible. Naturally, food played an important part so each evening after the performance he would treat us to Cantonese or Pekinese 'banquets', to a Mongolian hot pot or a Szechwan barbeque. Guided tours of the National Museum were organised for us, where we discovered the extraordinary wonders of Chinese art and the many thousands of treasures which had been brought from the Chinese mainland when Taiwan was founded. On days off we also ventured off on our own, although this meant avoiding the 'minders' who usually accompanied us everywhere. Taiwan was a tightly controlled country in every way, and visitors were meant to see only those things they should see. Our minders were usually young men, obviously soldiers, and were passionately patriotic. Apparently, the huge army Taiwan possessed was not only to protect the country from an attack from the Chinese mainland; Taiwan was also seriously planning to invade, and occupy, the mainland. I think that rather unrealistic ambition has been abandoned in time, but scare tactics, involving military manoeuvres, have taken place until very recently.

Taipei in 1974 was a grey, dour workers' city devoid of any charm or attraction, although it has improved with modernisation since that first visit. However, we found it interesting and typical of a side of Chinese modern-day life, while one could still enjoy the night markets, when the drab streets would come to life with stands and stalls, open-air restaurants decked with lanterns and enlivened with music. We tried every sort of local specialty, although only a couple of the company attempted the snails and snakes and various other unidentifiable items. As virtually no one spoke English we were encouraged to look around on other diners' tables, or even to go into the kitchens, to make our orders. We became fond of these people as we had been attracted to the Hong Kong Chinese; but rather than the sing-song Cantonese, these northerners speak Mandarin, with its harsh guttural sounds, and they also have a host of unattractive habits, such as constant belching and farting, hawking and spitting, grunting and snoring, all of which I believe is common in mainland China!

The last stop on our 1974 tour was in the Philippines. Our flights had been delayed, leaving us to arrive very late in Manila, around midnight. However, the welcome was warm, we were garlanded with frangipani wreaths and after fighting through hundreds of bemused Japanese tourists in the airport we were hustled into a large coach. Manila was one venue where we had to find our own accommodation and to pay for this. As usual on these occasions, the British Council came to our assistance, recommending a reasonably priced hotel in downtown Manila, which they used regularly for their own guests. As I gave the address of the 'Casa Pension' to our promoter I recognised a flash of alarm pass over his face.

The bus drove down Roxas Boulevard from the airport, the main entrance to the city, but once 'downtown', the driver turned off into a smaller street and then still further into the backstreets, where he stopped in front of a small hotel with a garish neon sign. We were obviously in a seedy area, the narrow darkened streets lit only by the neon of a scattering of bars. The hotel appeared to have closed for the night, but the bell brought to the door a uniformed man with a machine gun slung over his shoulder, who was expecting us. He handed me a list of the room numbers and slouched off. Taking the precaution of asking the promoter, with the bus, to wait, we ventured inside; turning on the lights in the first bedroom brought forth a loud scuttling sound and the sight of a couple of six-inch long, very black cockroaches nestling in the pillows. Shrieks followed from the other rooms as the dancers found themselves surrounded by dozens of the beasts, roused by the noise and the lights. We were soon back on the bus, giving the driver instructions to take us to one of the large tourist hotels, where thankfully we found rooms despite the lateness of the evening.

The Cultural Centre of the Philippines was at that time, and possibly still is, the largest and best performing venue in South East Asia. Imelda Marcos, the president's culture-loving wife, was the driving force behind the construction of this impressive building jutting out into Manila Bay. It houses not only a huge theatre, but a theatre and dance school and a national museum. I believe it also disguises a large underground defence centre for the government. The fit-up and the lighting took a good seven hours, but the equipment was superb, the crew highly trained and efficient. We learned, however, that these qualified technicians, in a prestige government run organisation, were earning the equivalent of about one hundred US dollars a month. There were more surprises that day; driving with a taxi from the hotel to the Cultural Centre, we passed a large open area at the side of the boulevard where huge crowds of people were standing, or huddling, in small family groups. They had a few possessions gathered around them while they watched a team of bulldozers razing the shanty town which must have been their homes. Apart from the roar of the machines, there was no sound and the people stood silently by, paralysed into inactivity. Asking the taxi driver what was going on, 'Madame Marcos Beautification Programme' was the prompt reply.

The company were now in top form and able to respond to the challenge of the huge stage and a more sophisticated audience. American ballet and dance companies visit the Philippines regularly while at that time there was also a semi-professional classical ballet company as well as national Filipino dance companies based in Manila. The British ambassador came to the first night and we were entertained with dinners and receptions by the very smart upper echelon of Manila's society. The British Council representative was anxious to hear how we liked the 'Casa Pension' and apparently was genuinely surprised that no one had mentioned the cockroaches before!

We had two days off between performances and couldn't resist spending some time at the hotel swimming pool, soaking up the sun. We would soon be back in the depths of the European winter, and we were, in any case, feeling the effects of a month of long-distance travel and demanding performances, as well as a packed programme of tourist activities. Some of the dancers had ignored any opportunities to explore the cities we visited, preferring to stay in the luxury hotels, making use of the swimming pools and even existing on a diet of club sandwiches provided at regular intervals by room service. This lack of curiosity was something Alexander and I could not understand, and despite the tiredness, we spent some time in downtown Manila. The city reflects the mixture of cultures which makes up the Filipino people; Malay, Spanish, American and Chinese. There are wide, modern boulevards and crowded, dirty backstreets and markets. Most stores, restaurants and even smaller shops employ guards with machine guns, which made

180

With our Filipino promoter in Manila. Alexander is on the far left, I am between our
Filipino hosts and Prue Sheridan is third from the right. Graeme Murphy and
Janet Verdon can just be seen behind us.

us uneasy walking around Manila. Martial Law had been imposed in 1972,
which apparently had brought some much needed law and order to the
country, while a curfew was still in place in 1974. Finally, after the last performance, we were ready to leave. Dancers Graeme Murphy and his wife,
Janet Vernon, who had worked with us throughout 1974, went on to
Australia (where they founded the Sydney Dance Company to win international acclaim), while the rest of us had an uneventful flight back to Paris,
and on to London, arriving in time for Christmas.

chapter
nine

─────────

The Growth Years
1975-1980

In many ways the company came of age as a result of that first tour to South East Asia – it was as if we had turned a new page to become a different sort of company. We no longer performed in market squares or under the Westway; we stopped the open-stage classes and rehearsals, the question and answer sessions with the audience and, as a result of the confidence the tour had given us, we felt ready to move on to bigger and better things, with stronger dancers and an enriched repertoire. If the Asian tour had been hugely exciting, it had also been extremely challenging; everyone suffered from jet lag, with the tiredness and irritability this inevitably caused. The heat, the humidity, the relentless roar of traffic, the noise from air conditioners, the extraordinary smells, the crowds of people pushing, shoving, shouting and chattering; all of this was a huge strain. While being constantly in demand for press conferences and interviews, as well as taking charge of the stage crews, supervising the scenery, the lighting, the sound, giving company classes and taking rehearsals, Alexander and I were also dancing four ballets every night.

Once back in London, we needed, above all, to catch up on our sleep, and then to get back to taking ballet classes ourselves. Dancers in London were fortunate at that time to have a choice of first-class teachers giving regular open classes to professionals. It took an American to provide us with the first real centre for dancers with spacious, light, airy, and well-heated studios. Gary Cockrell came to London as part of the cast of the original *West Side Story* company, and after the long West End season, opted to stay. He acquired one of the then recently vacated warehouses in Floral Street, once used by the Covent Garden Market, turning it into the Dance Centre, a mecca for dance students and professionals with a day-long schedule of classes, including classical ballet, modern dance, jazz and Indian dance; auditions were held there while details of jobs on offer were posted on a huge noticeboard at the entrance. Visiting ballet masters and company directors could drop into a class at any time and be certain of meeting colleagues, or finding dancers they might need, be it for the corps de ballet or for principal dancer positions. The Dance Centre was also in the heart of Theatreland and the dance world, with the Royal Opera House and the Coliseum only a stone's throw away. Dancers from The Royal Ballet and London Festival Ballet could join classes between rehearsals, as well as dancers from the musicals at Drury Lane or the Palace Theatre. Even visiting companies, such as the Bolshoi Ballet, used a studio for their company classes and rehearsals.

Also close by, in St Martin's Lane, nearly opposite the Coliseum, is the ballet shoe shop Freed of London, a resident there since 1929. Ruled over by the indomitable Mrs Freed, who bossed everyone, customers and staff alike, it was, and still is, the preferred supplier of ballets shoes and practice clothes for dancers all over the world. The heroines of the shop were the sales assistants, Ellen and Michelle (the latter ultimately to become a director of the firm), who patiently and efficiently served the varied lot of customers, be it a young student trying on her first pair of pointe shoes, or a star ballerina needing twenty pairs of shoes by the following week. Freed came to my rescue many times, posting express parcels of pointe shoes to remote corners of Europe. Just around the corner from Freed, in Cecil Court, was the Ballet Bookshop, a direct descendant of Cyril Beaumont's famous book shop in Charing Cross Road. The Ballet Bookshop (subsequently known as Dance Books) was, and is today, directed by ex dancer John O'Brien and book lover David Leonard – although the shop has now become a publishing house and online retailer and is no longer in central London. At the time when the Ballet Bookshop was based in Cecil Court, it became a meeting place for dancers and balletomanes, many who came simply to browse through the exceptional collection of new and second-hand books.

Before the arrival of the Dance Centre, teachers gave classes in studios scattered all over London: Audrey de Vos probably had the most pleasant studio in Notting Hill Gate; Idzikowski had by now moved out of the Kensington church hall, giving classes over a refuge for homeless people in Covent Garden; Cleo Nordi taught in a tiny space on top of Earl's Court Tube station, while Anna Northcote had the largest studio, in West Street in central London, but it was dark and airless, freezing cold in winter, heated with a single paraffin stove. There were more teachers in the Covent Garden area; Errol Addison, once a dancer with the Diaghilev Ballets Russes and star of West End variety shows, with Kathleen Crofton, a former member of Anna Pavlova's company, taught in a building in Great Newport Street, the Max Rivers Studios. It comprised of a warren of small rooms and studios for actors and musicians, while on the top floor two rooms had been joined together to create a dance studio. Kathleen Crofton, who still wore a 'Pavlova' hairdo, parted in the middle and drawn down and back over her ears to make a small bun, taught a strictly traditional classical ballet class in which she demonstrated the exercises while incongruously whistling a suitable tune. She had many followers, as did Errol; portly and jovial, he was accompanied on the piano by his brother, Cyril. Errol claimed to give 'balletic enjoyment' classes, hoping to keep up the spirits of the many unemployed dancers whose only chance to dance would be the daily class. In the 1970s Anna and Errol had moved to the Dance Centre, together with Eileen Ward, Brian Shaw and David Blair, all ex dancers or teachers with the Royal Ballet. The classes were packed and the standard high, and with a teacher one knew and trusted, it took just a couple of weeks of daily classes to feel back on form.

It was at one of those classes, on a January afternoon, that my eyes fell upon an impressive looking dancer standing against the barre. Good-looking, tall and strongly muscular, I could only guess he was a Russian 'star' visiting London, as English male dancers of that era were rarely so powerful looking. Alexander joined me at class the following day and discovered he was Keith Rosson, a former principal dancer of The Royal Ballet, who had just returned to England after a few years working in South Africa and the USA. Keith was looking for work, and as none of the major companies appeared to have positions available, he agreed to join us for the next tours. Although Alexander was still dancing actively, it was clear that his multiple duties as director and choreographer made it difficult for him to continue dancing classical roles, with the technical demands these posed, so he was looking for ways to limit his roles to those with which he felt more comfortable. Beginning with Keith, I had the good fortune to start working with a chain of partners –

Keith Rosson with Margot Fonteyn (left) and Galina Samsova taking applause after a
performance in Barcelona in 1966. Keith and Margot Fonteyn appeared as
guest artists with London Festival Ballet in *Swan Lake*.

experienced, international principal dancers – and working with them was always stimulating, and mostly highly enjoyable. It was, above all, an enormous thrill to work with Keith, someone who had partnered Margot Fonteyn, Svetlana Beriosova, Galina Samsova and many other leading ballerinas of the day. He was not only an exemplary partner and a tireless worker, but was great fun to be with. He was also keen to try as many new roles as possible and seemed to enjoy working in the more relaxed and convivial setting of a small company.

Keith was a true product of The Royal Ballet, having gone through the school to join the company corps de ballet where he spent his first year 'dressing' the stage, waiting to have the chance to really dance. However, he soon made his way through the ranks, arriving at principal dancer status, dancing all the major classical ballets with the company's ballerinas, while also being chosen to dance in more contemporary works by John Cranko, Roland Petit and George Balanchine. Writing of his first performance in Balanchine's *Apollo*, Richard Buckle enthused in *The Sunday Times*: 'There have been other casts for *Apollo* at Covent Garden, and the big news is that Keith Rosson was tremendous as the god. I wouldn't have believed it of one so Herculean. He really let himself go, which is a rare thing to see a Royal Ballet dancer do. His arms yearned upward in prayer, his eyes flashed holy fire. As a result Balanchine's old ballet seemed the best thing that had happened in years.'

We were also joined that season by a talented eighteen-year-old, Katherine MacKenzy, straight out of the Royal Ballet School, and an American dancer, Rory Foster, a tall, elegant dancer, a former member of American Ballet Theatre. We toured that spring and summer throughout the UK, France, Switzerland and Belgium, including dates in Brussels and Geneva. Keith was also performing with the New London Ballet, led by former stars of London Festival Ballet, Galina Samsova and André Prokovsky, but returned to us in the autumn for a new tour to South East Asia.

The Far Eastern impresario, Donald Moore, had been keen to bring the company back to Asia in 1975, but negotiations dragged on over the months while he was occupied with a huge tour of *Disney on Parade*, involving hundreds of participants and tons of equipment. As a result of the delays, some of our bookings had fallen through, and it was looking difficult to finance a company of the same size as in 1974. It was decided, therefore, to take a smaller group of just six dancers, and with Prue and Katherine, Keith and Rory joining the two of us, we had a small but strong and competent group. The promoter in Manila was laying down conditions: 'No modern or electronic numbers, no repeats, strictly classical ballet,' were his orders, and the other promoters were also requesting a more classical programme than on our last visit. Rather reluctantly we mounted a suite of excerpts from *Swan Lake*, another from *Les Sylphides*, as well as several classical pas de deux. Alexander had choreographed one new ballet in the spring, *Castles in the Air*, to Jacques Ibert's *Divertissement*, proving to be an instant success and a good addition to the repertoire.

With Keith Rosson in the 'Peasant pas de deux' from *Giselle*, on tour in 1975.

The tour was not without its problems and its dramas. Keith had warned us that he was not a good traveller by air, but we had not imagined the trauma which the long-haul flights would cause. Fortunately, he brought along a good supply of Valium, while Prue sat next to him on the long flight to Singapore, reassuring him every time the plane hit the slightest quiver of turbulence. On arrival in Singapore, we were whisked to the hotel in a comfortable and air-conditioned bus, and we hoped that the worst was over.

Unwisely, in hindsight, but understandably, the dancers all decided to set off sightseeing. Keith walked boldly from the cool lobby through the sliding glass doors to be hit by what must have felt like a wall of 32ºC heat and 100 per cent humidity, sending him reeling back into the hotel lobby where he fell flat on his back. A heart attack was suspected and the hotel doctor was called for while we all assembled in Keith's room. The Chinese doctor dutifully made all the checks – blood pressure, pulse, heartbeat, etc. – and we all sat quietly watching and waiting until he announced, 'Sir, I've been sitting here for half an hour and you are still alive. I don't think there is anything wrong with you.' Turning to Alex he added, 'One hundred dollars, please.' However, he did prescribe some more Valium.

The performances in Singapore went off successfully, after which we travelled uneventfully, if rather tensely, on to Manila. After our arrival, we made the same mistake, setting off from the hotel, thinking that a walk in the open air down Roxas Boulevard towards the Cultural Centre might be a good idea, as we had the rest of the day free. For some inexplicable reason I decided to take with me my large leather handbag, containing not only my passport but all the group's air tickets, having left cash and valuables in the hotel safe. Walking on the outside of the pavement, with my bag slung over my shoulder, we were chatting so intensely I didn't notice a taxi sidling up beside us until a man leant out and grabbed my bag. I hung on as hard as I could, but was soon being dragged down Roxas Boulevard on my stomach, besides the speeding taxi. My assailant was hanging on too, leaning over me and laughing at my pathetic attempts to win back my bag. At last I gave up when the car sped into a side road.

There was a police station nearby, so with a bloodied skirt and filthy face and arms I was ushered into the police chief's office. Here we found a scene like something from a Hollywood B-movie; the police chief sat back in his chair, feet crossed up on the desk in front of him, a cap slouched over one eye and a cigarette dangling from his mouth. He was surrounded by a gallery of mugshots on the walls, each portrait with a title; 'wanted for murder', 'wanted for robbery and assault', and so on. Showing little interest in our story – 'It happens every day' was his only comment – he passed me a huge book of the more notorious local criminals' portraits, asking if I recognised any of them – an unlikely possibility.

In the event, our travel agent from Tottenham Court Road proved to be a miracle worker, sending us replacement air tickets within two days, while the Australian Embassy gave me a new passport almost immediately. Despite the drama, and although I was bruised and bandaged, we performed the next day when I danced my first Black Swan from Act 3 of *Swan Lake*. I had not wanted to dance this extremely challenging pas de deux, as there was little time for rehearsals in London, but it was one of Keith's most successful roles and it was difficult to refuse. He supported me gallantly through the pas de deux, but it will always be associated with that nightmare in Manila and I swore never to dance it again.

Each evening, after our performances, we were treated to receptions by the elite of Manila's society, including friends and family of the Marcos's, who were still in power at that time. These people all lived in Makati, the residential district on the fringe of the city where the luxury villas, as well as the huge commercial centres, were encircled by a tightly guarded walled enclave. The company was wined and dined, while being incessantly photographed, and our two tall, blond, handsome male dancers were undoubtedly the star attractions besides the glamorous, bejewelled Filipino hosts.

Manila was also the only venue where we had problems with payment. On our many national and international tours, there were often worries that we might have trouble getting payments, especially on international tours when it was necessary to demand cash, and in US dollars. It was virtually impossible to get this in advance, and sometimes local promoters did not turn up, tried to rewrite a contract, or to put off paydays. On the Asian tours we found the Chinese, whether in Hong Kong or Taiwan, to be unfailingly

honest and reliable. In Europe, there were occasionally problems with late payments, especially in France and in Italy, but the funds did always turn up in the end. In fact, we are still awaiting payment from just one theatre, and this is in England, where the management of the time went into liquidation shortly after our visit, leaving huge debts unsettled.

Keith with two of our Filipino hosts at a reception in Manila.

Another 'line-up' in Manila, this in 1975. The company dancers are (from left) Prue Sheridan, Rory Foster, Keith Rosson, me, Katherine MacKenzy and Alexander.

Back in Manila, in 1975, the promoter did not turn up at the appointed time for settling our fee, but on reaching him by telephone, the meeting was rescheduled for the following morning. As it was our second visit to the Philippines, and our relationship with him was very amicable, we were not too concerned, but the following day's appointment was also not kept and we had to fly out that afternoon. When attempts to contact him proved to be unsuccessful, we knew some drastic action had to be taken. There wasn't very much we could do, only threaten; so we left a message to say that if he did not turn up with our payment in full by lunchtime, we would inform the British ambassador, the British Council and call a press conference. That worked, bringing the promoter to arrive at the hotel shortly afterwards, some-what out of breath and looking very serious.

So, on to Hong Kong, to perform this time at City Hall, under the aus-pices of what was then called the Urban District Council. The theatre was essentially a concert hall but boasted a good-sized stage with all the necessary facilities. Hong Kong was still British at this time, and the City Hall was run very much like a British town council building; rules and regulations abounded, but the locals who ran the offices, with delightfully old-fashioned names like Agnes and Violet, were full of Chinese vitality as well as being thoroughly business-like. Keith still caused us concern, and when we asked at City Hall if a doctor was on hand they soon had an ambulance at the stage door to whisk Keith, sirens blazing, across town for a total check-up. He was returned to us with a clean bill of health – and a prescription for more Valium.

Following the two performances in Hong Kong there was an extra date in Macau, the tiny island just a few miles across the mouth of the Pearl River, which belonged at that time to the Portuguese. Macau is reached by a regular hydrofoil service from Hong Kong and we were met on arrival by a diminutive elderly man with an interestingly wizened face, Mr Gomez, and at his side a huge bear-sized man in a brown cassock, Father Lancelot, a Franciscan monk. Both were Portuguese born but like many old Asian hands, had with time acquired almost Asian features and skin colouring. This unlikely couple were responsible for the cultural life of the island and proved to be exceptional characters. Mr Gomez had been the governor of Macau and on retirement had remained in what must have been Government House with a small staff of servants. It was a weatherboard, colonial-style building with a gabled roof and wrap-around verandahs, typical of Macau; as if a part of Portugal had been dropped onto a tropical island, the whole creating a muddled mixture of styles and cultures, recalling the great days of the colonies, when East met West. A maid was making up some camp beds on the open verandah. 'This,' said Mr Gomez, 'is where you can sleep.' We knew it was impossible – fun enough for a holiday, but the humidity was around 100 per cent, we would be surrounded by unknown insects, and possibly even animals, and we were tired and travel worn. So, as diplomatically as possible, we asked to be moved to a modern hotel.

The following day, the performance was to take place in a large hall in Father Lancelot's college. There was no stage, but we were to perform at one end of the hall with the audience seated on chairs in a semicircle around us. As there was virtually no stage lighting, and no way of hanging any scenery, the performance day was an easy one, leaving us time for sightseeing. Macau was one of the few places where mainland Chinese might have a chance to cross the border from Red China. From Mr Gomez's verandah one could look across the narrow strait of water to a kind of no-man's-land patrolled by armed soldiers, obviously posted to stop people leaving the country rather than stopping intruders entering. However, refugees still did occasionally make the treacherous crossing, either by swimming or in small boats, and invariably they would bring with them family heirlooms; small items of value to sell in Macau in order to start their new lives. Macau, therefore, was full of second-hand shops and antique shops packed with jade and silver, jewellery and ornaments at bargain prices. Browsing through these shops trying to imagine the history of all these treasures was a fascinating way to spend a couple of hours.

There remained a serious problem to be solved before the performance; the 'stage' floor was of highly waxed teak wood. On arrival we asked for the floorboards to be scrubbed with a strong cleaner to remove the wax, hoping to be able to use powdered resin on it, as was the normal procedure. The Asian stage floors had caused problems in general, as the teak wood is particularly hard and mostly very slippery, and as the theatres did not have the linoleum dance floors which were just starting to come on the market in Europe. Coming back to the theatre that afternoon, for the company class, we tried sprinkling resin on the washed floor. It simply skidded on top of the surface; next we tried a more abrasive cleaner, with a bit of grit in it; someone claimed that Coca-Cola was a foolproof, if sticky, solution. With an added sense of urgency we sent out for a dozen bottles of Coke. The surface of the stage was starting to look, and smell, a mess, and it still had the slipperiness of a skating rink. There seemed to be one remaining possibility – to dance barefoot, although this would look rather incongruous for a Swan Queen in a tutu. Even this last resort hardly helped, and every step was fraught with danger. With only a couple of hours to spare, we enlisted help from Father Lancelot, to find us a very large carpet. These are few and far between in Asia, as most houses and public buildings have plain wooden floors, but we had seen one, a huge Chinese-style carpet, in the lobby of our hotel. It took a little persuasion, no doubt a number of complimentary tickets, but we got our carpet, which gave us just enough space for a quickly revised version of the programme, one with a lot fewer pirouettes and big jumps than usual, but hopefully not many in Macau noticed.

To add to our problems, it was during this performance that Alexander started to feel ill, and by the time we reached the final ballet he was flat out on the dressing room floor. Keith, now luckily recovered from his jet lag and health problems, proved to be a real pro, taking over Alexander's role, improvising with abandon, quickly making an about-turn on exiting to reappear in his own role and saving the day. At dinner that night, in the long dining room of Mr Gomez's residence, he told us that we had fulfilled one of his long held wishes – to bring ballet to Macau. We would have wished to have been able to give him a better performance.

The company returned to Macau on one other occasion, in 1979, to find the island had changed dramatically in those few years. Portugal had finally severed ties, leaving Macau to officially become part of China. However, the Red Chinese saw the sense in keeping Macau open to visitors, especially those from Hong Kong, and in encouraging them to use the numerous casinos and gambling halls which were now being constructed on prime sites on the waterfront. Gambling was forbidden in Hong Kong itself, but enthusiastic gamblers from the British colony would swamp Macau each weekend, playing the tables and the fruit machines for twenty-four hours a day. This brought with it a definite advantage for us, as the largest of the casinos now possessed a well-equipped theatre, also offering us accommodation at the luxury hotel in the same complex. However, the Vietnamese boat people had discovered Macau, creating shanty towns in the backstreets, where these immigrant people lived under rough shelters of plastic or cloth; pitiful beggars filled the streets and struggled to survive in the gutters and on the pavements. When we left Macau in 1975, Mr Gomez had said solemnly that we would not see him again, and as we learned later, he already knew he was terminally ill. Four years on, by which time both Mr Gomez and Father Lancelot had disappeared, Macau had become a different sort of Asian backwater.

In 1975, the company left Macau for Taiwan, on the last leg of what had become an eventful tour. Unfortunately, despite Adam Chang's warm welcome and generous hospitality, there were more problems in store. During the second performance in Taipei, both Prue and I slipped on the treacherously slippery stage floor. This happened to me on the first steps of the *Don Quixote* pas de deux, when my leg slipped away beneath me and I felt the ankle twist and crunch. Keith was able to keep me upright, helping me to carry on through the pas de deux and on to the end of the performance. In the dressing room after the performance Prue, who had succumbed to a similar accident, joined me in watching in horror as our ankles swelled and puffed up; travelling on to the southern Taiwanese city of Taichung the following day, we could only commiserate with each other while keeping ice packs on the sprains. With only six dancers there was no possibility of cast changes, and it took us both a long, slow couple of hours to warm up the injuries with the simplest of exercises until the mobility came back and the pain subsided a little. As often happens in such cases, once we were into the performance 'something' took over, the adrenalin soothed the pain, and the injury was almost forgotten. With a smaller, less slippery stage, we were able to complete the final performance, and a couple of days later we were both back to normal.

In Taipei the following day, Alexander discovered his arms and chest covered in red spots; German measles? Chickenpox? Shingles? It looked like one or the other, and shingles could have been possible as a result of all the stress, but we couldn't tell. He was insistent on not calling a doctor, being wary of the possibility of ending up in a Taiwanese hospital, and as we had another day in Taipei when I was scheduled to teach a master class we could only hope that he would recover before our departure.

There were about twenty students in the ballet studio the next morning, obviously well trained and eager to work. The two-hour session which was planned was a little longer than the usual ballet class, but it seemed to go off well and was followed by the little flutter of applause for the teacher which has become the normal procedure. More dancers came into the studio laden with boxes of food, whereupon everyone settled down on the floor to dig into a huge picnic of rice and noodles, meats and vegetables. I thought this a charming idea and was happy to join in, thinking how different they were from Western dancers, who often prefer to go all day without eating anything much. Then someone asked: 'More class?' 'You want some more class?' Oh yes, they wanted another class, but firstly they would all have a quick nap. Stretched out on the studio floor, they immediately passed out for about ten minutes while I attempted to work out what on earth I could do for another couple of hours, hoping that my ankle would hold out.

Soon the meal was cleared away with the dancers back on their feet, ready to start again. It seemed a good idea to challenge them a little, so the girls stayed in their pointe shoes to try the more difficult pointe exercises, while the boys could work at the big jumps and more challenging steps, which usually come at the end of a ballet class. They attacked all of this gamely, even with considerable enthusiasm, until more boxes of food and pots of Chinese tea were brought in. I thought I'd better eat or drink a little to revive myself before the trip back to the hotel, when the only dancer who spoke a little English approached me shyly with, 'Could we do just a little more class, please?' I suppose they thought it might be a once in a lifetime occasion and they'd better make the best of it. Although I was seriously tired by this time, as the lack of verbal communication meant I had to demonstrate every step, and show every correction, I could hardly refuse. Fortunately, I had brought with me a couple of music cassettes with music from *Swan Lake* and *Les Sylphides*, allowing me to teach them some of the traditional classical repertoire, although this entailed yet more demonstration on my part. By the time they had learned most of Act 2 of *Swan Lake* everyone had had enough, and I was finally able to escape, after being presented with flowers and gifts and showered with thanks.

The taxi which took me back to the hotel was one of the many older, decrepit models often used by taxi drivers in Taipei, and the trip was not without incident; on the top of an overpass, the car screeched to a halt while the driver jumped out of the car to throw a blanket over the flames leaping out of the engine. More frighteningly, he had locked me into the back seat with no means of escape. He was determined to keep his fare, dead or alive! Back in the hotel, Alexander was still seriously 'spotty', but these looked as if they were fading. Terrified he might be stopped from travelling if this was noticed at the airport, we applied a good covering of make-up the next morning, and to our great relief, we were off to the airport and on our way back to London.

In 1976 Keith decided to throw in the towel, to stop performing and to complete a Royal Academy of Dance teacher training course. It was not easy for him, with teachers twenty years his junior, without any comparable background, telling him the right and the wrong way to teach dance. He did complete the course, continuing to take our company classes whenever we were in London, besides his other teaching commitments. We found a new leading man in Frederic Jahn-Werner, a Monaco-born, New-Zealand-raised son of a Dutch family who had been a soloist with the Australian Ballet and the Dutch National Ballet. Alexander immediately set to work to create *Voices*, his first 'serious' ballet since the 1974 *Visages d'une Femme*. Using George Crumb's atmospheric score, *Ancient Voices of Children*, a song-cycle of poems by García Lorca portraying games of love and death, *Voices* became one of his most successful works. Visually, it was inspired by the surrealist paintings of the Belgian artist Paul Delvaux, and the ballet evolved as a dream-like fantasy work, some of it almost in slow motion while other scenes were powerfully athletic.

From left: Prue Sheridan, Nicola Sanina and Katherine MacKenzy in Voices, 1976.

196

'Ric', as Jahn-Werner was known, had a good training in contemporary dance, as well as classical ballet, and was well suited to the new work, as were Prue and Katherine. Using more of the wonderfully danceable music of Louis Moreau Gottschalk, we also added a new closing ballet to the repertoire, *Pasquinade*, and performed both new works during the winter and spring tours in the UK and in France, after which Ric left us to join London Festival Ballet, notably creating the role of Tybalt in Nureyev's *Romeo and Juliet*. He later became assistant ballet master, together with Patricia Ruanne, at the Paris Opera Ballet with responsibility for Nureyev's ballets. We were kept busy that season with a series of lecture–demonstrations in Saint Quentin, in northern France, visiting kindergartens, tough technical colleges, schools for children with special needs and retirement homes, all over the slightly grim, rundown city. It was hard work giving three or four mini performances a day, transporting the company, costumes, sound equipment and all that was necessary from place to place, but although it was seriously challenging, it was made immensely enjoyable thanks to the excellent organisation of the city's cultural department and the often all too frequent meals, receptions and hospitality.

Discussing the finer points of classical ballet with a young audience in
Saint Quentin, northern France.

Katherine MacKenzy dancing an excerpt from *Les Sylphides* in Saint Quentin.

Back in the UK, in June, we took part in the York Music Festival for which Alexander had been commissioned to collaborate with the composer Elizabeth Lutyens on a new opera–dance work entitled *One and the Same* together with the excellent Vesuvius Ensemble, and the well-known soprano Jane Manning. It was not an easy job; Lutyens, as we found with other composers, had very fixed ideas of how she imagined the choreography, with little regard for the technical considerations, especially as we were performing in the rather sterile surroundings, and on the marble floor, of the university hall.

Two new members joined us in June – a French couple, Christine Lassauvageux and Francis Pedros. Both came from Bordeaux, where they had been members of the ballet company at the opera house, before moving to Belgium to the Ballet Royal de Wallonie, a company with a good reputation. Both were excellent dancers; Francis had a high, springy jump and Christine was a steely technician. They also had natural stage presence, lots of French charm and were versatile interpreters. Together with Prue and Katherine, we now had a solid core to the company, to which we could add more male or female dancers according to the demands of the repertoire. It developed into a happily collaborative period of around five years, full of activity and of creativity. Another new acquisition was a full-time administrator; Maggie, an Australian former dancer, who, despite dressing in long, flowing skirts and wearing strings of Indian beads, was a determined worker and full of enthusiasm. With an office assistant in Hilde, a German-born woman living locally, who spent her days bashing out hundreds of letters on an ancient Remington, we had a busy office, releasing me to concentrate on dancing.

During 1975 we had also discovered a much needed stage manager/lighting designer with whom we could work happily and with confidence. While we were setting up the stage at the Theatre Royal in Lincoln, we realised the theatre's technical crew consisted of just one man who did everything; he unloaded, set up the scenery, focused the stage lights, racing up and down from the lighting box to the dress circle, up to the gallery and back down onto the stage to do this. As I plotted the lighting cues with him I soon recognised that his skills – with the rather outdated equipment – were far ahead those of the usual provincial technician. During the performance, Alexander and I passed on the cues for the lighting changes between exits and entrances on stage as was usual; this was obviously not an ideal solution, but we had worked out a fairly foolproof system over the years. The following evening Nigel surprised us by saying we need not do this as he was aware when the cues would occur, and when that evening's performance went off faultlessly we realised we had found an exceptional technician, skilled both technically and artistically.

Nigel Clarke worked with us for many years; he came and went, obliged to keep his connection with the theatre in Lincoln, but accompanied us on all of our important tours. An exceptionally imaginative and sensitive lighting designer from whom I learned much, Nigel was not always easy to work with as he had a quick temper and even walked out on occasions. But he always came back and despite his impatience, and even fury, especially with French and Italian stage crews, enjoyed his international travels. Later he was asked to supervise the construction of the backstage facilities of the new Opera House in the Royal Cultural Center in Amman, Jordan and those of the huge new Academy for Performing Arts in Hong Kong. Tragically, he died at a much too early age.

In July 1976 the company made a first tour of Italy, promoted by the cultural organisation ATER based in Modena, which shortly afterwards created the highly successful Aterballetto ballet company. As is usual in Italy, the day-to-day organisation was all a bit chaotic, leaving one unsure if the stage would actually be built in time for the performance, the lights rigged and the sound operating, but it was easy to enjoy the summer atmosphere on the coast in Rimini, performing in the main square in the quaint mini state of San Marino, or in the historical cities of Piacenza and Modena. After performances in Milan we then drove north to southern Germany to take part in the summer music festival in Passau.

Hardly back in London, there was a London season at the Collegiate Theatre, attached to University College London (now known as the Bloomsbury Theatre), to prepare. We revived *Circuit*, *Nepentha* and *Visages d'une Femme* for this season, and included *Voices* and *Pasquinade*, as well as Prue's ballets *Quintette* and *Derivations*. Alexander still found time to mount a new, full company work, *About Face*, for which Shostakovitch's *Piano Trio in E minor* was the starting point. The music, full of references to folk music, which Alexander always loved, has many dramatic and darker undertones. The composer wrote the piece in a moment of despair during his many battles with the Soviet regime, and in the ballet my role was one of an outsider, at odds with the regimented group and destined to be a loner; it became one of my favourite roles, in a strong, emotional ballet.

An unexpected success of the Collegiate season was *Visages d'une Femme*, of which *The Observer's* critic Alexander Bland wrote: 'Christina Gallea gave a powerful performance in a slightly Gallic style – all stabbing toes and venomous wrists – with Alexander Roy, the choreographer, and Jean-Marie Dubrul, a massive figure with a *Kojak* coiffure, as her well-contrasted suitors. It was effectively designed and, like the whole programme, well lit.' The origin of the set design would not have been dreamed of by the London critic. It was only at the dress rehearsal for the second programme that Alexander realised the whole programme was danced on a bare stage and against a plain backdrop, either a black backcloth or a blue cyclorama. It seemed a matter of urgency to incorporate some more interesting visual images, and *Visages* was the work that would benefit most from this. He remembered we had a box of silk parachutes which we had acquired from an army surplus store in our storeroom and rushed back to North House to dig them out. Something had happened to them – whether they had been nibbled at by insects or rodents, or if they had just withered with age, we did not know, but they had turned into something spidery and web-like, as dusty and powdery as if they had come from Miss Havisham's house; perfect, in fact, for *Visages*. Draping them on some upright poles, to form a nest-like surround to the dancing area, we had an unexpectedly effective set.

Jean-Marie Dubrul, the newest of my international partners, was a French dancer we had known from Paris where he had danced with several companies including that of Janine Charrat. Jean-Marie and I danced together in most ballets of that London season and he was a superb partner in a typically polite,

French manner. In view of the fact that he worked with us for just a short rehearsal period, he was unexpectedly dramatic and moving in *Nepentha*, impressive in *Voices*. But Jean-Marie left us at the end of the London season as he was actually only on holiday from a French ballet company and, in any case, it was still not financially possible for us to keep any of these leading men, always much in demand, on long-term contracts.

Voices, shown for the first time in London, was also well received, with Katherine Sorley-Walker writing in *The Daily Telegraph*: '… derived its image influence from Paul Delvaux's paintings and sustained remarkably well a mood of slow fantasy. Its measured pace and hypnotic stage pictures were sensitively interpreted.' Reporting for BBC Radio London, Bill Dolman gave a vivid description of the opening of the ballet: 'It is the most intense work of the evening, a series of images of innocence, of love, of sexuality; parts of it are very erotic, and it is a ballet which is capable of several meanings. For example, we see a young girl playing with a large rubber ball, like a slow motion film, when a figure emerges from a mirror at the side of the stage, a terrifying wraith-like, faceless figure, watching the girl. It moves over to her, makes contact, after which the girl's movements with the ball are sensual and erotic. What is the figure? A doppelgänger? A fantasy in her mind? Suffice it to say that it is a haunting image which remains with you during the ballet, a figure I found menacing in the extreme. The figure was danced by Prue Sheridan, technically superb.'

Of *Castles in the Air*, the *Evening News* wrote: 'Dance can be lots of fun, and Alexander Roy's *Castles in the Air* is just that.' The other 'lighter' ballets, *Pasquinade* and Prue's ballets *Quintette* and *Derivations*, were all well liked and Francis Pedros ran away with praise from everyone. There were, of course, the usual grumbles: 'It could be a useful little company, if only...' The condescending tone continued to be used by those who could not accept the concept of a company's repertoire being almost uniquely the creation of a sole choreographer. Although this was quite usual on the Continent and in the USA, it was still expected of British companies to serve up a varied programme by different choreographers. At a meeting with Jane Nicholas at the Arts Council (whose policy demanded such a mixed repertoire), I suggested that this was like going into a supermarket to pick a choice of ballets off the shelves – all suitably approved and stamped by the Arts Council. Astounded, I suppose by my boldness, she made some quick notes on her writing pad, but it was still many years before the organisation changed their policy. The season at the Collegiate took place in August at the height of a heat wave; audiences were sparse but the critics had come in their numbers, many to see both programmes. The exposure to this scrutiny was necessary as one can easily become blasé and used to the almost always favourable press in the provinces, while the good reviews we received in London were of the greatest value in attracting more and better bookings in the UK and abroad.

Francis Pedros (jumping) in Prue Sheridan's ballet *Quintette*.

Voices on stage at the Collegiate Theatre in 1976 with (from left) Prue Sheridan, Christina Lassauvageux, Katherine MacKenzy and Jean-Marie Dubrul.

202

Alexander in *Voices*.

Katherine MacKenzy (centre) in *Housewarming*.

With Prue Sheridan (left) and the company in *About Face*, in London in 1976.

We did appease the Arts Council sufficiently to obtain two more productions grants, one for a new work by Prue entitled *Between the Lines*, an abstract dance work in a mixture of contemporary and classical styles, as well as a ballet from Terry Gilbert, whom we had known from London Dance Theatre, and who was enjoying considerable success as a choreographer working with several leading opera companies. Terry created *The Last Day of Summer* for us; a 'pretty' ballet, all chiffon and Brahms waltzes which was not really 'us', but it was a well-crafted work and was performed for some years. In the spring of 1977 there were more new works; Alexander mounted *Housewarming* to music by Francis Poulenc, Prue created her first 'serious' ballet, *Virginia Creeper*, about the relationship between a mother and two daughters, and Terry Gilbert gave me a solo, *Street Dancer*, to Benjamin Britten's unaccompanied cello suite. All of these were performed in London, at The Roundhouse, along with a revival of *Fanfares*.

During the next three years, and despite all the turmoil in the UK at that time, both politically and economically, we performed and toured more and more, visiting good-sized theatres as well as the smaller and medium-sized venues. There was very little competition for us as, besides the major companies with their regular touring commitments in the larger cities, only the New London Ballet shared some of our venues. But this company, despite adhering to the Arts Council guidelines, was forced to close in 1977. Fearlessly, we travelled as far as Bangor and Aberystwyth in Wales, Dundee and Inverness in Scotland, and everywhere in between. Basically, we were prepared to perform wherever we were wanted, as this was our raison d'être, as was the necessity to earn as much as possible from bookings to cover the running costs and balance the budget. We were now playing in larger venues, such as the Birmingham Hippodrome, the Nottingham Theatre Royal or the Bradford Alhambra, where the company was increased to twelve dancers and we added a small group of musicians to accompany us, instead of the usual recorded music, which the Musicians' Union did still allow us to use on tour. This very militant organisation made problems for many companies, especially overseas ones visiting the UK, who were accustomed to using recorded music. Some were obliged to hire an entire orchestra whose members sat backstage while the performances went ahead, accompanied by taped music, possibly electronic, or perhaps by a single musician or small ensemble. They were lenient with us, possibly accepting the fact that we had no alternative, except, of course, in the larger venues.

It was also in those major theatres that the company attracted some interesting attention. Lord Goodman, always outspoken, international lawyer, advisor to prime ministers, chairman of the Arts Council from 1965 to 1972, and director of the boards of most of the major theatre and opera companies in London, came to one of our performances in Nottingham. 'Why doesn't this company get Arts Council subsidy?' he was heard to shout out in the bar, 'It's a disgrace!' Apparently our dealings with the Arts Council didn't sift through to him at the time, but possibly his presence inspired the local critic to write in his review: 'All I can say from one showing at the Theatre Royal last night is that the keepers of the state purse ought to beg, borrow or steal to let British audiences relish a lot more of this splendid company. It's got fire in its belly, joy in its soul and technique to the tips of its toes.'

During one of those tours in the Midlands, my mother (who had remarried and settled in London) phoned early one morning at breakfast to tell us that there had been a fire at North House during the night. The fire brigade had responded swiftly, but the blaze, which had started in our living quarters, had brought the glass roof crashing down, completing the destruction of all our personal belongings, while flames had swept up the old lift shaft to the upper floors. A huge solid wooden door to the dance studio had held back the fire to the main part of the house, and the offices, storerooms and the studio were saved and untouched. It remained a mystery how the fire started, but sifting through the glass and the rubble in what had been our sitting room, where Katherine miraculously found my wedding ring, we also found a bottle of liqueur and some cigarillos – items we had never owned. So, it appeared that there had been a break-in with a party which had gone badly wrong. Obviously, it was a huge shock and caused enormous disruption, but performances went on, as did rehearsals, amidst the dreadful smell of water-soaked burnt wood; we found a spare room to sleep in and cooked in the dancers' green room. Fortunately, we were not often in London at this time and were glad to be away and on the road.

After the fire at North House in 1977.

In September we received another production grant from the Arts Council to mount a condensed version of the popular classical ballet *Coppélia*. It was a big decision to make, especially for Alexander, for what could be called an artistic compromise. However, it was obvious that we could not perform our more serious ballets – *Voices, Visages d'une Femme, About Face* and *Circuit* – in most places on tour in Britain. They could not be presented satisfactorily on smaller stages while they posed challenges for provincial audiences, where ballet was often still considered as an entertainment for children and families. It was also obvious that with the continuing difficult economic times for everyone in the country, we needed to find works which would be sure to attract audiences. The tours to South East Asia were also a boost for the company, becoming regular additions to the touring schedules, while here again we were constantly requested to add traditional works to the repertoire for local audiences which were starved of classical ballet.

Keeping the theatrical element as well as the classical choreography was a requisite for us, and *Coppélia*, with its popular, strong storyline, was a natural choice. It is possible to perform the entire second act, the most interesting of the ballet, with just three principal dancers, as well as half a dozen extras to play the parts of the mechanical dolls in Dr Coppélius's workroom. To this we added some excerpts from Act 1, which introduced the characters and set the story. The ballet provides a good meaty role for Swanilda, the local village girl who tricks Dr Coppélius by dressing in the clothes of the beautiful mechanical doll he has built and pretending to come to life. Delibes's music is charming and our arrangement of the ballet formed a good first half to the programme. Christine was a natural soubrette Swanilda, Francis a charming, philandering Franz, and with some persuasion, Alexander grew to be fond of the cranky old Dr Coppélius. There was an added bonus in attracting audiences by inviting the best local ballet school to provide us with six of their students as extras.

Building a set which we could tour was the main problem and it was obvious that we could not consider the usual traditional village square for Act 1 or Dr Coppélius's workshop for Act 2. So we opted for an original solution and used some simple scaffolding, meant for building in a children's playground, and painted it all in bright primary colours. This was all on wheels, so could be moved around to form a tiny house, a bay window or the walls of Dr Coppélius's workroom. Best of all, the scaffolding was all donated to us by a firm called Kidstuff. The production was an immediate success, increasing our bookings, attracting good audiences and remaining in the repertoire for several years.

Alexander as Dr Coppelius, with Christine Lassauvageux as Swanilda in Act 2 of *Coppelia*.

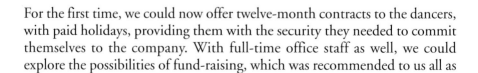

For the first time, we could now offer twelve-month contracts to the dancers, with paid holidays, providing them with the security they needed to commit themselves to the company. With full-time office staff as well, we could explore the possibilities of fund-raising, which was recommended to us all as the panacea for our financial problems. Of course, this left hundreds of theatre companies fighting for limited resources and as in most cases of sponsorship, donors prefer a company who can splash the news of their generosity to as wide a public as possible. Small companies touring mainly in the provinces cannot compete with those in major theatres in the capital. However, we did have some luck with Marks and Spencer, who made cash donations towards our regional touring for several consecutive years; a cross-Channel hovercraft company offered us free travel to and from France, and when this company folded, possibly due to their over-generosity, we obtained very good reduced fares from one of the ferry companies. In fact, if we were lucky in arriving at the ticket counter to find the right man on duty – he claimed to be a great ballet fan – he would slip us a dozen return fares, with two vehicles, for about twenty pounds. There was more generosity from Mercedes-Benz, who had a policy of selling used trucks and minibuses at much reduced prices to companies such as ours, and we were able to benefit from this largesse on a couple of occasions.

We also received gifts of materials and even a washing machine, but almost the best present of all was a photocopier. At this time, it was considered necessary to write personal letters to theatre directors and local promoters, and Hilde had churned out thousands of such letters in English, French and German with admirable zeal. The only alternative was a hand-operated duplicator, requiring 'inking' with a thick, gooey, black paste. This was inevitably a messy job, requiring special protective clothing and rubber gloves, while the machine would often spatter ink, spoiling dozens of pages of paper. It could in no way replace an important letter, but a photocopier could produce multiple copies of not only letters, but press releases, programme inserts, itineraries and so many items that we needed daily.

There were other things occupying us all in the office; establishing an official base at North House brought with it contacts and obligations, not only with the Inland Revenue, but with the Department of Health and Social Security, the Department of Employment, Companies House, company name registration, theatrical employers' registration, multiple different insurances, Actors' Equity, the Musicians' Union and even the Chamber of Commerce and Industry. There were endless forms to fill in, dues to be paid and visits to make; in many ways the earlier gypsy life had its advantages.

As always, it was a relief to escape to the Continent, and in particular to make a tour in the south of France in the early spring. We stayed in one-star hotels, with sagging mattresses and a single WC to share with the rest of the floor, but the rooms were clean and warm. We stopped in the *routiers* restaurants which dotted the *routes nationales* across the country, where one would share a table, or even a bench, with truck drivers and travelling salesmen; but we ate the best of French family cooking and enjoyed joining in their conversations with stories of trips as far as Scotland, Austria or Andalusia, while getting their recommendations for the best route on to the next town on our itinerary. There is a string of theatres, small opera houses, stretched like a necklace along the coast of southern France, from Perpignan, almost on the Spanish border, by way of Béziers, Montpellier, Nîmes, Aix-en-Provence, Toulon and reaching to Nice. A little inland there are also smaller theatres in Narbonne, Arles, Salon-de-Provence and Draguignan, and by programming these together we could fill a good two to three weeks of touring.

Many of the theatres, although owned and funded by the local municipalities, were run by a Monsieur Aymé, who was also director of the opera house in Nice and the summer theatre, the Théâtre de la Verdure. We never understood why he engaged us, year after year, to perform in his theatres, as audiences were always modest in numbers, often the case with dance audiences in the south of France. Perhaps we simply fulfilled his quota of dance for the season, as there were virtually no other companies touring at the time; even the 'Stars from the Paris Opera Ballet' were kept busy in Paris under their new director, and were no longer able to make sorties into the provinces. However, other directors, such as those in Perpignan or in Aix, seemed to be generally fond of us, happy to see the company expanding and developing, something they would check on each year, investigating a new vehicle or a new stage set. These theatres were also well patronised with audiences who returned year after year. For us, it was a wonderful way to break up the long, grey English winter, as the early spring sun was already warm, the outdoor cafes busy, and life seemed very much easier in the south of France.

All those towns have old medieval centres, where the theatre is usually situated, often surrounded by a flower market, sharing an impressive square with the town hall, or towered over by a huge Gothic or Romanesque cathedral. In other towns, the theatre might only be accessible through a fish or vegetable market, through rounded cobbled alleyways, with an entrance tucked away almost invisibly, such as the one of Aix-en-Provence, one of the oldest in France. This building was originally used by Louis XIV for playing tennis, but it was transformed into a theatre in the eighteenth century. These theatres had been left virtually untouched for a hundred years or so, as had the town centres, but they were part of an 'old' France which was soon to change, and which had to change, and we were fortunate in having experienced it at this time.

Travelling from one town to another was inevitably enjoyable; in February the almond trees would be in flower and the mimosas heavy with their musty golden blossom. It could rain, soft but insistent, swamping the vineyards and leaving huge puddles across the narrow tree-lined roads, which would lash the minibus. Sometimes, the bitter mistral wind would howl across the plateau at the mouth of the River Rhone, tearing at the trees but assuring us of continuing sunshine and blue skies. On days off we visited the Camargue, with its meandering little roads, passing herds of black bulls and flocks of flamingos. We visited and clambered all over the roman aqueduct, the Pont du Gard, near Avignon, and discovered Les Baux-en-Provence, high in the hills behind St Rémy where olive groves and clouds of black birds irresistibly recall the paintings of Van Gogh. A medieval fortress town, Les Baux was destroyed by a revengeful Cardinal Richelieu for its Protestant beliefs, and it remains a ghost town, so ruined one can hardly believe it was man-made, but rather that the mistral has carved the curious shapes out of the ochre-coloured earth, whipped by the rain and scorched by the sun. It would be the perfect setting for *Le Sacre du Printemps*, and a ballet festival was held there, in the open air, for many years.

On one such tour, on a Sunday, the company left Béziers en route to the central province of the Auvergne, arriving at one of our favourite restaurants, famished, at midday. On the door, a notice stated firmly *'Fermé le dimanche'* – a Sunday closing we had not reckoned with, but we could see the patron inside at Sunday lunch with his family. There were many times when we were grateful for French hospitality, and once again this Sunday the owner took pity on us, calling a stubble-jowelled cook from the dark reaches of a back-room kitchen to discuss a possible menu. Almost apologetically, he offered mixed hors d'oeuvres, *pâté en croute, boeuf en daube*, made with the rich dark meat of the Camargue cattle which had marinated for a day in the equally rich and dark wine of the Languedoc, followed by vegetables, salad, cheese, fruit and ice cream. We feasted like kings, thinking – Dundee, next month, will be different.

Those last years of the 1970s brought more and more touring, especially in the UK, while adding more ballets to the repertoire: *Masquerade*, to Khachaturian's suite of waltzes and mazurkas amidst the intrigues of a masked ball, *Peter and the Wolf*, a popular follow-up to *Coppélia*, and *Soirée Musicale*, to Benjamin Britten's arrangement of a Rossini overture. This was a sparkling, challenging technical ballet, good as a closing work, while Prue gave us *Charades*, a charming suite to the music of the eccentric British composer Lord Berners. Touring in the UK remained difficult. While a sort of revolution had taken place in London (with the arrival of the miniskirt and Mary Quant, hippies, long hair, smoking pot, the pill and 'love-ins', and with it a new wave of music, theatre and films), in the provinces, in Welshpool, or Wolverhampton, there was still bingo, Blackpool for the summer and the Berni Inn on a Saturday night.

In the bed and breakfasts, or the theatrical digs, we were squashed into twin- and triple-bedded rooms, beds with purple nylon sheets, sitting on worn carpets and piles of dust under the beds. If there was heating, it was procurable only by inserting coins into a meter, while it was not feasible, or advisable, to leave a gas heater on at night. We queued in the corridor in the mornings to get a turn in the only bathroom, showers were unheard of, and as a bath was only allowed once weekly, this had to be booked in advance. Brown bread and coffee were almost unobtainable, and a request for a boiled egg in place of a 'good English breakfast' resented. We were grateful for the Berni Inns, the only place to get a reasonable steak and a salad, and when they went out of business there were at least the Chinese restaurants, which stayed open after the performance, although an order for sweet and sour or a chop suey might be accompanied by chips.

The theatres were often cold and even dirty, a fact which made Francis, on arriving at the theatre, spend an hour in the dressing rooms with a bucket and a cloth, while Alexander would refuse to let the truck be unloaded before the backstage area had been cleared of rubbish and cleaned. Some new theatres were being built; they were modern buildings, council owned and run, but probably designed by the local council architect with little understanding of the needs of theatre, or the people who worked in them. Ken Dodd, Britain's best-loved comedian, famously described the new Pavilion Theatre in Rhyl as an 'early Portakabin with a dash of mock Wimpy'. However, we were happy with the new, clean theatre in Rhyl, which had a good-sized stage and where the dressing rooms, looking out onto the Irish Sea, were spacious and heated. There were theatres and towns to which we returned gladly, in particular a chain of new theatres around London in towns such as Stevenage, Guildford, Redhill, Bromley, Croydon and Hayes, with the added advantage

Masquerade with (from left) Alexander, Christine Lassauvageux and Francis Pedros.

Prue Sheridan as The Wolf, and Francis Pedros as Peter in the 1977
production of *Peter and the Wolf.*

213

that one could drive home after the performance. We were also the lucky ones among the touring community with our regular tours to continental Europe, as well as our visits to South East Asia, although we had limited these excursions to every second year.

In 1977, Donald Moore had closed his office to leave Singapore, which left us to organise our own tour, and as we already had the necessary contacts, this proved to be easy enough. Revisiting Singapore we played this time at the huge open-air National Theatre, seating 3,500 people. Once again we dashed in and out of showers all day, although here the management had taken the precaution of giving the stage a roof, even if the spectators were left in the open. The stage was so wide that we were forced to make a quick 3-metre sprint out of the wings to arrive at a suitable spot to start each entrance. However, where the audience at the Goodwood in 1974 had been the elitist expat crowd, the National was truly a people's theatre, offering a wide-ranging programme of performances at minimal seat prices.

A first visit to Jakarta had taken months of correspondence as the organisers had apparently never invited an overseas company before. Performances were given in a pleasant outdoor theatre, from where we heard, for the first time, the extraordinarily haunting call from a nearby minaret, the sound of the muezzin calling the faithful to prayer. There was another moment to remember from that balmy evening performance, when during *Pasquinade* Alexander, posing as a statue on a pedestal, difficult enough in the equatorial heat, was joined by two curious fruit bats that silently circled around his head, only to leave the stage with him at the end of the scene. Apparently, more than 4,000 people attended the performance that evening, many of them seated on the grass in front of the stage; doubtlessly, it was for most of them their first experience of Western classical ballet.

Nigel had come with us to Asia this time and spent the performance in a small glassed-in cabin with the lighting crew at the back of the auditorium. He attempted to 'run' the performance at the lighting board while inhaling clouds of the marijuana his Indonesian colleagues smoked continuously during the evening. When we all gathered around the hotel swimming pool after the performance, Nigel, stripped to his bathing trunks and still decidedly high, continued to entertain all the company, singing and dancing until the early hours.

In Taiwan, Adam Chang outdid his hospitality in taking us for a hair-raising bus trip into the mountainous centre of the island, to visit the country's most exclusive tourist resort, the Sun Moon Lake. Accompanied by his assistant, Mr Chen, a stop was made at every temple on the way, where Mr Chen dutifully made offerings to the gaudy statues, lighting bundles of incense and tiny candles. Mr Chen was also the keeper of the finances. Whenever it was time to make us a payment, Adam Chang would produce a large leather attaché case which would be passed on to Mr Chen, who would open the lid to reveal its tightly packed contents; piles and piles of US dollars, worthy of a Mafia godfather or a Hollywood gangster film. After carefully counting a bundle of hundred-dollar bills, Mr Chen would pass these to Adam Chang, who would ceremoniously hand them on to Alexander, only for them to end up in my commodious handbag. Perhaps the strangest of the places we visited over the years touring in South East Asia was Sarawak, part of Malaysia, but across the South China Sea on the island of Borneo, which it shares with the independent state of Brunei. We were aware that Shell had oil drilling stations in both of these countries, along with settlements like small towns housing British workers and their families. Oil had been discovered off the coast of Borneo in 1929 and Britain, who then occupied Borneo, was quick to exploit the valuable find. Sarawak became part of the Federation of Malaya in 1959, but Brunei fought to retain its independence as a nation state under the rule of its sultan. The oil soon brought prosperity, especially to Brunei and its sultans, but the drilling and the exploitation is still in the hands of the Dutch–British Shell company. As we discovered, both settlements boasted attractive club houses, with theatres and well-organised programmes of entertainments.

On our first visit in 1977, the company flew from Singapore to Kuching in Sarawak. From there we changed to a two-engined plane, to be squashed between a motley crowd of locals for a rather haphazard flight to Miri. Our trunks of costumes caused some delay in loading and finally were left behind for a later flight in a larger aircraft. Behind my seat was a crate of cockerels that crowed defiantly at the revving engines; apparently they were prize fighting birds on their way to an important meeting. Across the aisle from me was a woman whose feet and arms, as well as her face, the only visible bits of her body, were covered in brilliantly coloured tattoos, while her ear lobes were weighed down with huge pieces of brass, leaving them dangling to her waist. Despite all the confusion of our departure, she seemed unperturbed, and I hoped this meant that her gods were looking after us. The flight took us over miles and miles of rubber plantations and thickly wooded jungle. If there was no sign of life, I could imagine the people living down there; the Iban, reputably headhunters, in their longhouses on crocodile-infested rivers, and surrounded by panthers and pythons, even man-eating plants. The plane shuddered slightly from time to time, dropped unexpectedly and then after swerving out to sea over idyllic looking secluded beaches, finally landed at Miri airport.

The expat life of the oil company employees is very similar in any country and most of those we met had spent time in Saudi Arabia, in the Gulf and in Central America as well as in Asia. They lived well, with their families and with servants, in pleasant wooden bungalows set in beautifully laid out parks and gardens. Their older children were provided with boarding schools in the UK, and all employees received regular long periods of leave. But they all worked hard and long hours, with the women not permitted to work and expected to provide a lively social life, with the theatre forming an important part in this. If the stages were small and technical facilities very limited, everyone helped with great enthusiasm and considerable technical expertise. For us, it was, above all, a fascinating experience being so close to the jungle, driving through flooded mud roads to ford a swollen river to cross from Sarawak to Brunei. Our hosts also spoiled us thoroughly, and were generous with their hospitality. Brunei national television filmed a short programme of *Coppélia*, the pas de deux from *Les Sylphides* and *Masquerade*. The sultan of Brunei had decreed that every household in the country should have a television set, presumably in order to keep in contact with his scattered and often isolated subjects, and despite being a Muslim country it was decided to show our film for Christmas that year. It was an intriguing idea, imagining the almost naked Iban in the jungle, as well as the demure headscarved school children we had seen on our drives, all watching *Coppélia* and wondering what they made of it.

The tour was to finish with a series of eight performances in Malaysia, arranged through the same impresario (we shall call him Mr R) we knew from our first tour. Totally oblivious to the notion of international time differences, Mr R would inevitably telephone London around three or four o'clock in the morning. At that time, 'living above the shop' as we did at North House, this meant stumbling out of bed to the telephone, with the possibility that it might be worrying news about an elderly family member, only to hear from Mr R with another proposition. Although concerned about his reliability, we had agreed to the tour, but became more and more worried by the fact that the contract had still not been finalised before leaving London. Innumerable letters and faxes remained unanswered while a charming, if useless, secretary would answer his telephone with promises of relaying our requests for news. Finally, the British Council in Kuala Lumpur gave us some startling news: 'Mr R has gone upcountry and can't be found.' Apparently, he had recently arranged a concert of a very well-known British pianist for the British Council, and while everyone was enjoying the music inside the capacity-filled auditorium, Mr R emptied the box office safe and disappeared.

Obviously, our tour was off, so our flights were rebooked to London, but, unfortunately, with a stopover in Bangkok. We arrived in the afternoon and were confronted with the complications of clearing customs with the trunks of costumes and finding overnight storage for them. Fighting our way out through the crowds and bustle into the blazing heat of the afternoon sun, we then bundled into three or four different cars and set off for our hotel in the centre of Bangkok. It is a long, straight road into the city, so we were surprised when our driver left the main road to turn off on to a much smaller road, appearing to head for the country. Our queries just brought 'OK, OK', but shortly afterwards the car rolled to a gentle stop. The driver appeared to speak no English and silently left the car, murmuring 'gas', walking off down a seemingly endless straight road, where as far as the eye could see there was nothing but paddy fields of rice.

There were four of us in the car, left debating; would he return with a posse to rob us, to kill us, or to take us hostage? It seemed obvious that the 'gas' story was a ploy to leave us helpless in the middle of nowhere. There seemed little point in leaving the car to walk anywhere, with or without our luggage – so we waited. Half an hour, an hour went by, while the sun settled closer to the horizon and a few lights appeared in the distance. Then our driver appeared, as a spec on the road, then closer, carrying what appeared to be a plastic carrier bag. It proved to be a sheet of plastic, scrunched up to make a bag, filled with petrol. Silently, he filled the tank, climbed in, reeking of petrol, and we all continued, somewhat shamefacedly, the drive on to Bangkok. The incident proved to be a good reminder of the difficulties of misunderstanding between different cultures, but also the dangers which can prove problematic in very foreign countries.

The same driver appeared to overlook one suitcase at the rear of his boot when we finally unloaded at the hotel, while the hotel clerk, the following morning, needed reminding that there was a large envelope at the back of the safe deposit box which he had not handed back to us. Driving back to the airport that morning, one image remained indelibly etched in my mind; of a small boy, curled up and apparently sound asleep, in a wheelbarrow which was parked in the middle of a roundabout. He was surrounded by the noise, the exhaust fumes, the sounds and smells of Bangkok and possibly that was where he lived, in a wheelbarrow. Each time, returning from Asia, I found myself asking what quirk of fate had allowed me to be born in a prosperous, Western society and not in the slums, in a shanty town, or on the streets of an Asian city. It is a humbling experience to see such poverty and feel so helpless.

Back in London, the following two years were busy touring ones, giving around one hundred and fifty performances annually. Much of our time was spent in the UK, where we visited many venues on a regular annual basis; Hayes, Stevenage, Winchester, Camberley, Scunthorpe, Hereford, also Guildford, Birmingham, Bradford and Northampton, all with programmes of short ballets, with *Coppélia* and *Peter and the Wolf* being the most in demand. We still made regular trips to France and to Switzerland, with occasional visits to cities like Brussels or Geneva where we could perform our more serious works.

We returned to Italy, notably to L'Aquila, in the Abruzzo region of central Italy, so sadly almost destroyed in the 2009 earthquake. At the time of our visits, L'Aquila was a typical, lively Italian city; its streets were lined with baroque and Renaissance palazzos and churches, opening into elegant piazzas. The early evening *passeggiata* brought everyone out into the streets with the timeless ritual of strolling from street to street, square to square, meeting, chatting, discussing the day's business. The Teatro Comunale is a good-sized opera house; although it always took some persuasion to make the local stage crew get started and to finish the fit-up in time, we greatly enjoyed those visits, promoted by an exceptionally active local music society.

In 1979 the company made a first visit to the island of Malta, playing in the lovely Manoel Theatre, built in 1732, and lovingly cared for by the government. The auditorium is a mini La Scala, ringed with row upon row of tiny boxes, all ornately decorated and fringed with tiny crystal chandeliers. We immediately liked the Maltese people, their warmth and their charm. If life was very simple at that time, the capital city, Valletta, is full of huge imposing buildings, churches and palaces and above all forts and defences, all reminders of the country's long, colourful history. Due to its strategic position at a midpoint in the Mediterranean, Malta's history is one of occupation, resulting in many wars and disputes. The country had only become a republic shortly before our visit, when in 1974 the British formally withdrew. Perhaps because of this newly found independence it was not always easy to negotiate with those in charge. They tended to lay down the law – they determined when we should visit and what they demanded of us, they chose the programme, the length of the performance, and in view of the modest fee they offered, made the organisation of our visit something of a nightmare. All the same, we returned in 1981, 1985, 1989 and 1993, each time with a box file full of letters and faxes, but glad in the end that we had made the effort.

Another legacy from the recent colonial past was a procedure of hierarchy, which we had already noticed in the theatre, with strict rules of formal behaviour, even in what was then a radical socialist state. The minister for culture invited Alexander and me out to dinner one evening in Valletta's best hotel. During the short drive from the theatre, he mentioned hesitantly that there might be a 'problem' on arriving at the hotel: the problem was apparently that the hotel had a strict rule of jacket and tie only, while Alexander was wearing a decoratively embroidered shirt he had recently acquired in the Philippines, usually worn in Asia to formal events, but which was totally lacking both the necessary jacket and tie. On arrival a short word with the maître d' only confirmed the rule, but the head waiter quickly offered his own jacket, an offer which was naturally accepted. Unfortunately, the waiter was a big, burly man, leaving Alexander with the jacket hanging to his knees, the shoulders hanging down his arms, and his hands out of sight. The ridiculous effect was only increased by the addition of the minister's wife's belt tied around his neck in place of a tie. At least we could now enter the dining room! For our return visit in 1981, Alexander choreographed a short ballet to Albinoni's *Adagio*, in honour of the women of Malta who had been so brave and who had suffered so much during the siege of Malta in 1942.

In 1979, our administrator, Maggie, left us to return to Australia and Deidre replaced her, arriving with a collection of pot plants which augured a long stay. Deidre had worked in the arts department of a London council and soon got to take over most of the administrative work, staying with us for several years. One event in 1979 stands out above all in my memory, when the New York City Ballet visited London, playing for three weeks at the Royal Opera House. I was not needed on tour during that period, while I was busy in the office organising forthcoming foreign tours. Each evening around six o'clock, I found it impossible to resist getting a Tube into town to join the queue for returned seats for that evening's performance. The company, its dancers and their repertoire were at a peak, although it was the last season when Georges Balanchine accompanied them, watching each performance from his favourite spot in the downstage wing. The quality of the dancing was unequalled anywhere in the world; exquisitely pointed feet, delicately placed heels, divinely steel-like legs, the supplest of backs, trailing tendrils of arms – and that was just the female dancers. The men, led by Mikhail Baryshnikov, but by no means overshadowed by the legendary Russian dancer, were strong and supple, exuding intelligence and control and all in a cornucopia of masterful ballets, both from George Balanchine and from Jerome Robbins.

Of course, London's ballet world came in force, especially on the last night when I sighted three of the 'Dames', Ninette de Valois, Marie Rambert and Alicia Markova, company directors Robin Howard and Norman Morrice, as well as the usual crowd of critics. De Valois and Rambert sat together in the stalls, gossiping and giggling like girls, and at the final curtain calls, the nonagenarian Marie Rambert – de Valois was no longer agile enough – pushed her way through the crowds to the barrier of the orchestra pit to shout and applaud Balanchine to the very end. It was a real moment of dance history to remember.

Two very different leading men joined us during that season; Ozkan Arslan was principal dancer with the Turkish State Ballet, where his wife was director. He had studied at the Bolshoi Ballet School in Moscow and had recently appeared as guest artist, dancing in *Giselle* with the Bolshoi Ballet, as well as appearing with London Festival Ballet and the Joffrey Ballet in New York. Ozkan was an impressive technician, extremely good-looking, but best of all he was a worker, an indefatigable one who could, and would, insist on rehearsing for hours on end. Ozkan performed with the Turkish company at the same time, but thought nothing of flying back and forth to London, and elsewhere, as we needed him. There was, though, a problem in that he would accept a performance with us, knowing he had one scheduled for the same day in Istanbul, or Ankara. This often left us not knowing if, and when, he would turn up, as on one occasion, when he made his way from Istanbul to Inverness, he entered the theatre through the stage door just as we were taking a final curtain call. He had imagined we would be able to simply reschedule the performance to await his arrival. However, much as we did enjoy working with him, it was likely that his absences would cause problems during the planned overseas tours of that year.

In the autumn of 1979, the Viennese dancer Peter Mallek joined us. Peter had led a very full international career, becoming principal dancer with the Vienna State Opera Ballet, the Eglevsky Ballet in New York, the Australian Ballet and London Festival Ballet. Peter and I danced the pas de deux from *Le Corsaire*, which was new for me, as well as the excerpts from *Les Sylphides* and *The Nutcracker*. Quite the opposite of Ozkan, Peter appeared not to need or want rehearsals, and could remain sitting in a chair, chatting while sipping a martini, until he actually heard the introductory music to his entrance on stage. Fortunately, his good early training and his vast experience stood him in good stead so he was a reliable performer. Peter was already planning to start his own ballet company, which he has directed ever since, apparently with the same relaxed, untroubled manner.

We visited Asia again at the end of 1979, performing in now familiar theatres in Taiwan and Hong Kong, including the new venue in Macau and the theatre in the Shell settlement at Seria, in Brunei. On the way back to Europe, the company then visited Bombay. It was all my fault adding India to the itinerary; my irrepressible desire to see new countries, experience different cultures and the fact that we could have a stopover in India, at no additional cost, seemed to make the visit an attractive, even sensible option. The only promoter, the Indian National Theatre, was a quasi-amateur organisation, formed in 1944 on a wave of post-independence emotion, with the aim of creating and building up a cultural life in the new nation. A dedicated team of workers and artists has existed ever since, despite almost non-existent funding, battling the regimented bureaucracy which stifles so much in the sub-continent. However, they were keen for us to come, as ballet companies had visited India in the past, notably Anna Pavlova's company in the 1930s and more recently groups from France. There was no alternative but to agree to the conditions – £170 per performance, from which we paid all expenses, including the hotel, while we were also offered a curious extra payment of 'smoke money' of 15 rupees (less than £1) per person, per day. This, no doubt, was a hangover from colonial days, when it may have been the only payment a worker received. Considering it a tourist visit, we even declined to add extra matinee performances, so we could spend a few hours sightseeing.

We arrived at Bombay airport at midnight and spent three hours trying to get out. The passports were checked minutely, the visas which had cost Deidre a month's work of haggling with India House in London were scrutinised, while the customs lists of the contents of the theatre trunks landed up on a long table manned by a team of three or four customs officers. Each read the list from top to bottom, queried certain details and then gave each sheet of paper a huge whack with a rubber stamp, added his signature and passed it back to us with instructions to hand it on to his colleague, who was seated next to him. This continued until we had the final signature and could meet our hosts from the National Theatre. There was an open truck on hand for the luggage and a battered looking bus for us, to which we were accompanied by a team of tiny, scrawny men each balancing one of the huge trunks or a pile of suitcases on his head. We settled into the bus for the drive of 18 miles to the centre of Bombay, along a long, straight road.

With time our eyes adjusted themselves to the inky blackness and the dim lights from our bus caught the edge of the road, sometimes a rough pavement, where there appeared to be small piles of rubbish, or blackened humps of rags or cloths. Then one noticed an arm, an exposed leg; the humps were in fact little groups of people, huddled together, bodies curled up feigning sleep. Hundreds or thousands of people lined that road; people with nothing, families with children but with no belongings – not a cooking pot, no food, nothing but the clothes they were wearing. These people had made their way from the country, where they were starving, in the belief they could find a better life in the city; whether they had just arrived or whether they had no choice but to stay on the side of the road, and to live there, one could only guess. As daybreak gradually lit the sky, we drove along a long curving beach-front to see more and more people, some slowly rousing themselves from a night spent on the sands, others forming a snaking queue in front of a single water tap. Arriving finally at our destination, we found a modern, westernised hotel where we tried to grab a few hours' sleep before that day's activities. We had a performance that night when we would perform *Coppélia* and *The Nutcracker* to an Indian audience; it seemed like madness!

Three days were spent in Bombay, performing in sold-out theatres, to the Indian elite, the prosperous middle classes who appeared to appreciate our performances and arranged receptions for us, even inviting us to their homes. We spent any free hours hurtling through the city in rattling, run-down taxis, often racing the wrong way around a roundabout to beat the traffic, or more often sitting in traffic jams, cars jammed up against each other, smothered in exhaust fumes in the 40°C heat, and dripping with sweat. This gives newspaper sellers the opportunity to ply their trade through the open car windows, and also the beggars, lepers, to poke their deformed stumps of arms into the car, or children with glittering brown eyes and gleaming white teeth demanding 'rupee, rupee'. One morning when we had left the stage crew to transport our scenery from one theatre to another, we were watching a turbaned snake charmer on a busy city square and became aware of a large ox-cart trundling past. Piled onto the cart were bundles of brightly coloured plastic tubing – our *Coppélia* set on its way through the streets of Bombay.

However, there were a few enjoyable hours at the silk market, where seated on silken cushions and drinking milky, spicy tea the merchant smothered us with bolts and bolts of brilliantly coloured materials, cascading down from the shelves which reached to the ceiling, and obviously did not let us go until we had made some serious purchases. In a jewellery shop full of beautifully crafted silver items we spent a good hour discussing politics and the state of the world with the owner, disturbed only by a tiny, elderly man, sitting on his heels while he scuffled around our feet, sweeping away imaginary bits of dirt. There is not much for a tourist to visit in Bombay, but if one has the courage to brave the crowds, the heat, the noise and the pollution, it is tempting just to wander through the markets, the maze of streets behind the main boulevards, where Victorian grandeur has been smothered in shacks and tenements, where cows wander at will across a four-lane highway, or to trundle through a vegetable market and find that despite the wretched poverty, the people remain lively and busy. However, the inevitable undercurrent of the smell of sewage follows one, mixed with the choking smoke of exhaust fumes, whiffs of spices and incense, and just when one has thought, 'I can cope with this, it has a fascination,' one can exit a restaurant in the early evening to find a family of rats, as big as cats, foraging on the footpath.

Our most frightening experience was, on one such walk through the streets of Bombay, when Alexander threw a few rupees to a group of street children who had been following us, and for whom one could only feel a terrible pain of pity. These children would have been orphans, or abandoned by their families who could not provide for them, leaving them to their own devices. Forming gangs, like packs of dogs, they live on the streets, begging and no doubt stealing in order to survive. In a second, half a dozen scrawny children jumped at him, clambering onto him, grabbing his clothes and reaching for his pockets while I screamed ineffectively. There were onlookers, shopkeepers, other pedestrians, but no one made a move or apparently was prepared to help us. Finally, we reached the corner of the footpath, where the children who were still clinging to Alexander jumped off, disappearing as quickly as they had come. We could only presume that we had reached the limits of their 'territory' and they didn't dare venture further.

Back in London, and after a brief Christmas break, we embarked on a new year which was to bring enormous changes to the company. It is true that this was happening in general in the UK. Mrs Thatcher's new regime brought in economic reforms to tackle the galloping inflation, soaring unemployment and the grip of the trade unions. Margaret Thatcher had no interest in the arts whatsoever and especially not in the theatre. She demanded reduced expenditure from the regional councils where the first to be slashed were the budgets allocated to the so-called arts and entertainments departments. The emphasis shifted immediately to money, management and marketing, the dreaded expression 'bums on seats' entered into every theatre manager's vocabulary and became their priority. In France, the situation was not much better; the country was suffering from major unemployment problems with factories and heavy industry becoming obsolete, causing huge migrations from the industrial north and east of the country to the major cities, or to the south of France, where more work might be available. Theatre-going, which had always been a minority interest in the French provinces, was becoming a luxury for the few, or, where dance was concerned, an occasion for the local ballet school to give their annual 'gala'.

In spite of all this, 1980 was a bumper year for the company; we gave 184 performances from January to December, the majority in the UK, but also in France, Switzerland and Belgium. The company continued to grow in numbers, with fifteen on the permanent payroll, plus freelance technicians, musicians, guest teachers, costume and scenery providers. Most importantly, Alexander continued to create ever more works, culminating in two premieres during the year, *A Smile at the Bottom of the Ladder* and our first full-evening production, *A Midsummer Night's Dream*. In order to fit in rehearsals for these two important ballets, the summer holidays were cancelled, with the promise to make them up at Christmas, and it was only thanks to the fact that we had a homogenous group of dancers, a team which had been working together for four years, that we succeeded.

In order to compete in this new world where marketing was all important, we hired a professional designer to produce the logo, a large, glossy brochure and new posters. Mercedes offered another, much larger, truck while we bought a brand new fifteen-seater bus. We commissioned a major workshop to produce the scenery for the two new productions, also engaging a bevy of seamstresses for the costumes. After three years, the piles of cement, sand, bricks, cement mixers and wheelbarrows which had surrounded North House and had been necessary for the rebuilding following the fire were cleared away, leaving us with a new apartment, enlarged storage and workshop space and a completely renovated house. It was a metamorphosis which opened out a completely new phase in the company's history.

chapter ten

_____

The Boom Years
1981–1987

Obviously, all this investment needed funding and we could not count on the Arts Council, sponsors, or 'angels', as the West End backers are known. We needed to raise the money ourselves, and fortunately had found a sympathetic ear in the person of the bank manager at the end of Eton Avenue. Armed with a briefcase bulging with contracts, budgets, calculations and estimates, I made an annual visit to see 'The Manager'. After an amicable discussion, during which I explained to him why we needed so many thousands of pounds ahead of the season – to spend on new productions, equipment and rehearsal costs – I needed to convince him that these funds would be repaid by the end of the season. Fortunately, the company was obtaining record numbers of performances and, in theory, the forecast looked favourable. But at that time, with interest rates on bank loans peaking around 20 per cent, there was every incentive to pay the loans back as fast as possible.

The manager checked that the deeds of North House were still in his safe, and the overdraft would be authorised. Apart from building up a new image for the company with glossy, attractive promotional material, it was essential to produce new ballets, strong works of ballet-theatre which could compete in this tougher, more competitive world. These new productions needed as much rehearsal time as could be squeezed into the already heavy schedule, and they needed attractive, but expensive, sets and costumes; we could only hope that these costly investments would repay themselves.

For the designs, we turned once again to the Arts Council, and made an application, on their recommendation, for the Young Designers Scheme for *A Smile at the Bottom of the Ladder*. An enthusiastic young woman designer came to watch rehearsals where Alexander spent several sessions with her explaining that the idea came from a novella written by Henry Miller, the story of a clown searching for love and friendship in the milieu of nineteenth-century Paris. This character is based on the painter Henri de Toulouse Lautrec, a man with tragic physical handicaps who often referred to himself as a clown. The ballet was set in Montmartre where Lautrec was a regular visitor to the cabaret of the Moulin Rouge, the circus and the bars and broth-els of the area. Lautrec recorded all these settings himself in his magnificent paintings, drawings and sketches as well as bringing to life the colourful characters with whom he spent his time. After several weeks, the young woman presented us with her set design; the stage, a traditional 'black box', with a window frame suspended on high and a modern bar stool. This, she claimed, was Lautrec's studio, a set which could also be used for the other scenes of the ballet. Neither traditionalists nor conservative in our tastes, we found this was taking minimalism too far. 'Did you want more elements?' she queried. Yes, we did, and a lot more as well. Writing a regretful letter we returned the cheque to the Arts Council, and that was, in fact, the last time we made an application for funding.

Alexander produced a design of his own; a versatile stage set which easily transformed from the artist's studio to the Moulin Rouge, to the circus, as well as to the more abstract scenes. We were fortunate in having a very competent technical stage manager, and found an excellent firm of scenery makers. The costume designs had really already been created by Toulouse Lautrec himself, but my mother drew up working designs for the seamstresses and we all had fun shopping for fabrics. Browsing through record shops, the only satisfactory way for us to find music at that time, we came across a film score by Dmitri Shostakovitch, *The New Babylon*; this music was written for a film taking place in Paris at exactly the same time, and is filled with echoes of the can-can, the waltzes and quadrilles, as well as the darker moments, which Shostakovitch wrote with so much power and emotion. *A Smile at the*

Bottom of the Ladder was challenging for the dancers, but we had an ideal Lautrec (whose handicaps became emotional rather than physical) in Francis Pedros, and a perfect La Goulue (the star of the Moulin Rouge) in Prue Sheridan; Christine Lassauvageux played the role of the clowness, Cha-U-Kao, while Alexander cast me as The Woman, who passes through Lautrec's life as his mother, Suzanne, the woman he idolised, and finally as Death.

With over 180 performances that season in the UK, often with a matinee before the evening performance, as well as dashes across to France and Switzerland, we were very pressed to fit in the necessary rehearsals, but *Smile* had its premiere at the Civic Theatre in Scunthorpe (of all places) in September 1980 and was then performed extensively throughout the UK. Several London critics came to see us in Bromley, with Ann Nugent writing for *The Stage*: '… Characteristically, this artist was sensitive and sad underneath the clown-like exterior and Francis Pedros left a vivid impression of pathos, while dancing with vivacious fluency. Roy's set, with its looped ropes, on high, its mixture of circus entrances, and grand salon furniture, was dominated by the all-important ladder; it was simple and effective. Choreographically, Roy has cleverly shaped his steps to show the strengths of his dancers. In style they alternated between exuberance and elegance; in approach they had an engaging vitality, and technically they looked more assured than at any time previously in the company's history.'

Alexander as the Clown in
A Smile at the Bottom of the Ladder.

A scene from *A Smile at the Bottom of the Ladder*.

No sooner was *Smile* premiered, than we started on rehearsals for *A Midsummer Night's Dream*, for which some tentative first scenes had been sketched in. Alexander had wished to create a full-length ballet for some time, and Shakespeare's plays were the ideal starting place to search for a suitable theme. With a cast of just ten or twelve dancers, we had to be inventive, and adaptable, and the *Dream* seemed to offer many opportunities with its three linked stories; the young lovers, the comic artisans and the fairy world. It was interesting to discover, in research into Shakespeare's own company, that at the time the play was written, his cast of actors was not much bigger than our company, and it is most probable that the artisans doubled as fairies, improbable as that seems. The main problem, as in all of Shakespeare's works, was that the cast included very few female roles (as they were always played by men) but a lot of male roles; a particular problem for us with the continuing shortage of good male dancers. It seemed feasible that some roles, such as Oberon and Puck, The King of the fairies, and the Fairy Messenger, could be played by women, providing they were strong dancers; so Prue was cast as Puck and Gillian Winn, a tall, powerful dancer who had been with the company for some years, as Oberon. I danced Titania, the Queen of the Fairies, and Alexander took on the comic role of Bottom. The lovers, Hermia and Lysander, Helena and Demetrius, proved easy to cast, and the two men doubled as artisans.

The ballet followed the plot of the play very closely, with Alexander and I working on the production collaboratively, scene by scene. After rehearsals he would then work until late into the night, arranging and rearranging the music and planning the next day's scenes, although, as always, he never actually choreographed until he was in the studio with the dancers. The choreography for the three contrasting groups of characters differed from the nearly purely classical dance for the scenes with the lovers, to a freer, more contemporary style for the fairies, Puck, Oberon and Titania, and a heavy style of character dance steps for the artisans, Shakespeare's 'rude mechanicals'.

Michael Bassett, principal pianist for London Festival Ballet for many years, was now musical director for our small music ensemble, and had made an arrangement of the Shostakovitch score for *Smile*; he now worked with the music we had chosen from Rossini's Sonatas for Strings and the Duo for cello and double bass to create a complete ballet score. Most choreographers who had tackled the *Dream* before us had made use of Mendelssohn's incidental music to *A Midsummer Night's Dream*, but this is too short for a full-length production, and we also felt that the full orchestral score was too heavy for what was seen as a very light, fresh production. Rossini's Sonatas for Strings, written when he was twelve years old, seemed to fit the bill perfectly.

This time Alexander did not hesitate to design the ballet himself, and although the main consideration had to be the practical one of creating a set which could tour easily and fit onto the many different shapes and sizes of stages we encountered on our travels, he did this with considerable success. The set was, perhaps unexpectedly, a white one; with a white dance floor, white side masking and backdrop, decorated with delicate green branches. A ruined archway stood in the upstage right-hand corner, forming the entrance to the palace, or a ruin to be found in the Athenian woods, where most of the action takes place, and a pillar, useful for Puck to hide behind, stood centre stage against the backdrop.

The lighting was all important, and here Nigel Clarke excelled himself, introducing dappled leafy moonlight, or bathing the stage with golden Grecian sunlight. My mother, having abandoned her earlier career as an artist and writer, now took over the costume design (and brochure design) for our

229

One of Anthony Crickmay's studio photos for *A Smile at the Bottom of the Ladder*,
I am here with Francis Pedros.

new ventures, creating stylised Grecian costumes for the lovers, gossamer light
in the palest green for the fairies, and for the artisans, we reproduced the
costumes Heath Robinson had created to illustrate the play, comically rustic
and marvellously original. For the pre-production photographs, necessary for

230

the press and other publicity months before the production was ready, we were most fortunate to win the collaboration of Anthony Crickmay, unarguably Britain's greatest dance photographer. Crickmay usually requested only two dancers for a photo session so Francis and I went to his studio, being photographed as Titania and Puck (in improvised costumes), and as Lautrec and La Goulue in costumes which were ready. Crickmay's photos opened many new doors for the company, attracting the eye of several international agents, as well as theatre directors, promoters and journalists everywhere, and we used them for all the years ahead.

Francis Pedros as Puck in *A Midsummer Night's Dream* in 1980. This photo attracted the attention of the theatre directors and promoters world-wide. Not only did it help to win us some valuable bookings, but was also used for posters, publicity brochures and programmes everywhere on our tours.

231

Having spent more time in the office over the past couple of years than in the ballet studio, I felt the need to devote some time to myself to prepare for the two new challenging roles and took off to Paris for a longish week of ballet classes. It felt as if I was returning to my student days, living in a sixth-floor attic room in a hotel in Rue Blanche, a stone's throw from Boulevard Pigalle, but chosen for its view over the roofs of Paris. My days were spent going to classes; Salle Wacker had closed by this time, and Madame Nora had moved to another studio in the Pigalle area which she shared with Daniel Franck, an up-and-coming young teacher who was still dancing with the Paris Opera Ballet. Sadly, most of her former students had not followed her, or perhaps changes in the dance world meant that professionals no longer had the time to attend classes outside their companies.

Madame Nora had also become a little eccentric, not arriving at the studio until about fifteen minutes after the scheduled beginning of class, by which time one of her regular students would have started the class with the rest of the dancers. Madame Nora would then insist that one sang or spoke continuously during the exercises, an unusual practice, which naturally was off-putting for new students and irritating for those who just wanted to do a good class. However, she did keep a nucleus of dancers around her, although none of them were active professionals, while she enjoyed going off with a few of them to a nearby restaurant for a light lunch, and to gossip about recent events in the dance world.

I did not attend her classes this time, having recently experienced the power of her fury when feeling slighted; it was quite a violent row, the kind of attack for which she was famous. It had come to her attention that we, with the company, had recently been in Paris for a few days and not attended her classes. Not only that; we had advertised and auditioned dancers without contacting her. This resulted in a string of telephone calls one Sunday afternoon in London when she arraigned me for the insult this had caused, 'after so many years, etc., etc'. She was correct that it was a slight, but we knew that the dancers would not have gained much from taking her classes during our short visit and we also knew that we would only find professional dancers of the standard we needed in other studios. Three times she slammed down the phone, only to call back five minutes later with another volley of abuse, while I apologised, pleading for understanding in view of the limited time we had had available.

Raymond Franchetti had taken over the role of star teacher in Paris in his studio behind the Moulin Rouge, with several daily classes packed with luminaries including Natalia Makarova and Mikhail Baryshnikov, dancers from an older generation like Zizi Jeanmaire, as well as *étoiles* from the Paris Opera. Taking two ballet classes a day was demanding, but set me back on track to tackle my new roles and I allowed myself a special treat of attending a performance of *La Bohème* where, at an exorbitant price and from the back of a box at the Paris Opera, I watched the magical partnership of Plácido Domingo and Kiri Te Kanawa.

Dream was premiered in the Hoe Theatre in Plymouth in November 1980 and then performed on a short tour to Switzerland, Belgium and France. The small theatre in Plymouth was useful as a try-out, but it was only really possible to see and feel how successful the ballet was once we were on the well-equipped and good-sized stages on the Continent. The reception and the reviews were overwhelmingly positive and we felt, with relief, that the hard work had paid off, and possibly the financial investment would as well. After a Christmas break, the company gave a few performances in England before a lengthy Continental tour.

Unexpectedly, several of the London critics came to see the *Dream* in Canterbury and in Westcliff, obviously intrigued as to how we would manage to mount the first British full-length version of the ballet with our limited resources. John Percival wrote in *The Times*: 'To put on *A Midsummer Night's Dream* as a two-act ballet is a bold enterprise at any time; when you have a company of only ten dancers, it appears positively foolhardy. But, with some doubling of roles and a firm refusal to acknowledge boundaries of sex, Alexander Roy carries it off surprisingly well in his new production for his London Ballet Theatre. The dancers are kept hard at work. Katherine Mackenzy, for instance, makes a convivial Snug, a timidly ferocious Lion, and between whiles promenades prettily as an attendant fairy... Prue Sheridan makes a capriciously dominating figure of Puck... For a small touring company this *Dream* is quite an achievement.' Curiously, we had met with some scepticism from the British theatre directors. Many felt that their audiences were not 'ready' for full-length ballets, especially not Shakespearean ones. They booked the *Dream* warily, often insisting on a second programme of shorter works, but they were proved to have underestimated their audiences as theatres were consistently full, and the reaction of the press and the public enthusiastic.

Not always so in France: suddenly our long-held happy relationship with theatres and audiences there was changing. We had successful performances in the larger cities such as Strasbourg, but elsewhere audiences appeared to be bemused by the storytelling of the *Dream*, while the press, on occasions,

233

Christine Lassauvageux as Hermia and Glenda Nichols as Helena in
A Midsummer Night's Dream.

Alexander as Bottom (centre), with the workmen in *A Midsummer Night's Dream.*

234

found us too English, too classical, and some even found us downright boring. But we did have some success with a performance on the outskirts of Paris, in Enghien-les-Bains, a prestigious spa town with an important theatre.

Alexander was adamant that he wanted Madame Nora to come, so he braved going to her studio the morning before our performance. She ignored him completely until the end of the class, then demanded to know what he wanted and denied any interest in the performance. Next, she taunted him with the impossibility of the travel arrangements, refused his offers to drive her or to send a taxi, until one of the pupils enthusiastically offered to drive her there. Feeling as much in awe of her as I had as an eighteen-year-old, and terrified by the prospect of her being in the audience, I chose a dressing room far from sight, on the top floor of the theatre. At the end of the performance, I heard the unmistakable voice shouting 'Where is Christina?' as she climbed higher and higher searching for me. And then she was there, four flights up, slightly out of breath but able to embrace me and compliment us on the performance. It was an enormous relief to have mended that rift, and although we seldom had the chance to spend time in Paris after that visit, we were back again, part of her 'family'.

In 1981 we enjoyed a long tour of France and Switzerland when Keith Rosson returned to the company as ballet master. There was still a lot of work to do on *Dream*; every scene needed polishing, especially those with the

On the road in 1981 – filling in time at Dover docks awaiting the car ferry to France.

Keith Rosson having found a corner backstage to rehearse, while on tour in France.

Backstage in costume as Titania, with Gillian Winn as Oberon.

artisans, where exactness of the movements of the five dancers of different shapes and sizes was essential; for the scenes with the lovers there was so much detail in the storytelling, with a great deal of precision needed for the very fast choreography. Keith was irrepressible, taking rehearsals during every free moment. He rehearsed on stage, surrounded by technicians and scenery, in half darkness during lighting rehearsals, and if the stage was really unavailable, he would gather the dancers together in the theatre foyer or in a large dressing room; he would even give a warm-up class in a corridor if no other space was available. For someone who had grown up in the closeted surrounds of the Royal Ballet, with all its privileges and advantages, he was remarkably free of pretensions, and interested only in working, polishing the dancers' technique and strengthening the ballet.

Fortunately, bookings for the UK poured in and, encouraged by the good response to *Dream* in Switzerland, we launched a major campaign to theatres and promoters in Germany, a country which the company had not visited for some years. The idea of a full-length ballet with a British theme was obviously attractive, winning us several performances during each of the following seasons. In 1981, there were also visits to Malta and Italy and another month-long tour of South East Asia; we were also able to engage a number of new British dancers for the company – Tania Fairbairn came from the Royal Ballet School and had been a member of the Scottish Ballet, Jonathan Rant was also at the Royal Ballet School and had danced with PACT in South Africa, and Leslie Bryant came from the Rambert Ballet School. All were versatile, attractive dancers and, what was becoming more and more essential with our heavy workload, good and responsible company members.

The tour to South East Asia included the most extensive tour of Taiwan we had made to date, with extra performances planned in a brand new theatre in Kaohsiung, an industrial city in the south of the island. However, as often happens in these cases, the completion date of the building was postponed, with Adam Chang not sure if our performances could take place. For this reason, he had hesitated in signing and returning the contract, assuring us on the other hand that if we could not go to Kaohsiung, he would add extra performances in Taipei. Confident that we could trust him, we did not worry unduly when the contract had not been returned by the time we left London.

Our departure from Heathrow was delayed due to a caterers' strike so we arrived in Hong Kong too late for the onward flight to Taipei, leaving us no alternative but to stay the night in Hong Kong and take a flight to Taipei the following day. International communication was always complicated in those days, and all we could do was to send a telegram to Adam Chang with the revised arrival time. Apparently he did not receive this, and so it was only after a telephone call from Taipei airport that Adam Chang met us the next morning, red-faced and panicking, waving the contract in front of him. He must have feared that we had decided against coming, but the local press had learned of our arrival, and as usual, had turned out en masse.

Just before leaving London we had received a telegram:

CONFIRM EVERYTHING RECEIVED PLEASE BUY 20 BOTTLE OF SCOTCH ME THANKS ADAM CHANG.

Each of us paraded through Taipei airport clutching two bottles of Johnny Walker, a fact which was confirmed on TV that evening, and on the front page of most of Taipei's newspapers the next day. Alexander had brought Adam Chang a present as well; before we left Taipei in 1979 he had given Alexander a music cassette, saying that he thought the music would make a good ballet. It contained two works by the French composer Darius Milhaud, and *Le Boeuf sur le Toit*, with its zany South American rhythms full of good-humoured fun, appealed to Alexander immediately. Besides all the other work we had squeezed into 1981, he had choreographed the ballet in two days just before our departure for Asia and it was premiered in Taipei and dedicated to Adam Chang.

The performances in Kaohsiung, a drab, smoky, industrial port town, did go ahead in a huge, super-modern theatre where we gave the first performance by a Western company. This brought about an amusing incident when the sound engineer asked Alexander for the performance tape in order to make a sound test. Shortly afterwards we heard extraordinary noises coming through the auditorium loud speakers and realised that the tape of the Rossini sonatas was playing at double speed. Alexander rushed up to find the engineer, whom he met on his way back from the sound cabin, obviously pleased with the results. Apparently he had never heard Western classical music before, and was unaware of the cacophony of jumbled sounds his tape recorder had produced playing at the wrong speed; in fact, to us, it sounded quite like Chinese music.

We performed *Dream* in all the venues of this Asian tour and it proved highly successful, the humorous elements being especially, and noticeably, appreciated. As it was not possible to take all of the scenery with us by air, we asked the promoters in each venue to provide the all-important Grecian arch and the pillar, sending photographs and detailed drawings in advance. This was done willingly and we were delighted to see how, in each venue, these items gained oriental curlicues, either in a Chinese or an Indian style or how, in Brunei, a bit of oil pipeline came in handy to produce the pillar.

Another special Asian situation arose on the last leg of the tour, when we gave four performances in Bombay. The preparations for the first performance were taking an interminable time, and it seemed as if we would never get the stage lamps rigged and coloured in order to start lighting. The theatre's stage manager was not a pleasant man, and we were seriously embarrassed by the arrogant and rude way he treated the stage workers. They were simple men, not trained technicians, but they were apparently used to working backstage, and it seemed to us as that a kind of Ghandi-style passive resistance had taken over. At lunchtime the stage manager left, announcing he would be back in an hour's time and we knew we had to take things in hand. Sitting down on the stage floor, among the technicians, and surrounded by rolls and rolls of Cinemoid colour sheets, we found some knives and scissors and started cutting the squares of colour ourselves. It was a simple, time-consuming job, but soon the men joined in, and although none of them spoke English, we managed to chat, or rather to mime, even enjoying ourselves, and finished the job by the time the stage manager returned. At the end of the performance, we wanted to give the technicians a small payment to show our gratitude and asked the stage manager where we could find them: he immediately offered to take the money to distribute it himself, an offer we did not take seriously. Fortunately, we were able to find the men before leaving the theatre.

In 1983, we made a final tour to South East Asia, performing in the Shell settlements in Brunei and Sarawak as well as visiting Singapore, where we gave two performances and recorded a film for Singapore TV. Major changes were happening in the region; both Hong Kong and Singapore now had their own large classical ballet companies, even Taipei had several ballet groups and the government was finally supporting the Cloud Gate Dance Theatre company which was winning ever more acclaim. The boom in the electronics industry in Taiwan was waning, due, no doubt, to competition from other Asian countries, so Adam Chang had been advised to restrict his 'largesse' as a patron of the arts. Foreign dance companies visiting Asia were now mostly part of cultural exchange events, organised at government level, and there was really no longer a place for independent groups such as ours.

We gave two seasons in London in 1982; a week at the New Wimbledon Theatre performing *Dream* in London for the first time, and a two-week season at the Bloomsbury Theatre in May with *Dream* as well as a triple bill made up of *Le Boeuf sur le Toit*, *Voices* and *A Smile at the Bottom of the Ladder*. A young South African, Clair Symonds, who had only recently returned from Iran, where she had been a member of the Iranian National Ballet and had just escaped the revolution, took over my leading roles in *Dream* and *Smile*. Clair won praise from the London critics and was well liked on the subsequent tours, where her partner was the Finnish dancer Alpo Pakarinen, a strong, Russian-trained dancer who had danced with a number of international companies, including London Festival Ballet.

At one of the performances of *Voices* I was surprised to find our old friend Eilean Pearcey in the audience. Eilean had become highly regarded for her work drawing dancers, done notably during performances and rehearsals; she had a special talent of catching movement with a few strokes and capturing the qualities of the individual dancers. She worked extensively with London Contemporary Dance Theatre, the Martha Graham Dance Company and all the visiting Russian ballet companies; Eilean also produced several series of drawings for us, done during our London seasons. This time she was accompanied by Paul Delvaux's widow, who was naturally interested to see *Voices* and to judge how her husband's paintings had influenced Alexander's choreography. Apparently, it was decided that Delvaux would have approved. Eilean had a talent for acquiring interesting friends; on occasions we would drop into her Kensington studio to find such people as the renowned patron of the arts Peggy Guggenheim, or John Drummond, then racing up the hierarchy of the BBC, having tea. Becoming something of an eccentric, almost buried in her studio under thousands of drawings and sketches, Eilean lived to become ninety-eight years old, and as a lifetime practitioner of yoga, was able to stand on her head almost to the end.

The Falklands War was at its height during this London season and undoubtedly many people stayed at home watching this evolve on TV, but possibly the out-of-the-way Bloomsbury Theatre – part of University College – was simply not a good venue. Audiences were thin and although we had some good reviews, the season seemed a difficult one. In fact, we had entered a new phase in the company's history, and not an easy one. Just when everything seemed to be going so well, the harmonious, homogenous group we had held together for five years or so broke up.

The French dancers, Christine and Francis, felt it was time to move on, to return to the Continent, and to find a new company before they were any older. As is often the case, it proved difficult to find a company interested in engaging them both so they returned to Ballet Royal de Wallonie in

A drawing of me in *The (Immoral) Story of a Small Town and The Visit of an Old Lady* by Eilean Pearcey, from 1969.

Charleroi, in Belgium. Francis went straight to the top of the roster, starring in several of director Jorge Lefevre's works, while Christine did well as a soloist, although she was soon to stop dancing and start a family, settling in Belgium permanently. On the demise of Ballet Royal, Christine and Francis opened, and have run ever since, a large and successful school, with Francis also developing his talents as an actor and drama director. Their departure was followed later in 1981 by Katherine and Gillian, and even Deidre, finding the workload in the office ever heavier, left us at the end of 1981. Fortunately, all these dancers remained personal friends and friends of the company, returning to perform in emergencies, for special occasions, as well as helping out with rehearsals when needed.

In the office we made a serious mistake in attempting to replace Deidre with a youngish man, a former dancer who had then obtained a degree in arts administration from Harvard University; he had approached us, offering his services, after a spell as administrator for a small contemporary group, formed and funded by the Arts Council, followed by administration for a touring group, a successful company of international principal dancers.

241

Warning bells should have rung, as we knew this company had folded in bankruptcy, but we accepted his offer to work for us, running the office and all that it entailed. On his first day with the company, he arrived around eleven o'clock, clutching a pint-sized mug of coffee and arranged his appointment diary; a meeting at the Arts Council, another at the British Council, lunch with a journalist, more meetings with regional arts associations, and evenings at the theatre, watching other companies. None of those meetings directly concerned our company, but he felt it essential to be seen and to take part. All that was needed, he explained, was for the company's image to become better known, when bookings and subsidies would come pouring in; he saw his role as the company's ambassador. He made up sheets of idealised budgets, waited for the telephone to ring, but spent a couple of hours at lunch while I made up lists of theatres we visited regularly and whose directors we needed to contact urgently.

Obviously, his stay with us did not last long but he did bring about one important change, persuading us that the twelve-month contracts we offered the dancers were no longer viable, for no matter how many performances we packed into the schedule, the income was not covering the running costs. It was a difficult decision, but we accepted the wisdom of it, although we feared for the dancers and how they could manage with shorter contracts. In fact, this system of limited seasons with short-term contracts was already becoming common and today is almost the norm, but it does pose enormous problems in keeping together those dancers one needs, and values, from one season to the next.

After twenty-seven years as a professional dancer, I felt the time had come for me stop performing and decided to take over the company's administration myself. As a result of our 'Harvard' administrator, the bookings had sunk from nearly two hundred performances per year to one hundred, so no more time could be wasted in attempting to fill up the coming season. It was also proving difficult to reform the company with the kind of dancers we needed, and many came and went over the next two or three years. The situation had changed from the earlier days when most of the dancers were of our age, or not much younger, and we worked virtually as colleagues. The dancers were now young enough to be our children and a different working atmosphere, a 'them and us' relationship, inevitably evolved. These young dancers were also of a generation with easy access to grants with entry into the vocational schools where the day was divided into academic work and ballet classes. Many were not really passionate about becoming a dancer, not determined to become a principal dancer and had never dreamt of becoming a famous dancer. On leaving school, they simply wanted a job, and were badly prepared for the demands to be made on them.

We engaged a talented nineteen-year-old who had literally never read a book, and a charming twenty-three-year-old with several years' professional experience, who never listened to classical music, believing Mozart was 'for old people'. In both cases, they danced *Dream* never having read or seen the play, and *The Magic Flute* never having heard Mozart's music beforehand. Fortunately, they both had other qualities, not only good looks and competent techniques, but they were intuitive dancers, naturally following a choreographer's line of thought and entering instinctively into a role. This is a talent which cannot be taught and must be cherished, but it is also a rare ability.

In 1983 we mounted a new full-length ballet, *Beauty and the Beast*, inspired by Jean Cocteau's 1946 magical film of the fairy story written by Madame Le Prince de Beaumont. The ballet was conceived as a true fairy story, very dreamlike; partly surreal, partly impressionistic. For the music

Prue Sheridan with Spencer Parker in *Beauty and the Beast* in 1983.

243

Alexander chose the string quartets by Claude Debussy and Maurice Ravel and other pieces by Debussy and Manuel de Falla. These very challenging scores required musicians of the highest standard and we were fortunate in finding the Fairfield Quartet, four very attractive young women who had been winning international competitions and making a name for themselves. There were now also some new dancers who would form the nucleus of a renewed company. If *Beauty and the Beast* did not enjoy the huge success enjoyed by *Dream*, it remained in the repertoire for many years and offered some rewarding roles to the dancers.

Caroline Heming, a strong and attractive dancer with several years of professional experience, danced the leading role and proved to be a valuable acquisition to the company, as did Sheila Styles, formerly of Sadler's Wells Royal Ballet, who replaced Prue, finally leaving after sixteen years with the company in 1984. Naturally, it was a serious loss but one we had to expect, and we felt comforted by Prue's move to Germany, firstly as dancer, but soon to become assistant ballet master for the company based at the prestigious opera house in Dresden, and finally as director of dance and principal choreographer at the theatre in Detmold.

Sheila, always a valued member of the Royal Ballet, was also an individualist from an early age, choreographing and always eager to work with small, creative groups besides her commitment to the Royal Ballet. While with us, Sheila continued working on different projects and with different companies, amazing us at the end of a lengthy tour by performing the following day with another company in a principal role as demanding as that in a full-length *Swan Lake*. During the years she worked with us, she was always a role model for the younger dancers, and constantly helpful in taking classes and rehearsals with the company.

We also found some younger dancers who proved to be valuable additions to the company; nineteen-year-old old John Broome, small and sprightly, who fulfilled many roles with success, including that of Puck, and later Papageno in *The Magic Flute* and Cherubino in *Figaro, Figaro*, also Antoinette Goodfellow, Colleen Barsley and Paul Payne, dependable, serious workers and excellent, versatile performers, all of whom have gone on to make successful second careers as teachers.

The number of our performances in Germany was increasing each season, and in 1984, the company made a first visit to Berlin, to perform in the International Congress Centre, a huge multi-purpose building in the centre of the city. Our truck was lifted from street level to arrive directly at the rear of the outsize stage, some 30 metres wide and 25 metres deep. Here we found the stagehands racing from one side of the stage to the other on roller skates, but all the technical equipment was the best and the most up to date.

The dancers could hardly imitate the stagehands when performing the *Dream*, and although we reduced the playing area by using two lots of stage curtains for the side masking, the dancers were still challenged – but they revelled in covering that stage with their biggest leaps and fastest runs. The Fairfield Quartet accompanied the performance and were seated on stage, but to the side of the action.

Rudolf Nureyev, with his programme of *Nureyev and Friends*, had played in the theatre on the evening before us, making our Berlin friends despair as to whether we would have an audience at all, but, unknown to us, our performance was part of a subscription series which brought in some 3,000 people, packing the auditorium; quite a surprise and a great return to Berlin for Alexander. With Caroline dancing Titania, Alexander as Bottom and a good-looking Dutch dancer, Hugo Bregman, as Oberon, *Dream* was a huge success, rewarded with a 15-minute ovation. My best memory is of the diminutive Colleen, as Puck, taking a solo curtain call, with the applause reaching a crescendo and echoing through the cavernous spaces of the theatre.

This performance and the others the company had given in Germany attracted the attention of several German agents, who started to compete with each other, enticing us to sign up to an exclusive contract. We chose the most important of them, a Salzburg-based agency with a long history of managing opera and dance companies, who offered us a good contract for touring in West Germany, Switzerland, Austria, Holland and Scandinavia from the 1985 season onwards. This was obviously an exciting development, something we had long hoped for.

In the meantime, the company completed the performances already booked while adding another new ballet to the repertoire, *La Ronde*, based on the play by the Austrian playwright Arthur Schnitzler. This hour-long work, a roundelay of romantic meetings and partings, was danced to music by Jacques Offenbach, mostly pieces from his operettas, brilliantly colourful and effervescent. Schnitzler's play is also a satire on the conventions and hypocrisy of Viennese *fin-de-siècle* society, inspiring Alexander to include some darker and more dramatic scenes in the ballet danced to Offenbach's cello duos, which brought depths to the work. The pivotal role of the Prostitute was particularly well performed by Claire Porter, who had originally joined the company straight out of school, and now several years later had become a self-confident actress-dancer. Claire went on to make a successful new career as an actress. *La Ronde* was instantly successful and made a good double bill with a shortened version of *Beauty and the Beast*.

Our contract with the German–Austrian management couldn't have come at a better time, with the loss of our Asian market and the ever reduced number of performances in France. It is true that dance was undergoing huge changes in France; the opera–ballet companies which had existed in virtually every good-sized city were being closed down and the classical, or the so-called neo-classical, companies had only managed to survive in Toulouse, Bordeaux, Mulhouse, Lyon and Nice. To replace them the Ministry of Culture set up 'Centres Chorégraphiques Nationales' in smaller and larger towns and cities across the country. These centres were, and still are, bases for small groups of contemporary dancers directed by choreographers of a new generation. Classical ballet was out and contemporary dance, strongly influenced by Merce Cunningham and his collaborators, was the new way forward. These choreographic centres were charged to work with local dancers, to organise classes and workshops, and to perform, not in the opera houses, but in new purpose-built modern buildings. The huge funding needed for this 'revolution' came from national and regional sources, leaving very little money available, and very little interest, in inviting foreign companies. With this change, the former traditional ballet audience had virtually disappeared in the regions in France, and those administrating the choreographic centres as well as the local journalists were of a newer, younger generation, with no roots in dance and no interest in our middle-of-the road style of dance, incorporating both classical and contemporary techniques.

The decline in our bookings happened gradually in the early 1980s until, in the 1983–84 season, we gave just nine performances in France with our traditional summer tour abandoned, when we faced the reality that the old-fashioned spa resorts were no longer popular as holiday destinations. However, there were some changes for the better; summer festivals sprung up all over the country with ambitious, eclectic programming and generous funding. France offers unbeatable venues for outdoor performing; in Roman ruins, in the grounds of chateaux, in city squares, or in the shadow of medieval cathedrals or castles. During the 1980s we performed in the Roman amphitheatre in Fréjus, on a stage encircled by the citadel of Sisteron, in the centre of Carpentras – with the cathedral walls as a backdrop – and on the Mediterranean at Sète, in the rightly named Théâtre de la Mer. Italy offers similar possibilities; in 1976 we had already made a tour of these summer venues, and in the 1980s we made two trips to Syracuse, on Sicily. We performed *Dream* in the magical settings of a Greek theatre dating from the fifth century BC, and on a subsequent visit performed *The Magic Flute* in the Roman amphitheatre of the third century AD.

For the performers, these open-air performances are not without problems; it is usually not possible to get on stage until the late afternoon when the summer heat has subdued, dressing rooms can be hundreds of metres away from the stage, with amenities such as water and electricity only very basic, while crossing from one side of the stage to the other backstage can entail crawling under the stage, or even leaving the theatre to rush down an adjoining street to find another entrance. For the technicians, it may well mean working during the previous night to avoid the daytime heat, and I once spent the entire night, in Carpentras in southern France, lighting the performance, together with the theatre's crew, only able to regain our hotel as daylight stopped our activities. For the audience, it can mean the discomfort of a couple of hours on stony, tiered seating with the vagaries of the weather, occasionally exploding with a summer thunderstorm or, in Provence, the whipping up of the violent mistral wind. But once the sun has set on a baking midsummer day, the cicadas have ceased their persistent chatter, performances start as darkness falls around 10 p.m., and an air of magic takes over. Natural stones or ancient ruins become part of the scenery, the star-filled sky adds another dimension to the stage picture and the enforced informality brings audience and performers together in a unique manner.

In the autumn of 1985 we made our first tour with the new management, twenty performances throughout Germany, Austria and Holland. Apart from the few performances in 1983 and 1984, we had not appeared in Germany for more than ten years. The towns and the cities had undergone huge changes during that period, and most of them for the better. However, we revisited theatres we had performed in twenty-five years before with American Festival Ballet which had remained unchanged – the old-fashioned lighting rigs still in place, the polished waxed floors still intact, all cared for as if they were national treasures. But we also performed in many brand new theatres, some multi-purpose halls, nearly always well equipped and well staffed. It made touring very easy; as did the hotels, well run and exceedingly comfortable, most of them with a restaurant open after the performance and happy to accommodate a company of exhausted and ravenously hungry dancers and technicians. Although we had working days of up to sixteen and eighteen hours, with just one or two days off during the month-long tour, it was amazingly easy to slip into a comfortable routine of travelling and performing. That winter was an especially hard one, when we spent many hours battling through snow, ice and fog. Travelling with three vehicles – a truck, a bus and our own car – we took the precaution of leaving in the morning at hourly intervals, so that in the event of a breakdown we, coming along at the rear, would be able to find anyone in trouble. What a boon a mobile phone would have been!

The subscription system is the backbone of the German theatres and our performances were organised within these annual series assuring us, and the agent, full houses wherever we performed. It has remained almost a ritual for the well-off German citizen to buy a series of six, or even ten, performances every year, in order to support the local theatre, but also as a social event where they promenade through the huge foyers and corridors, sipping glasses of champagne. Many arrive at the theatre not even knowing what they are going to see that evening; an opera, a ballet, a play? But they are the most receptive of audiences, unexpectedly open-minded about new and different ways of performing and the company was always rewarded with overwhelming enthusiastic applause and long, detailed press reviews.

Back in London, one morning in February 1986, a telegram arrived from the national Artists' Agency of the German Democratic Republic asking if we would be interested in performing at the Komische Oper in East Berlin in January 1987, as part of the 700-year anniversary of the founding of the city of Berlin. It was a totally unexpected but enormously exciting offer for Alexander to return to the theatre in Berlin where he had experienced his first major professional success, and to be able to do this with his own company. A few weeks later a gentleman from the East German Artists' Agency turned up in our office with a contract for four performances; he had come to finalise appearances not only with us, but also with the Royal Ballet, Ballet Rambert and the London Philharmonic Orchestra – we were in good company! After sifting through piles of photographs and reviews, the programmes were decided upon; the company would perform the triple bill of *Le Boeuf sur le Toit*, *Voices* and *A Smile at the Bottom of the Ladder*, as well as the full-length *A Midsummer Night's Dream*. We immediately decided to invite back some of our former dancers who had been so successful in the same triple bill programme – Francis, Gillian and Prue – as none of the current company knew this repertoire.

The idea of performing my original roles in *Voices* and *Smile* for this very special season was too tempting, so I gave myself six months to get back into condition. However, shortly before we left London for our 1986 German tour, the dancer who was to play Titania in *Dream* unexpectedly dropped out leaving me little choice but to take over this role as well, and straight away. I was fortunate in having as a partner Carl Myers, who had recently left the Royal Ballet where he had been a principal artist for several years. This messed up my careful build-up for a return to the stage, but these things rarely go to plan and I had the chance to dance the twenty-odd performances of *Dream* during the 1986 tour of Germany and Austria.

Rehearsals for the season at the Komische Oper went ahead over the Christmas period, with Francis coming from Belgium, Prue from Germany and Gillian squeezing in time between her commitments in London. Amazingly everyone remembered their roles, making remounting the three complicated works on a new cast infinitely easier. Finally, we were ready to leave; the truck went ahead by road with careful instructions to our technicians, who were driving, of how and where to cross the West–East borders in Germany, and with advice not to stop, under any conditions, on the motorway between the East German border and Berlin. We warned them that this would bring the VoPos alongside immediately, resulting in confiscation of the truck and possibly even prison for the drivers.

For the company, the East German travel office in London had issued a single document in lieu of individual air tickets for the flight to East Berlin; something which seemed curious, especially as we had a complicated route from Heathrow to Copenhagen, and then on to Prague, where we would pick up the East German airline, Interflug. East Germany had no rights to fly their national airline into the UK. Checking in the next day at Heathrow, the Dutch airline, KLM, immediately refused to let us fly, insisting that we needed individual tickets. There was no alternative but to rebook the flight for a day later, a change of plans which robbed us of an extra day in Berlin for stage rehearsals. January 1987 was a record-breaking winter, and once the train had crawled back to central London, Alexander and I were forced to wade, knee deep in snow, along Bond Street to the East German travel office, where they finally issued the tickets.

This was not the end of our travel odyssey, as the following day the flight left London late, due to problems caused by the weather, arriving in Copenhagen at exactly the time we should have been boarding a flight to East Berlin. I dashed out of the plane as soon as the doors opened and fortunately the Berlin flight, an Interflug plane, was parked at the next bay. As expected, there were two very official looking East German security men stationed at the entrance to the plane, their long leather coats and wide-brimmed hats pulled well over their faces, images familiar from so many Cold War films. We couldn't afford to miss this flight and I charged up to them, requesting they hold the flight, explaining we had to reach Berlin that day in order to perform at the Komische Oper, and that we were guests of the government. Presumably they were expecting us, so when the Danish airport staff wanted to close the flight they dourly stated 'We delay this flight' and no one dared oppose them. Even our baggage was transferred in time and we left

Copenhagen in the Interflug aircraft, which was a third-hand, battered and bouncy machine, with luggage racks that were simple net baskets over our heads. No wonder they didn't have permission to fly into the UK! During the flight the two East German security men sat with their backs to the cockpit, grimly inspecting the plane-load of passengers.

Fortunately, our truck and our technicians did arrive in East Berlin on time and would have been at the stage door of the Komische Oper at the arranged hour if the weather hadn't caused so much disruption. Overnight, the diesel had frozen making the truck immobile. Apparently, there were no breakdown services, but a telephone call from the hotel brought forth the entire stage crew from the Komische Oper, who pushed the truck a good kilometre, or more, through the icy, snow-bound streets to arrive at the stage door. To our great relief, we arrived to find the stage set and ready for our performances. Inspecting this later in the day, after our arrival, Alexander was approached by an elderly stage technician who had been watching him walking around the stage and the backstage areas, remembering the theatre from all those years ago. 'Good to see you, Alexander,' he offered warmly, and, yes, he had worked on stage and remembered the performances of *The Devil in the Village*.

It is a beautiful opera house, all white and gold, but if the auditorium was in a fairly good condition, the state of the stage was disastrous, with huge gaps in the floorboards which even the dance floor could not disguise. The lighting board, situated at the back of the stalls, could have competed with the most antiquated of French boards, consisting of hundreds and hundreds of hand-operated levers and wheels. The theatre and the country had simply run out of money, and as we were later to see, everything was gradually deteriorating and falling into ruin; the roads, the buildings, even the official prestigious ones such as the opera house. Fortunately, the stage crew were excellent and fired with enthusiasm to make this unique theatre festival a memorable one.

We gave the triple bill for the first two performances, winning ovations and Alexander was met at the stage door by fans clutching photographs and programmes from his earlier days in the theatre – an extraordinary experience. During the day before the first *Dream* performance, several of us were invited to a reception by the British ambassador; in between the small talk, the ambassador called Alexander to one side and asked how we were managing with the fee from the East German Artists' Agency, as the Royal Ballet and others were badly affected by receiving payment only in East German marks, which were effectively useless. The ambassador was astounded to hear that we were being paid in sterling, in cash, something we had been offered from the outset, and without which the visit would never have been possible.

It was also during the reception that Alexander unknowingly downed a glass of whisky (which he usually never drinks), having mistaken it for apple juice, when it was offered on a silver platter by the embassy butler.

Back at the theatre, where the technicians had been busy with the changeover for the new programme, a television crew was ready in place and waiting for an interview; Alexander's photo was on the front page of the Berlin newspapers with the headlines shouting 'Back to his roots'. The East Germans were obviously eager to make the most out of his visit. Seated in the stalls with the TV cameras and microphone, he was encouraged to reminisce about his time in the theatre and, in particular, his work with Walter Felsenstein, the legendary director. He said later that it was thanks to the whisky that he managed to talk non-stop for twenty minutes; perhaps it was also the whisky that left him rolling in the snow in front of the stage door with Tom Schilling, the ballet director at that time, with whom Alexander had worked at the very beginning of his career in Leipzig, an event which Sheila reported to us on stage as she arrived at the theatre from the airport.

Sheila had briefly left us to rejoin Sadler's Wells Royal Ballet, but now came back to the company, flying in for the *Dream* performances and to dance Titania. However, a casualty of the uneven stage floor meant some fast recasting, leaving Sheila to dance Hermia, and me to dance the role of Titania – not something I had planned for, especially in view of the fact that I had also been injured the previous evening, coming down from a lift with my foot firmly wedged in a hole in the stage floor. Once again, I was grateful for Carl's masterful Royal-Ballet-style partnering, and for Sheila's professionalism.

Dream was televised the next evening and the TV film was later shown throughout Eastern Europe, including the USSR, and also in West Germany. However, our fees for the television film were paid in East German marks, and the only way to use these was to do some shopping in East Berlin, something which had become even more difficult since our visit in 1964. Fortunately, the dancers found a Polish tourist shop selling handicrafts and were able to do some sightseeing – visiting the Wall from the 'other side', which they were informed was to protect the country from invasion.

On our last evening in East Berlin, Alexander and I wandered out of the hotel at midnight onto the Alexanderplatz, a huge Soviet-style square, ringed by grim concrete buildings. The temperature was down to –20ºC, and the tips of our noses were numb with the cold. The Karl-Marx Allee joined the 'Alex', an immense avenue of apartment buildings for communist party officials and elite members of the government where, incongruously, huge crystal chandeliers could be seen inside the small box-like, impersonal looking apartments. It was impossible to imagine that all of this was to change within a very short time.

Back in the UK, the company continued performing and touring, now giving around one hundred performances annually. Conditions were difficult; cutbacks continued to limit theatres' and councils' budgets, the exchange rate fluctuated, inflation was high and expenses soared. However, the German tours gave us a sense of security and we were able to plan new works and new tours. It was during this time that one of those chance happenings brought about another huge, and welcome, change to the company. I was in the office one afternoon, when the advertising department of an annual international theatre directory phoned to say – as they often do – that the publication was about to go to print, but they 'just happened' to have a half-page of advertising available, which they were offering at half price. I must have been feeling generous, so agreed to take this, sending on the usual design, with Crickmay's photo of Francis as Puck, and some current details about the company – and promptly forgot all about it.

About six months later, we received a letter from an agent in San Francisco to say, having seen our advertisement, he would like to bring the company to the United States – and would we be interested? Gary Lindsey was an agent specialising in dance companies, and had been involved in bringing Ballet Rambert to the States some years previously; he handled a number of important American companies, and his credentials were exemplary. Yes, we were interested! Having just invested in one of the first fax machines, we were now able to put this to use, sending sheaves of material to Gary, while coming into the office in the mornings to find the floor littered with pages of information, contracts, programme suggestions, and later schedules and tour lists. Our first American tour was scheduled for the autumn of 1988 – but first we went to South America.

chapter eleven

South American Adventures 1987

One had always heard hair-raising stories of the dangers of touring in South America; Anna Pavlova with her company, Diaghilev's Ballets Russes and the Ballet Russe de Monte Carlo did tour the continent extensively in the first half of the twentieth century, but more recent visits from European companies had become rare events. Even in the 1980s stories abounded of crumbling stages and corrupt promoters leaving dance companies stranded, without the means of returning home. Nevertheless, we felt that the survival tactics we had acquired from our many international tours would guarantee our safety anywhere in the world. Over the years we had received offers from several South-America-based promoters, but most of these initially enthusiastic approaches fizzled out, or were thwarted by the most common of South American problems – earthquakes, revolutions or rogue impresarios.

In 1974, during our season in Paris, a distinguished looking gentleman approached us backstage, introducing himself as a Brazilian-based impresario from Sao Paolo, as well as the representative of a very large international communications company. He had not been invited, so obviously we were flattered by his offer to represent the company in South America. As we were staying in a small hotel near Montmartre, he suggested meeting in a bar on the Boulevard Pigalle around midnight, an unlikely venue for a business talk, but, still high on post-performance adrenaline, Alexander and I duly waited in the brightly neon-lit, rather sleazy Pigalle bar. The Brazilian arrived a little after us and we were uneasy to see that he was accompanied by four burly heavies who took up positions at each of the exit doors. However, it was a stimulating conversation; he appeared to be genuinely enthusiastic about the company, and cited a number of well-known companies and artists he had already presented in South America. Agreeing on the basis of a business agreement, we promised to send each other the necessary information and material for further negotiations. The gentleman was then bundled into a huge black Mercedes and sped off into the night. We never heard from him again.

Finally, in 1981 a reputable firm run by German émigrés in Buenos Aries showed serious interest, offering to book a lengthy tour to include not only the major cities in Brazil, Argentina and Chile, but also exotic sounding venues in Peru, Bolivia and Ecuador. Obviously, they wanted to see the company first, and one of the partners, visiting Europe, made a stop in London. Deidre collected him from Heathrow, whisked him up the M1 to see a performance that evening near Leicester, and after discussing details on the drive back to London, Alexander and I entertained him at a midnight supper at North House before driving him back to Heathrow for his flight to Argentina. Negotiations progressed over a few years slowly but surely filling a box file, however, when another of the firm's directors died, it was decided that the agency could not take on the workload of what was becoming a long and complicated tour. In 1987 the signed contracts for performances in Ecuador, Columbia and the Caribbean island of Aruba were sent on to us (the Argentinean promoter even relinquishing his commission), with details of possible additional performances in Mexico, Guatemala and Jamaica. We still needed to finance the fares, the salaries, touring allowances and all the additional expenses but, with some ingenuity, we found an airline willing to offer us cut-price flights, and with an additional week's booking in Bermuda, the tour appeared to be feasible.

The evening before our departure the company was invited to a send-off reception at the Colombian Embassy. Any misgivings about dealings with the South Americans – and the final negotiations had been prolonged and painful – were dispersed by the warmth and charm of our hosts. Walking back to the car in Belgrave Square, I remember being aware of an electric stillness in the air; an extraordinary feeling that something unusual was about to happen. Putting it down to 'travel fever', we went to bed full of anticipation for the day ahead. The Great Storm, or the hurricane of October 1987, hit London around midnight. North House rocked on its foundations, the lime trees lining Eton Avenue crashed across the road, the garden walls tumbled down and north-west London was totally blacked out. I didn't dare let the thought cross my mind: is this some sort of an omen?

Driving to Heathrow the next morning, the extent of the damage was horrifyingly visible. In Hyde Park the power of the storm had ripped out the huge oak trees, hundreds of years old, leaving them lying helplessly on their sides, and had thrown smaller trees into rubbishy heaps. With many roads still blocked, the taxi picked its way across London and on to the airport. Despite disrupted road and rail transportation, the van with the trunks of costumes and scenery, as well as all the company members, arrived at the appointed time, everyone buzzing with excitement about the trip ahead. We had with us nine dancers, a stage manager and three very large flight cases containing everything needed for the two different programmes we were to perform. Luggage allowances went by weight, so by reducing our personal luggage to 10 kilograms per person we could (just) get the trunks accepted as personal luggage and be assured they would travel with us. The 10 kilograms personal luggage allowance was an unlikely target, but we needed only summer clothing and knew that airlines are usually generous to groups like ours.

The flight to Ecuador involved a change of planes in Miami. No one had prepared us for the arrival at Miami airport; we only wanted to change planes, we did not want to enter the USA, emigrate to the USA, and certainly not defect to the USA. The airline, the travel agent and our South American promoter had assured us that a US visa was not necessary for a simple change of planes within the airport. The Miami immigration authorities thought otherwise. Arriving with an hour's delay, due, no doubt, to the aftermath of the hurricane, we had just forty minutes to the connecting flight to Guayaquil. It seemed possible that we, at least, would make the flight, leaving the luggage to follow on later.

The arrival hall was also the transit hall and at least a thousand people were lined up in thirty different queues, trundling through the immense building, laden with boxes, bags, suitcases and children. It looked as if the entire population of the Caribbean was attempting to enter the USA on that particular day and no one, absolutely no one, was interested in our plight – that we had only forty minutes to catch a flight to Guayaquil. In fact, hardly anyone seemed to speak English; Spanish was used by the numerous officials herding us into snaking lines and stuffing sheaves of forms into our hands.

Our desperate pleas for assistance, and our incredulous queries as to the necessity of such an ordeal, were dismissed as incomprehensible.

After two hours of queue shuffling we reached the immigration officers' counters and were immediately impounded. Twelve of us were locked up in an empty room, and essential visits to the toilets, or in search of food, could only be made accompanied by an armed security guard. It was then decided to grant us a 'visa waiver' (this later became an automatic procedure) as well as rebooking us onto a later flight. However, first we had to clear all the baggage through US customs, into the USA, only to check it all out again for the new flight. There were no trolleys, no porters, no assistance of any kind, so we shunted the huge flight cases along endless corridors and heaved them onto the customs inspection benches. Blank, disinterested faces rebuffed our breathless pleas: 'We don't want to enter the USA, this is all just for TRANSIT!' The tutus were picked at, the donkey's head from *Dream* was laughed at, and the pointe shoes were marvelled at. It was all good-tempered, but we had been on the go for eighteen hours and found the exercise pointless and exasperating. Finally, we were rechecked in, relabelled and were on our way out of the US of A.

We touched down in Guayaquil at 2 a.m. on a breathless, equatorial night. The South American aircraft had been aged and cramped and we were glad to be back on terra firma. Clutching a telex received in London just before our departure, 'Theatre director will meet you at airport with transportation,' we looked around eagerly for some sign of a welcome, some assistance after a very long, very eventful day. The airline office in Miami had promised to telex ahead to the theatre director informing him of our new arrival time. However, like most airports throughout the world, this one was deserted and desolate at 2 a.m. How were we to get ten travel-worn company members and several large flight cases of theatre equipment out of the airport? Would we find the hotel open when we got there? Where was the theatre director? And did anyone speak English?

The forecourt of the airport was a little more lively, and we were soon propositioned by a dozen taxi drivers. At least, they claimed to be taxi drivers, but the state of their vehicles and their sweaty, unshaven appearances did not invite confidence. We had no choice, and when I discovered a battered pick-up in a dark corner of the forecourt, and had woken the sleeping driver, we could only take the risk and pile into three taxis, load the luggage on to the pick-up and hope we would all turn up together at the hotel. I noticed too late that none of the taxis had meters, and as we hadn't done any bargaining beforehand, we spent the trip attempting to revive our flagging brains for arguing in Spanish, which surely would be necessary at the end of the trip.

Miraculously, we did all turn up at the same hotel, which was open, and invitingly bright and modern. The night porter was charming, the fares modest, and the sullen faces of our drivers brightened at the sight of real US dollars. We settled gratefully into the pleasant rooms and I returned a message from the theatre director to call him on arrival. It was 3 a.m., but I suspected he was not over-surprised by the delayed travel arrangements. He also reminded us that there would be transportation at the hotel at 8 a.m. to take us, the theatre equipment and the stage manager to the theatre. It was a short night but we slept soundly.

We had no idea what to expect of the theatre in Guayaquil, as all the usual requests for technical information had been persistently ignored; we did not even know if our technical requirements had been received and understood. In those days before fax and email, telex messages were the only way to make satisfactory communication with countries such as those in South America. The postal system seemed virtually useless, and international telephone calls passed through a chain of buzzing exchanges, involving minutes or even hours of waiting, resulting in fading, crackling, often unintelligible conversations. I can't imagine how telex actually worked, with a thin tape of paper emerging from the sort of machine used by secret service organisations in the Second World War, and messages in Spanish seemed to materialise almost indecipherably. The British Council representatives were our saviours, mostly because their telex machines appeared to be the only ones that worked efficiently, and the rep in Quito, to whom I had turned, had given us detailed notes about the theatre there. However, all he could say about the theatre in Guayaquil was, 'STAGE 12 METRES WIDE X 8 METRES DEEP FACILITIES UNKNOWN.'

The Teatro del 9 Octubre – most Guayaquil addresses appeared to commemorate a date in the country's colourful history – was situated in a busy street in the downtown area. The theatre has a huge, cavernous auditorium, and, although it is now mostly used as a cinema, it has been used by theatrical touring companies for many years. Anna Pavlova visited the theatre with her company in 1917, arriving in Guayaquil with all sixty-five company members on a cattle boat from Costa Rica. Although her visit was a sell-out success, conditions must have been horrific, as was the city itself at that time; filthy,

257

poverty stricken, rife with swamp fever, hardly a suitable venue for the celebrated ballerina and her famous company.

Approaching the stage down an endlessly long aisle, almost ankle deep in discarded sweet wrappers, it only gradually became apparent, through the gloom of the dim working lights, that the stage, although of a reasonable size, was completely empty. Not only were there no stage curtains, and no stage lights, there were not even any bars for attaching these, nor pulleys or ropes to raise and lower them. The dressing rooms which surrounded the rear of the bare stage in a semicircle, in the fashion of the old Italian opera houses, looked as if they had had little use since Pavlova's visit. A damp, musty smell pervaded everything, and I thought in horror of unpacking the costumes in such conditions. Everything on and around the stage was covered in years of dust and neglect, and obviously no one had believed sufficiently in the reality of our arrival to make any preparations. Or was it simply the *mañana* mentality and that Latin or Hispanic tendency to do nothing at all until it is absolutely unavoidable?

We had brought with us a new set of stage curtains for the *Dream*, made up of pristine white scrim – or gauze – especially lightweight for air travel. We were dreading exposing this expensive new acquisition to the dirty, humid conditions in the theatre, but initially it looked as if we wouldn't be using any scenery at all. A shy, South American Indian was introduced as the stage manager, and although our command of Spanish was very basic, it proved once again that the theatre is the most universal of worlds, and we managed to communicate with our limited vocabulary, backed up with some vivid miming and lively demonstration. The stage manager was obviously bright and willing, if very limited in his experience, due, no doubt, to a chronic lack of technical equipment. He had a gentle air of confidence, and fortunately we had nearly three days before the opening performance. There seemed to be nothing more we could do and so we left him with our stage manager, who was looking increasingly desperate, and a motley crew of helpers, together with our drawings and notes, while we escaped outdoors.

Once out into the heavy, humid air, we found downtown Guayaquil was a busy commercial centre, the streets full of banks and shipping companies as well as numerous dusty, old-fashioned, very rundown bars and cinemas. The country's largest city, it was just as seedy as one expects of an equatorial South American port town. In fact, Guayaquil had only recently recovered some sense of permanence after surviving centuries of earthquakes, fires, revolution, attacks by pirates and even infestation by termites. However, the general atmosphere was lively and good-tempered, although the backstreets clearly lacked rubbish collection and even sanitation. Tourist guides now warn of pickpockets and muggers in Ecuador, but in 1987 there was none of that feeling of unease; one felt safe, although contact with the locals remained distant. There were none of the stalls and peddlers or pavement kitchens which enliven the streets in Asia, and no one seemed too interested in foreigners.

The following morning we approached the theatre anxiously, but were amazed to find work on stage in full swing; hanging bars of rough timber were in place above the stage, the dressing rooms had been totally repainted, while crates of stage lamps were being unpacked and hung, the cables snaking through the auditorium. The dancers, after a day off, were able to do their morning class and to rehearse at the nearby Casa de la Cultura, while we continued to supervise progress on stage. The curtains were unpacked and gingerly hung into position, the stage lamps were rigged – with some problems – and brought to life, the costumes unpacked and passed on to a motherly señora for pressing. On the day of our first performance, the dancers dribbled into the theatre, sporting their tropical sun wear and dark glasses, blissfully unaware of the awesomeness of the conditions on stage just forty-eight hours earlier.

The rest of the day, with class and rehearsals, continued as normal, except for the startling reminder of that horror of international travel – jet lag. I always expect at least half the company to be affected at some time during a long overseas tour. I have known grown men to break down in tears with homesickness, and the gentlest of people to fly into violent rages. It is impossible to rationalise the attack with the person at the time; it is always unexpected, and mostly totally out of character. Naturally, the change of climate from a European winter to a tropical, equatorial country can make the effects much more severe, and in this case jet lag struck right at the end of rehearsal, about two hours before the performance. We had been fortunate in having the use of a linoleum dance floor which the theatre had acquired for the recent visit of a group of Russian dancers. It was in a good condition, so we were surprised when one of the dancers slipped and fell during rehearsal, and alarmed at the violence of her reaction.

She shrieked, she shouted, she wept inconsolably while everyone rushed to her assistance and she was carried to the dressing room. Cold water was applied, someone raced to the nearest cafe to find ice, while someone else made tea. The source of the pain, the ankle, was stroked, massaged and band-aged. She continued to shriek and to weep, then she resolutely declared she was not dancing. We had an hour and a half before the curtain, no time to rehearse the string of understudies which a replacement would call for. We coaxed, we applied ice and lineament. The ankle looked normal, it moved, it could even be stood on, but the tears and the shrieks continued. Everyone was now in a high state of tension, but the rest of the company silently started their own preparations for the performance. We hung on, hoping she might just come back to normal, managing finally to calm her with some sweet tea and an aspirin, as well as an assurance that she could just walk through her role that evening. In the event the recovery was total, and nothing more was heard about the ankle that evening or during the rest of the tour.

The performance of *Dream* was followed the next evening by a double bill featuring our version of *Coppélia* (where we were joined by some local dancers to play the roles of the dolls) and *La Ronde*. The Offenbach music and the lively humour of *La Ronde* seemed to win the audience's favour and both performances, played to packed houses, proved to be successful, much to our relief. The next day we took an eight o'clock flight to Quito, the capital of Ecuador, perched over 9,000 feet up in the Andes. The flight takes only thirty-five minutes, and the plane literally never stops climbing from sea level to reach Quito, nestling among the high, remarkably green Andean valleys. Feeling quite dizzy from the rapid change of altitude, it was a relief to be met on arrival by a charming, efficient welcome party, and to be whisked away in cars and a bus to the hotel. However, climbing the stairs to our hotel room, I found my heart thumping as if it would jump out of my chest, and I couldn't help remembering how athletes at the Mexico Olympic Games had trained at altitude for months to become acclimatised; and here we were with just seven hours to the performance!

The hotel was in old Quito, originally an Inca city and rebuilt by the Spanish in 1534. While Guayaquil resembles a South American port town in a B-movie, Quito belongs to another age. The Spanish-style colonial buildings have deteriorated with a certain dusty refinement, and the people are quiet and shyly friendly. Walking along the narrow, cobbled streets, all running either uphill or downhill, to the nearby theatre, it soon became noticeable that the secret of coping with life at 9,000 feet is to slow down. We imitated the leisurely pace of the locals around us, but soon came upon the huge exterior of the Teatro Bolívar. Posters pasted around the theatre confirmed that it was now used principally as a cinema, but I knew it had an impressive history of receiving visiting opera and ballet companies, including the Ballets Russes, Pavlova's company, the Grand Ballet du Marquis de Cuevas, and more recently, several North American dance companies. The interior of the Bolívar came as a shock; it had a huge auditorium capable of holding 4,000 people, all ornately decorated, gilded and glowing with seats in slightly faded but plush red velvet, somewhere between a baroque cathedral and a 1930s movie palace. Excesses of curlicues competed with huge painted Roman pillars, and if everything seemed dulled with a century of Andean dust, the effect remained remarkable, as indeed was the theatre's existence in such an unlikely setting.

The scene on stage was just as unexpected; everything had been prepared for our arrival, the lamps ready for focusing, the bars ready to hang our scenery, a team of smiling helpers to iron the costumes and the rest of the day went as smoothly as possible. For the dancers, the main challenge was to cope with the altitude, and here again everything had been taken care of, with Red Cross workers stationed in the wings during the rehearsals and the performance, with oxygen masks at the ready to which the dancers would rush between their appearances on stage. The audience that evening was a more sophisticated one than in Guayaquil and gave us a great reception. The British ambassador, who came on the opening night with a party, seemed bemused to find us there at all, and he confirmed that we must have been the first British theatre company to visit Quito.

On that first day of our stay, one incident stood out; during the afternoon, a good-looking young man approached Alexander in the theatre, asking for an interview for a local magazine. Arrangements were made, but while waiting for him in the stalls the following day, Alexander became aware of some heated arguing and shouting at the back of the theatre, and was informed that the man was not a serious journalist, but a trouble maker, and he had been sent away. This was an incident which made more sense in the light of later events.

There was a welcome free day following the second performance in Quito, so a bus excursion was organised through the mountains to Otavalo, where the weekly market would be held. The bus was small and rattly and the road bumpy and potholed; the scenery, as we rolled along the tops of the Andean range, was disappointingly ordinary and could well have been a country road in France or Italy. There was a little farming, some scattered villages where one could see women washing their linen in shallow streams, and very little traffic. It took about two hours to reach Otavalo, where we found a really busy, bustling small town packed with people and produce. The locals are Otavaleños, originally a pre-Inca tribe with a thousand-year heritage as farmers and artisans, and we were delighted to see that they really do wear their picture-book clothing of vividly coloured skirts, blouses and jackets, and an extraordinary assortment of headgear including, of course, endless variations of the South American bowler hat. Their colourful and imaginative clothing was curiously at odds with their very reserved and almost morose behaviour.

It was difficult to judge whether this was just shyness or if it was possibly an animosity towards strangers, as we were almost the only tourists there.

The market goods on offer were quite extraordinary; huge freshly slaughtered carcasses were laid out on rough wooden planks, the glazed-eyed heads thrown into plastic buckets. One of my best memories is of Sheila Styles, our principal dancer, dressed somewhat incongruously, but ever the ballerina, in an ankle-length black lace dress and stilettos, picking her way among entrails and innards tumbling out onto the pavement, all under a beating midday sun which rendered an almost unbearable stench. We hurried onwards to little shaded alleyways, where women sat haphazardly, many with huge bundles tied over their shoulders. Some sold beans, brightly coloured in red, yellow, purple and as large as bananas; also huge tomatoes and aubergines, peppers and varieties of vegetables I had never seen before. Other stands were selling local pottery, jars and vases and figurines of Inca or Aztec gods. I bought an attractive figurine of a small dog god in terracotta and a more frightening devil-like creature of Aztec appearance in black clay. Of course, no one spoke English, but the market traders' Spanish was clear, and spoken so slowly to make communication easier than expected.

My most treasured acquisition was a poncho made from soft Andean llama wool. This is an indispensable garment for the Indians, used not only as an all-weather garment, but also as a mattress, a pillow or a bedcover. It can also be folded to make a baby harness to be carried over the mother's back or used as a container for carrying animals, dead or alive, vegetables or other produce. It became an essential travelling companion for me, and since the visit to Ecuador, accompanied me on every tour; it has been sat on and slept on, always useful for grabbing those vital extra moments of rest, stretched out on a dressing room floor or on a backstage table, and, of course, marvellous for cuddling up on aircraft, coaches, cars and in draughty waiting rooms.

Laden with our new possessions, we returned to Quito, stopping off on the way at a pleasant lakeside restaurant. The only unusual thing to happen on the drive back was that the bus was stopped twice at roughly built roadblocks, when all our passports were checked by what appeared to be military police. We had settled down for an early night in anticipation of the six o'clock call to leave for the airport when we would take a flight to Cali in Columbia. At some time during the night, I became aware of rumbling sounds and increasingly loud noises coming from the square below our hotel rooms. The hotel was situated on the city's main square and almost directly opposite was the Government Palace. Peeping through the shutters, I realised that something unusual was happening; the large square was packed with people. They were carrying banners while singing and chanting, while others appeared to be attempting to enter the palace. The main gates were blocked by two small tanks, and guarded by rows of soldiers. In my altitude-dazed, over-tired, somnolent state, I presumed it must be some kind of South American fiesta and went soundly back to sleep. The following morning only the tanks and the guards remained while I had almost forgotten the sight of several hundred, or thousand, people crowded into the square under the glare of the street lamps. There was little time to wonder if it was only a dream, as we were off to the airport.

The theatre directors, two charming, cosmopolitan brothers, had assured us that we would be met at the airport and given their assistance to complete all the departure arrangements, as indeed was stipulated in their contractual duties. Departures and arrivals at international airports are the most dreaded moments of international touring; each country and each airline has its own set of rules concerning baggage size and weight, different sets of regulations regarding customs documents and declarations, unexpected airport taxes and exit fees. Even with the best advance information, coping with these as well as a party of sleepy, disorientated dancers and technicians, at unwelcome hours of the day or night, is a nightmare. In this case, we had arrived with time in hand; everyone was awake and no one had lost or mislaid their passport. However, neither of the directors or anyone else from the theatre was to be seen. As it was seven o'clock on a Sunday morning there was little point in attempting to call the theatre, but seeing the hall fill with travellers it was becoming urgent to carry on with the check-in.

The initial response was immediate – the flight cases were too large to be sent as personal luggage and would have to be sent as freight. This came as a real shock, as we had arrived in Ecuador with the same airline only a few days earlier without problems, so we attempted to reason with the check-in clerk; we pleaded, we cajoled and we demanded to see his superior. The elaborately uniformed, moustachioed, thick-bellied superior officer rejected our pleas with immediate disdain and disinterest. The problems of freighting involved not only extra expense, but even more importantly, the probability that the cases would not travel on the same flight; in this case we knew that this was the only flight from Quito to Cali for a week. Years of touring have allowed me to polish my technique at beguiling and persuading over-zealous officials, even weeping and sobbing to accomplish our needs in an emergency, but having exhausted my repertoire we finally accepted the fact that the flight cases would have to be freighted.

The pick-up from the theatre had long since left, the freight office was half a mile from the terminal, at the other end of the airport, and there was no transportation available. Fortunately, the cases were on wheels, but dressed in what I considered to be my 'good' travelling clothes, and in high heels,

Alexander and I, accompanied by the stage manager, started to push them there. Inevitably (we were still in the Andes), the rough, unsurfaced road went steeply uphill to the freight office. It was decided that Alexander should rejoin the dancers in the terminal, while my minimal Spanish might be needed once we got to the freight office. It was. While we continued arguing and filling in multiple import–export forms, Alexander was rounding up the dancers, who, by this time, had drifted off into the shops and cafes all over the airport.

Then suddenly someone saw the theatre director, in an animated conversation with friends, and clearly oblivious of our predicament. However, as the flight for Cali was being announced, he burst into action and took stock of the situation. I am not sure what kind of traditional South American formalities were exchanged, but the stage manager and I were soon speeding back to the terminal, a pick-up with the trunks hot on our heels, while the Spanish being exchanged was fast and furious. Back at the terminal, the theatre director rushed in with us in tow, doors opening for him, smiles and bows greeting us as we collected a final group of dancers who had been left sealed off behind glass doors in the departure lounge, like a desperate column of refugees. As we rushed across the tarmac, the plane's engines roaring, I noticed the trunks being loaded into the hold. Climbing the stairs into the plane, I saw the relief on Alexander face; he'd already been recasting *Dream* for six dancers, in practice clothes, and, of course, without scenery!

Once we were airborne, I started to assess our progress so far; we hadn't encountered an earthquake – surely the most frightening of possible South American disasters – but the London hurricane wasn't a bad substitute, and we had survived that, intact. We hadn't been caught up in a revolution, another common South American occurrence, or had we? On arrival in Cali, we learned that the events which took place outside the Government Palace in Quito the night before had been an attempted coup, just a minor revolution by South American standards, and we had escaped on the last plane out of the country. A general strike had been called and was carried out almost immediately following our departure, all ports and airports were closed, roads were blocked and a state of emergency declared. We had just avoided that, and even more miraculously, we had, so far, been paid in cash, in US dollars, promptly and without problems. We weren't doing too badly.

There was a curious postscript to our visit to Ecuador; the newspaper review from Quito was awaiting us when we returned to London and it was more than usually interesting. The writer, reviewing the performance of *Dream*, described the 'spirits and the fairies' which had appeared in the depth of the night stirring up magical events in the city. It was apparently a kind of coded report, not so much about the performance, but an attempt to beat the censors in what was a hard-line military dictatorship by using the spirits of *Dream* as a symbol of the desired revolution!

———————

I was not looking forward to our visit to Colombia; the negotiations had been long and tedious with a bad-tempered local organiser. The initial plan had been to give two performances in each of Bogotá and Medellín, the country's largest cities, and one in Cali. However, the wars with the drug barons were at their height – there was almost civil war, with daily fighting, people being gunned down with alarming frequency, and when a curfew was declared in Bogotá and Medellín, the performances were cancelled. Apparently the Cali Cartel had not yet reached the heights of its notoriety, and the city was considered calm enough for life to continue with some normality. The telexes flashed back and forth between Bogotá and London, but there was very little we could do to protest at the loss of four fifths of our contractual engagement, as it was obviously a case of force majeure. As the date of our visit drew closer, we grew more and more concerned at the lack of information and communication from the Colombian promoter. We had requested some basic details – the name and address of the theatre and the hotel, the time of the performance, when we would be paid, whether our technical requirements could be met, etc. However, as in Ecuador, our letters and telexes remained unanswered until we finally received a reply: TO BE BORED BY MANY RECOMMENDATIONS EVERY DAY PLEASE PLEASE NO MORE PROBLEMS STOP NO MORE PHONE STOP... Fortunately, the British Council representative was not so easily bored, and once again, came to our assistance with all the necessary information.

The flight from Quito to Cali was only thirty-five minutes and we were met by a lively business-like woman from the local arts association to transport us to the hotel. The drive into town was along a long, straight road lined with small shops and workshops, and the hotel, a large art deco building, was blissfully cool and air-conditioned. However, everyone was quite adamant – we should not leave the hotel at any time. We would be collected by bus the following morning and driven to theatre, three blocks away, and returned to the hotel when required, as it was much too dangerous to venture outdoors on foot. The thought of spending the entire day and evening in the hotel, even with the distractions of a rooftop swimming pool and restaurant, seemed like imprisonment to us, but the dancers, still reeling from the six o'clock airport call and the ensuing dramas at Quito airport, were disinterested in Cali, and happy enough with the rooftop alternative.

Alexander and I changed into our simplest and least foreign looking clothes to venture outside into the heavy, humid air. It was a Sunday morning, and if the streets were deserted, they seemed safe enough; we passed a cathedral and the main square, soon finding a park by a river, full of families enjoying a normal Sunday morning. We joined them on the grassy surrounds of a bandstand, and listened to a brass band concert while lively children played on the grass around us. However, later that day we saw another side of Colombian life; two exquisitely groomed ladies, members of the board of the arts association, arrived in a huge, glistening black limousine to take Alexander and me for a drive, to see the sights of Cali. My first impression on seeing them enter the hotel lobby was of two walking Christmas trees. Not only were they dressed in the most expensive designer clothes, but they were laden with flashing, glittering jewels, rings and bracelets, necklaces and earrings; it was quite a breathtaking sight. We joined them to reach the car, parked in the hotel driveway, and were only just seated when the car was pounced upon by a group of very rough young men; they banged on the windows and shook the doors, they shouted abuse while our hosts continued talking quietly to us about the drive they had planned. The chauffeur managed to speed away, leaving the men to scatter, still shouting, while leaving us rather shaken. I couldn't help wondering why they had dressed so ostentatiously for a simple drive?

Cali, which we were only able to see from the safety of the car, appeared to be a modern, prosperous city with new and impressive high-rise blocks, full of banks and shops. It was some years later that it became known that the prosperity of Cali was built on drug money. The sun was sinking as we reached the outskirts of the city to admire the magnificent villas and haciendas, standing in attractive parks and gardens. Not far off was a row of hills, grey and muddy brown, and with the sun in one's eyes it was difficult to make out what was there in the distance. Our query was met with 'that's where the poor people live', and gradually one could make out the rows and rows of rusty, corrugated iron lean-tos clinging to the sides of the hills, with walls of plastic sheeting glinting in the rays of the setting sun. It was our first glimpse of the horrors of the barrios, shanty towns apparently lacking electricity and sanitation, located far from the city centre; out of sight, out of mind, but the homes of millions all over South America.

The following day in Cali brought more surprises. The Municipal Theatre is a jewel of a nineteenth-century opera house, in excellent condition, where we found in the dressing rooms autographed photos of illustrious performers who had preceded us: Caruso, Pavlova, Isaac Stern, Leonard Bernstein and many more. Our performance drew a capacity audience, the stage was a good size, the lighting equipment more than adequate, the *Dream* set looked good and the dancers were on top form. Where the audience in Ecuador had been a homogenous mixture and seemingly classless, the Cali theatregoers were definitely upper class and dressed accordingly, the performance probably being the excuse for a social get-together. Again, where the former had been spontaneous with their applause, and voluble with their enjoyment of the performance, the Colombians were initially reserved, enough so to have me spending the first scenes becoming more and more nervous while sitting in the electrician's control box, almost in the dress circle. However, they were a sophisticated audience, they reacted in the right spots with polite applause, and roused themselves to 'bravos' for the final curtain calls.

We were glad to be off the following morning when we said goodbye to some unexpected new friends at the hotel. I had sometimes wondered about the fate of those dancers who respond to advertisements in the UK trade magazine *The Stage* for 'good dancers required for long contracts in South American circus'. Well, they were here in Cali, a group of five or six English girls, some even ex-fellow students of our own dancers. They had a month to spend in Cali, followed by more months in cities throughout South America. The circus performed in huge indoor buildings so was really more of a variety show, needing accomplished dancers, and they were reasonable happy, if badly frustrated at being cooped up in the hotel for all their off-duty hours. As has long been the case – and Anna Pavlova was perhaps the first to take advantage of this – the promoters had discovered that English dancers are the most reliable and the hardest workers.

The company was now off to Aruba and the Caribbean, allowing us to feel that the easier part of the tour was now ahead, although there was one piece of unfinished business to attend to before leaving Colombia. The Colombian promoter was to come to Cali, to meet us, and more importantly, to pay us. I was almost not surprised to receive a message just before the performance to say he had not been able to come but would meet us the next day in the airport when we changed flights in Bogotá. This was the moment I had been dreading; on overseas tours like these, we clearly stipulated in the contract that payment must be made no later than the interval of the performance. This was something I had learned with interest from Margot Fonteyn, who on her many international engagements insisted on cash payment in her dressing room before the performance, even if this meant dancing with a wad of dollars sewn into her tutu; no doubt she had learned from experience.

We were in a quandary; should we state our case to the local organiser that the promoter was not keeping to the terms of the contract and that we could refuse to perform? Our dealings with him had not been easy, and we had little confidence in his reliability. Fortunately, the British Council representative was at the performance, making us fairly confident that the promoter would not risk his reputation in this way, and cancelling a performance was something we did not take lightly and we had never done before. We decided to take the risk, in spite of some garbled instructions as to how and where we could meet in the arrivals hall of Bogotá airport. Here, surely, was one of our greatest fears becoming a reality. On arrival in Bogotá, I left the rest of the company in the transit area and, with great trepidation, made my way to the meeting point. Despite my fears he was there, clutching one of our publicity brochures to identify himself, and sweating profusely. A quick handover of a bulging envelope seemed a risky thing to do, but I was almost beyond caring, just anxious to get back to the others and onto our flight. This took us over the full length of Colombia, to the border with Venezuela, and then we were over the Caribbean and descending towards one of those turquoise ringed islands so familiar from travel brochures.

Aruba, part of the Dutch Antilles, is one of the last of their colonial outposts. The difference in atmosphere was evident as soon as we reached the airport terminal, which was partially open air. The immigration officials welcomed us with smiles while our hosts were already waving from a public area overlooking the customs hall. The theatre equipment was whisked away and we were soon in a coach on the way to the hotel, with a free day ahead of us. Everyone seemed so happy and relaxed, and we were overjoyed to find the hotel a sumptuously luxurious one, situated in a park of palms and tropical plants, directly behind the beach. It was packed with American honeymoon couples – for which the island had become famous – and we picked our way around them and through pathways fringed with flowering frangipanis and bougainvillea to the whitest and finest of sandy beaches. The sun blazed down and if a gentle breeze fanned the beach, the bright turquoise water was warm and soupy. It all seemed like heaven.

The local arts association was experienced in promoting dance companies, receiving regular visits from the best companies from the Netherlands, so our performances went smoothly and we enjoyed that special Dutch warmth and hospitality which made the whole visit a pleasure. There was one breathtaking moment the day following the performance, when Alexander and I battled our way through a tropical downpour which turned the roads into torrents of water, to arrive at the main bank in the town centre. We had been able to speak to the bank manager at a reception the previous evening, explaining that we needed to send some funds off to London, and he confirmed that this would be possible from his bank the next day, but that he would not be there due to a business trip to Caracas.

We handed our pile of dollars to the clerk behind an iron grill at the bank, and the man – a local person, rather than a Dutch one – seriously counted and recounted them, stacked them into neat piles and then pushed them out of sight. He leaned towards us, looking very serious. 'And how did you come by all this money?' he demanded. We almost gasped; he was obviously suspecting us of drug smuggling, or some equally criminal act and now, with the bank manager unavailable, we could very well be in trouble. This was, after all, a colonial outpost, possibly flexing its muscles, dreaming of independence and resenting the presence of so many Europeans. Fortunately, we were carrying a briefcase containing all the contracts, the correspondence and the programmes, including those from the previous evening's performance in Aruba; with these we were able to convince him that the funds were legally obtained, and we had the right to send them off to our bank in London. But it was a nasty moment.

Following Aruba, we spent a week in Bermuda, performing in a small very English-style theatre while being billeted in luxurious mansions belonging to the island's elite. The local ballet society is an extremely active one, inviting American ballet companies on a regular basis, but obviously was pleased to have found a British one able to make the trip. However, this visit did bring us back into the real world with a jolt. The head of the family who had offered accommodation to Alexander and me returned to the island a day or so after our arrival. He had rushed to New York following the calamitous events of October 1987 to find that he had lost the major part of his fortune on Black Monday; tragically he died of a heart attack just a day after his return.

Finally, after nearly a month, we were on our way back to London, but with a stopover at JFK Airport in New York. I remember sitting in the airport's cafeteria, looking out towards that great metropolis, knowing that the following year, at the same time, we would be in the United States, and more unbelievably, touring with the company across the country. At that moment it seemed nothing could stop us fulfilling more and more of our dreams.

chapter
twelve

The Boom Years, Continued
1988-1991

As a young dancer, one of my greatest ambitions was to dance with Ballet Theatre (now called American Ballet Theatre), a company which seemed to encompass everything I idealised in my profession: a repertoire which stretched from the purely classical, by way of the meatiest of dramatic works, created by the legends of contemporary ballet, Antony Tudor and Agnes de Mille, to the high jinks of comedy ballets such as Jerome Robbins' *Fancy Free* or de Mille's *Rodeo*. My paragons were dancers such as Nora Kaye, who could transform herself from a regal Black Swan to the histrionic Lizzie Borden of *Fall River Legend*, and those glamorous women with glittering classical techniques and warm, colourful personalities such as Violette Verdy and Lupe Serrano. However, in the 1960s it was obvious that I would never be able to finance a journey to New York, nor obtain the legendary green card, with its permit to work in the USA, as the country was overfilled with talented, well-trained dancers who were battling to find work in a ballet company. Chance brought me the opportunity to do the next best thing when, in 1959, I was able to join American Festival Ballet, an American company based at that time in Europe.

As I have already described in earlier chapters, it was here that Alexander and I met, forming the partnership which brought about the formation of our own ballet company. Despite all the international tours we undertook, we had never dreamt of being able to visit the United States; very few British dance companies did, apart from the Royal Ballet's regular visits to New York, and occasional ones to Washington. Ballet Rambert had made one extensive tour, as had London Festival Ballet in the 1950s, an adventure chronicled by Julian Braunsweg in his notorious book, *Ballet Scandals*. So it was with great excitement that we prepared for the first coast-to-coast tour in the autumn of 1988, a seven-week tour with thirty performances, performing the full-length production of *A Midsummer Night's Dream* and a double bill of *Beauty and the Beast* and *La Ronde*.

The company was made up of ten dancers, plus the two of us, whereby Alexander was also dancing, and two technicians. Gary Lindsey provided a touring manager, who prepared all the technical details for the theatres we were to visit, as well as arranging our transportation from airport, to motel, to the theatre as required. Gary also took care of all national and international flights, booked the accommodation, provided the publicity and publicity material, and paid us a good fee. There was obviously an enormous amount to take care of, and we were spoiled in needing to do little more than turn up in time to get on the bus. I kept a detailed diary of that first tour, which does perhaps best tell the story of the impressions and the experiences we had in a new country as vast and as varied as the USA.

20 September 1988

We were waiting in the company office for the taxis to take us to the airport when at 10.35 a.m. the news arrived from Jacqui at the US Embassy – where she had been since day break – that her visa had come through. The taxis were ordered for 10.45 a.m. She is a late replacement and for a couple of weeks we have been waiting with some anxiety, to see how amenable the US Department of Justice will be approving issuance of a last-minute visa for an alien. Somehow I always thought it would be OK, but then I am an irrepressible optimist. However, one wonders why do they leave it literally to the last moment?

The BA check-in proved to be extremely smooth, despite our travelling with fifteen large blue metal trunks, containing everything we need for the performances – scenery, costumes, props, make-up boxes, ballet and pointe shoes, tapes and cassettes, lighting colour sheets and gobos (metal templates for special effects) – plus another fifteen personal bags. Fortunately luggage to the States goes by numbers, and not by weight, and miraculously we were within our allowance and so everything could all travel in the same plane with us. The one major problem was that with all the excitement, I neglected to check where the allocated seats were for Alexander and me, and whether they were located in a desirable spot. It was a jumbo and we ended up with the smokers at the back of the plane, so things couldn't be worse. The crew changed us to good window seats on row thirty, but within minutes someone else was claiming rights to these and we ended with bulkhead seats in row forty. I was glad enough to have the comparative isolation, especially with an empty seat next to me, but Alexander was thrown into despair, and miserable at the proximity of a large grey bulkhead, and more grey walls and curtains as the only view.

The eight-hour flight was just about bearable, relieved by a good movie and time to sort out the pages and pages of the itinerary, but landing was delayed in Chicago by the tail of Hurricane Gilbert licking the air with fearsome rainstorms and a blanket of thick grey cloud. Immigration scrutinised our passports with distrust. Customs tried miserably to be business-like with the international customs carnet we offered them, but they had obviously never seen anything like it before, and porters for our thirty bags and trunks were unobtainable. However, we were through in an hour to be met by Dabney Forest (can there be a better American name?) with a large coach and a likeable driver, Jack. The motel was nearby, the Sixpence Inn – very nearby, and I can say from first-hand knowledge that a plane lands at Chicago O'Hare every sixty seconds, and each of them comes about 10 foot over the Sixpence Inn. Our first American dinner had to be hamburgers and French fries at Denny's, but the salad was good and service terrific.

20 September

We crashed out at 9.30 p.m., planes or no planes, but woke at 2 a.m. (8 a.m. London time) ready to get up. Extraordinarily enough, it was blissfully quiet, despite the airport and the surrounding highways, allowing us to doze until 7.30 a.m., when it was back to Denny's for breakfast and non-stop coffee. We drove towards Chicago and saw glimpses of the huge skyline behind multiple lanes of traffic. In the midst of an area of terrible urban decay, derelict warehouses and old factories, Dabney materialised. We picked her up with the dance floor, rolls and rolls of linoleum which Gary Lindsey has provided for the tour. Around 10.30 a.m. we set off on the 94, 230 miles to Menominee, Michigan.

So this is the Midwest. I had always believed it to be Utah or Kansas, or somewhere more remote, but here we skirted the Great Lakes and Menominee is right on the edge of Lake Michigan, and, apparently, IS the Midwest. We planned our arrival in order to have a day off, to sleep off the jet lag, and to settle down before the touring begins, and we spent this day in Menominee, still in a daze. It is a very small town. A single main street with a large number of empty shops, boarded-up shop windows, signs 'To Let' or 'To Sell' on every block. At 4.30 p.m. on a Tuesday afternoon we wandered around in small groups, bumping into each other, in the otherwise empty and desolate streets. There was an eerie sense that some disaster has hit the town, emptying it of inhabitants. What has happened to Menominee? Fortunately, the hotel, which is in the centre of downtown, is first class; we have huge rooms and a good restaurant, which we share with a scattering of travelling salesmen. There's not much choice, so we're in bed by 9.30 p.m.

21 September

Menominee High School auditorium – pretty awful! It took about three hours to find out which, if any, of the lights were working; to repair these, to patch them into the system, and so on. We had very little help, a few shy school boys, and our two technicians seem pretty helpless; but we do have Dabney, who, apparently, can do most things. However, the stage is a good size and there were about 700 in the audience – very attentive and receptive, and to our relief the humour of *Dream* came across well. The theatre's tape recorder packed up halfway through the play (*Pyramus and Thisbe*) in Act 2, but fortunately our system of having a back-up cassette playing simultaneously (silently until needed) proved its worth and we were able to switch over to this, almost unnoticeably. We were given a reception in a local restaurant, and Alexander, Dabney and I had dinner with the organiser, a very large, expansive and enthusiastic woman. Hopefully, Gary has given us a 'simple' theatre as a try-out.

22 September

On to Iron Mountain and it really is mining, hillbilly country. A small but comfortable motel and another high school, the stage up a flight of stairs: there we were met by a crew of rehabilitated alcoholics, young men, including a Native American – and found a very small stage. We ate in a nearby diner and were overwhelmed, as we are each time, with the friendliness and the fantastic service. We gave a better performance – a full house – and were given another reception, this time backstage with dips and warm, sweet wine.

23 September

A very beautiful drive through forests of beech and maple and fir – the maple leaves turning the most amazing shades of gold, russet and the deepest reds – mile after mile. Ironwood is right at the top of the USA, near Lake Superior, and here they have six months of winter with 10 feet of snow. We were glad it's only September. The iron boom started here in the 1880s and ran out in 1936, since when Ironwood has been struggling to stay alive with tourism, but life here seems very backward and I suspect people have a hard time to get by. A 'real' theatre this time, a little gem of a 1920s variety theatre. Backstage conditions were atrocious and help minimal. There were more outsize, enthusiastic women who arrived with boxes of doughnuts and sandwiches, Coke and coffee. The second programme was scheduled and I worried about *La Ronde*. I suspected that *Beauty and the Beast* was probably already over their heads, and on the tiny stage would not look good. *La Ronde* appeared to lift their spirits and there was some good applause, spiced with loud whistles of approval.

But – we were told of complaints, with people walking out, finding the sexual overtones shocking and irresponsible. The local vicar had a quiet word with us and warned us that should we perform this in the South, and we are to visit Mississippi and Alabama, we risk being lynched and strung up on the main street. The chief problem is a simulated striptease, which the Maid performs on a table, trying to attract the attention of the Young Man. She does have flesh-coloured tights on, but apparently this is going too far for the American audiences, as is the scene with the Actress and the elderly Count. We promised to make some modifications, but were stunned by this reaction.

24 September

On to Calumet – once the most important copper mining area in the US. Another old theatre, built in 1900, at the peak of Calumet's prosperity, and this one has been restored and is kept in beautiful condition. It is a mini opera house with a great atmosphere, and once received celebrities such as Caruso and Sarah Bernhardt, during their American tours; Bernhardt's dressing room is now a tourist sight. However, the stage is small and raked (sloped) backwards – not easy, but we gave a good performance to a capacity audience, all helped by a reasonable lighting rig and some bright university students to help backstage.

25 September

An 8 a.m. start and another drive through endless forests and lakes to Ishpeming. It was another high school but a decent stage and well equipped. A real one-horse town, and practically comatose on a Sunday – but the town is obviously more prosperous than the ones we have visited so far. Despite all the dancers' tiredness, they did a good class and later, an excellent perform-ance. Much to the organisers' relief, the theatre was sold out and after the performance they gave us another reception – which we wriggled out of, as there was nothing but carrot sticks and dips to be seen. We found a pizza to take back to the hotel and slept, for the first time, right through the night to 6 a.m. But why do they have Eastern Daylight Time here?

26 September
We had a long 500-mile drive right across Minnesota to Moorhead, on the border of North Dakota adjoining Fargo, and to a motel, way out of town, stranded on the highway between a row of restaurants and supermarkets. The trip was made easier than feared by the beauty of those endless miles of autumn forests, until we arrived out on the plains and the farmland, which was clearly suffering from a summer drought. We had the first evening without a performance for nearly a week but an early night was spoiled by a relentlessly loud TV in the neighbouring room. It was probably from some of the dancers – who are inexhaustible.

27 September
Performance day in a 'real' theatre – one of MW's (the American technical director we are yet to meet) 'A' classified theatres. It is large, modern and well equipped, and is within the state university. We did class in the morning, bussed the dancers back and forth to the hotel, rehearsed in the afternoon and, as the result of a perfect 'theatre day', gave an excellent performance: a good finish to the first week.

General impressions: America is so old-fashioned in many ways – archi-tectural design, as far as we have seen so far, 1970s style in simple things like door handles, taps, light fittings, carpets and linens, also the shops and restau-rants, and amazingly, the telephone service. As I remember, as a child, it was necessary to call an operator to obtain every call, and so it is here today in the world of privatised telephone companies – extraordinary. Unexpectedly, the theatre equipment is also very old-fashioned. All the theatres we have visited so far have simple two pre-set manual lighting boards, something one hardly sees any more in the UK, where computerised boards have taken over. Manners are almost quaint, and Americans are much more polite than we are in Europe. Much of the country is very rundown – roads with huge potholes, a lack of pavements, electric cables strung out along streets and buildings in city centres, and in small towns, people poorly dressed and many men hanging around, obviously unemployed. All of this may only to apply to the regions we have seen in this first week…

Main concerns: the usual – our technicians become scruffier and more difficult by the day. Dabney says they would never get work in the US. It is really a pity none of our 'good guys' could come or wanted to stay away from the UK for this very long tour and we have two 'unknowns', badly chosen, as it turns out.

28 September

Day off – in Moorhead. We yearned for a late sleep-in, but this was impossible, as I had to get to a dentist; in the event, a brief, painless and very low-cost affair but the day did not improve with cold, rainy weather. Moorhead downtown consists of a couple of main streets, a pleasant post office and an even more impressive bank which, unfortunately, did not keep the funds Gary has sent for our first week, but sent them back to him! Otherwise a reasonable shopping mall and a single restaurant – in the midst of wasteland, empty buildings, a scattering of a new buildings, no town centre, no plan and so, no town. We found a group of three shabbily dressed Native Americans and a drug addict vagrant sheltering in a bus shelter; all a bit sad. A restful afternoon and another three-hour stint trying to work out the rest of *The Magic Flute* (to be premiered on our return to Europe).

Dabney left today (she has just been filling in until MW's arrival) and we await him with interest, wondering how our techie 'bumpkins' will cope with a professional technical director, less patient than Dabney, as they seem pretty uneasy. MW has just been lighting a New York season for the Trisha Brown Dance Company.

29 September

An early start with a drive to Fargo airport and we said goodbye to our driver, Jack, who has been excellent, if slightly prima donna-ish in his ways. The check-in is unbelievably simple with no interest shown at all in the number, size or weight of the luggage. The bumpkins made a lot of fuss about having to look after the boom box (a portable cassette recorder, needed for rehearsals and a back-up for performances). We changed planes at Minneapolis, and after a delay, flew on to Detroit, where MW awaited us. As I half expected, he is an American version of Nigel; highly strung and a bit neurotic. But where Nigel manages with just a few handwritten technical notes, MW produces sheaves and sheaves of technical info – stage plans, lighting rigs complete with every lamp, its size, wattage and colour – individually produced for each venue.

We drove on to Holland, Ohio and stayed in the usual highway motel. I have discovered that should I have to get up in the night, it is unnecessary to put on any lights, as the bathroom will be in exactly the same position, and at the same distance from the bed, as in the last motel, and the one before that.

30 September

The Franciscan Life Center in Sylvania is a religious-run arts centre and college, situated in a beautiful park and the theatre is adequately large and very pleasant. The friendliness and helpfulness were again overwhelming ('no problem' to every query) and we also got help with a couple of trips to town where I cashed in all our traveller's cheques (with considerable trouble) so the company can get their per diems – as Gary's money is still missing. We took a short walk through the park before the performance and found a quiet corner where the departed sisters are buried. There was a quite extraordinary atmosphere, a spiritual quietness in this spot, which allowed us to stand 3 feet away from a group of rabbits that were grazing on the juicy grass. The *La Ronde* programme (revised version!) went down successfully and without problems. We finished the day with the now inevitable reception, with dips and lukewarm wine ('White or blush?').

1 October

We set off in the dark at 7.30 a.m. to get to Akron University Theatre by 10 a.m. This was our first union house and the pressure was on to finish the fit-up, totally, in four hours. There was a HUGE auditorium and the usual very wide, flat stage. The crew, an army of them, were excellent and everything went to schedule. MW had to take over to get the lighting finished within the final fifteen minutes when, as threatened, the crew dropped everything and were off. Looking at the stage from the auditorium, Alexander was approached by a small, white-haired man enquiring if we have roles for elderly dancers. With some surprise, Alexander gradually made out the features of Jerry Burr, an ex-dancer from our days with American Festival Ballet – almost thirty years ago! We had a lot to talk about and went out to dinner with him after the performance. He's settled, not too happily, into the dance faculty of Akron's university and is on the way to receiving a professorship. However, life in a regional dance department, with an associated company, sounds far from ideal – for a real 'old pro', anyway.

2 October

Warren, Ohio – a great barn of a theatre and the sponsor was none other than David Holmes (now minus Anne-Marie), whom we remember from Audrey de Vos's classes in London. They must have been the first Western dancers to travel to the USSR (in the 1960s) to study in Moscow and came back demonstrating wildly acrobatic lifts – with Anne-Marie held at arm's length above David's head, and much to de Vos's disapproval! The poor man is now stuck in this very small Ohio town, running a large school and giving a few performances a year (mostly of *The Nutcracker*), with the assistance of a few teacher–soloist dancers. It's becoming clear that there is a very fine line here between professional and non-professional companies. It was a matinee performance and we drove on later, in the dark, along winding, hilly roads and across the border to Warren, Pennsylvania. This MUST cause confusion? Another awful meal – this whole week since leaving the Upper Peninsula has been awful – and dead tired, we fell into bed.

3 October

This small Pennsylvania town is exactly as I imagined – some stately old homes and a neat little town centre with quaint old-fashioned shops, and blissfully, a nice cafe–restaurant to which we made several visits during the day. More problems with Gary trying to send us some money and finally this is solved with the promoter giving me the fee cheque, which we can cash, if and when we can get to a bank. The theatre is an old variety house, lovingly restored. Unfortunately, backstage has not been restored and conditions are pretty awful. I had tried to implement a new system of starting the dancers' class and rehearsals at 2 p.m. – giving them a free morning by pushing the techies to be finished by 2 p.m., giving them a free afternoon. Curiously, the dancers were ALL late, some not turning up until 2.30 p.m. – so the system proved unsatisfactory, and Alexander is proved right in insisting that they have to get going in the morning or they'll not get going at all! The theatre was sold out (as most so far); a very conservative, mostly elderly lot, and then yet another reception from which we escaped early, skipped dinner and got to bed. Alexander sleeps soundly, but I had the usual problem of being disturbed by noisy laughter and TVs, and knowing it's the dancers – sometimes I hate 'em all.

4 October

A visit to Niagara Falls had been planned for some time – although we are always wary of combining sightseeing with a working day. However, everyone was keen so we drove the short distance from Buffalo, which seems to be a very large, industrial town, and across the Canadian border to the falls. Hideously commercial – nothing but motels and souvenir shops – and the Falls are seen from a distance by the spray. I wished they were Victoria Falls and that we were in darkest Africa – all the same, on approaching them I involuntarily gasped at the hugeness of the amount of water, the unbelievable power of it tearing over the edge and crashing down and down with unimaginable speed. Quite terrifying, but the whole thing is spoiled by the surroundings; car parks packed with coaches, thousands of people milling around, gaudy neon lights, loudspeakers and raucous music. We were glad to get away after an hour and to make our way back to Buffalo airport.

Then, of course, the worst happened, and we were held up at the USA border. An unfortunate woman, a Jamaican apparently, was nabbed by customs or immigration – who had a beanfeast with her bulky handbag. Out came a blonde wig, a pair of silver stilettos and a variety of suspicious looking implements – probably connected with drug-taking. She was in trouble – and so were we, as everyone else wanting to get through was being ignored. With just twenty minutes to spare before our check-in time, I pushed MW forward to make a request to let us through – which was done in haste.

The dance floor had already been taken to freight and our check-in was again blissfully easy, and the flight went smoothly via Detroit, to Memphis, Tennessee. We arrived in the South – and it is warm, and there are black faces everywhere, and that Southern drawl is more than one ever believed possible. Our new bus driver was young and black, and very smart, but he did drive the bus as if it was a sports car. We collected the floor from cargo, ate in a Highway Steak House, and drove on past Gracelands – his house, his aeroplane parked nearby, his garden and his museum. Niagara and Elvis all in one day! We drove on to Helena, Arkansas, and the Holiday Inn.

5 October
The weather is unseasonably cool, but still pleasant enough for us. The theatre is modern, big and very pleasant. There is a decent dance studio, where we worked in the morning, and I was then able to get a lift downtown, to the bank, and finally to get some cash. The wide, empty streets with one-storey shops are just what I imagined the deep South to be. Back in the motel in the afternoon, I got an unexpected phone call from a theatrical agency in New York – I know the name well – asking if they can represent us. The Far East? Australasia? Japan? How did they know where we are? Alexander has been rehearsing *The Magic Flute* with the dancers, as time is catching up with us and the premiere is shortly after our return to Europe. He has also been having more trouble with the bumpkins, who are getting stroppier, and sloppier, by the day. However, a full house, a good audience and a proper dinner afterwards in a downtown restaurant – real Southern food, blackened catfish.

6 October
A long, very interesting drive through the cotton fields of Mississippi to Mobile, Alabama – the cotton now fortunately harvested with machines. The country is similar to southern France and some parts have the same red soil. Suddenly, we came to flat farmland, with the occasional subtropical swamp, and there is a lot of very poor housing, even shacks, in this, the poorest state in the US. Mobile is a city of 300,000 and has been, at some time, a real

town. The old theatre is in the town centre and we called there first to unload and then to the hotel – a beautiful real luxury hotel. Bliss! We were on the ninth floor with a great view looking out, I presume, over the Gulf of Mexico – and we had a surprise welcome of a bottle of sparkling cider and choco-late-covered strawberries! I had the first of the master classes to teach to some local dance students and was driven to the dance studio by the organiser of the local sponsor organisation: a very smart young African–American, who when we passed the local golf and country club mentioned: 'Well, that's one place I can't go to; I'm just their token black, you know.' (And we thought that segregation had come to an end in the USA?) The class for a dozen kids went well enough, despite some problems with a (good) pianist who had never played for ballet before. But the studio was excellent and we are able to rehearse there tomorrow. We had dinner with the organiser and the attractive dance teacher from the uni. – more good Southern food – too much – too good…

7 October

Performance day in Mobile – we spent the morning rehearsing *Flute* in the uni. studio, and with some difficulty managed to finish the long scene at the end of Act 1. Some of the dancers, and all the boys, have managed to forget most of the choreography since leaving London! In the theatre, the old equipment and the theatre lighting worked well, the performance went well – 80 per cent of 2,000 seats sold, a very generous reception, real Southern hospitality.

8 October

We planned our first late sleep-in – ruined by a fire alarm shrieking out at 8 a.m. Grabbing my handbag and Alexander the case of performance tapes and our more precious documents, we started to race down nine flights of stairs. I had to pick up a small child who had been abandoned on the way – while her enormously fat mother struggled down clutching a new pair of shoes, a new dress and a large decorated basket! Odd. It was a false alarm, and we regained our room for breakfast and finally checked out at noon. We had an hour to wander through the remains of downtown – a ghost town of abandoned offices and buildings, and boarded-up shops. There were signs of some new initiative to bring life back to the city with a few trendy boutiques. Otherwise, what is open, like a rundown Woolworths, is obviously only for the poor blacks. We had an afternoon rehearsal and made a start on the finale of *Flute*, and after some long goodbyes, as it seemed everyone had made lifelong friends in Mobile, we drove on to Meridian, Mississippi.

9 October

As part of The Lively Arts Festival we gave a matinee performance at 4 p.m. All the male dancers were grumpy and class and rehearsal brought about some outbursts. This is an extraordinary theatre, almost a sort of temple and doubtlessly an old variety theatre, but more a sort of Moorish palace extravaganza – quite something! Also unusual – and apparently the norm here – was the popcorn. The vendors arrived an hour before the performance and the smell of roasting popcorn filled the theatre. Everyone in the audience seemed to have a bag and while they munched through Act 1 of the *Dream*, the roasting went on in the lobby. We nearly came to grief with the theatre's tape recorder, which played slower and slower and threatened to give up completely – it made it, but only just. We must see that Gary provides a machine next time as it's no use bringing ours with the different voltage here. We ate in a real restaurant – one founded in 1870 by Germans, and still German run. But we were back at the motel – marooned on a highway, miles from anywhere – at 8 p.m. and what do you do ? There's nowhere to go and nothing to do. The yanks eat and watch TV – it's their way of life and explains a lot.

10 October

Four hundred miles right across Mississippi and Georgia in glorious scenery, very like France, and with just a few small towns, some of which have retained their town centres and some sort of town life. We spent an hour in a huge mall in Dothan (it seems as if malls here have replaced both city centres and tourist attractions such as museums and galleries), but we did find the first health-food shop and the first bookshop. The motel at Valdosta was again way out of town, on the highway, but fortunately had a restaurant – and we were greeted with huge baskets of fruit and local goodies by the sponsors.

11 October

Another time difference as we are back to Eastern Time (this happens every couple of days) and so we have to get up an hour earlier, which seems hard as, I must admit, we are damn tired. I had a 10 a.m. class with local dancers at the state college (of Georgia): about fifteen dancers of very differing ages and standards, but with some helpful teachers and a pianist who coped well. The company class followed – spirits are low with some distinct grumpiness. I guess jet lag is kicking in after the initial excitement, and they resent having to rehearse *Magic Flute* as well as everything else – but then that's the way the cookie crumbles, as they say here! I took the class very gently and they thawed, gradually. Our performance was the opening of the local theatre season here and a huge buffet was given afterwards in the lobby for all the audience, with fountains (literally) of champagne (so called), warm and sweet, as usual. The performance went well, after all, with all 1,200 seats sold. We skipped dinner and settled for cheese crackers and beer in the room (all that was available in the motel coin machines) and were asleep by midnight.

12 October
We drove right across Florida to Jacksonville for a flight to Boston, during which I read, with interest, over the shoulder of the man sitting in front of me, a magazine article dealing with the problems for the successful manager motivating the work force! We were collected in Boston by an amiable black bear of a man known as Jesse, and drove to a nearby hotel in anticipation of a real day off and a visit to Boston. Alexander did want to rehearse but I managed to convince him of the necessity of this free day – remove all excuses for complaints and let them get in some sightseeing, when they can.

13 October
Boston was VERY cold and I hastened to buy a winter jacket. But it is a 'real' town and an overwhelming relief after three weeks in the sticks. A very pleasant city, too, with a good mixture of new and old buildings and some beautiful skyscrapers, imaginative and almost inspiring! We drove on to Manchester in the afternoon, near Concord, New Hampshire, where we are to perform, and to a pleasant motel. It is, however, as usual, in the middle of nowhere, surrounded by highways.

14 October
The technicians overslept (for the first time, I must admit), so we drove on to the theatre in Concord without them. The town was a mill town some fifty years ago but is now pretty desolate and the theatre a somewhat ramshackle place, but with a good crew. One thousand two hundred seats all sold out and the sponsor was happy. They have had regular visits from companies from New York – Trisha Brown Dance Company, Pilobolus and others – but have never sold out before.

15 October
We drove back to Boston and flew across the whole continent to Seattle on the west coast. We flew backwards in time so the eight-hour flight still arrived in daylight, but we had another two-and-a-half-hour drive to Bellingham, Washington. It should have been shorter, but the driver took a wrong turn and we spent half an hour looking for a place to turn the coach. These drivers don't appear to use maps, relying on signs, and they also don't calculate in miles, but in time – a three-hour drive, for instance. And they're usually right.

16 October

A 10 a.m. class with local dancers – the usual mixed bunch, but keen and enthusiastic, and an excellent pianist. Company class followed in a very pleasant studio. (It's amazing how many good ballet studios we're able to use.) I continued with the Three Ladies from Act 1 of *Flute* while Alexander sorted out the rest on stage. The Performing Arts Centre in the university is beautifully situated with a stunning view over the huge bay, and the theatre is big and well equipped. The performance had been sold out for some time, and as it was a matinee we could go out to dinner afterwards. It was also Alexander's birthday, so we invited Caroline, Nicole and Darius – the 'grown-ups' of the bunch. A nice evening.

17 October

After a morning class, we drove 300 miles to Corvallis, Oregon with some difficulty – this driver was decidedly bad on directions !

18 October

Morning class in the theatre lobby and we moved on stage to rehearse the dreaded scene with the ropes in the *Flute* (it is finally cut). The mood is better, but some of these newer dancers are going to be short-lived with the company, as they are trouble makers. Another sold-out house, another reception – which was a bit painful, as it had been a long day, and from which we escaped asap.

19 October

An early start to Eugene airport, and on to San Francisco, where we finally met Gary – rather as I expected, a small black moustache, quiet, a little shy, very pleasant. We collected the dance floor from cargo and drove on to Modesto. This is California? Desolation! Our motel is one of the most basic, right on the highway, and all we can visit is a not-very-good mall. This is farm country, hillbilly land, rough and tough. This is something different. We grabbed a pizza in the local pizza parlour and were fascinated by the enormous women – rolls of fat under their chins, around their middles, down their arms; bulges and lumps on their bottoms and their legs of gigantic proportions, pudding-shaped faces that could be anything from thirty to sixty years old. We have seen a lot of obesity so far, far beyond anything in Europe, people hardly able to waddle, needing two seats in a cafe, or in the theatre, even a nun needing two walking sticks to heave herself along. But here in California – it's still worse. There were also a lot of very battered, wild looking men – lots of Mexicans, and poor white farm workers. And there is the dust – everywhere. They are suffering badly from drought, and the dust is in the air – and it covers everything.

284

20 October

The theatre is in a high school – and it's also rough and tough. We are advised to lock up the costumes and to treat the teenage natives with respect. MW had a 'delightful evening' with the resident stage manager the day before so we let him get on with the fit-up. The whole place is the pits.

21 October

A 7 a.m. start and 200 miles to Bakersfield, through cotton fields, orchards and along a long, straight highway. The theatre is situated in the state college on the edge of town, and the hotel 30 miles away on the other side of town. We decided to forget about the hotel and after a quick lunch in a mall made for the theatre. I had a 1.30 p.m. class with some local dancers and the company could take advantage of the sun and the warmth and the pleasant parkland all around the theatre; the temperature is in the nineties – and we appeared to be virtually in the desert. The local dancers turned out to be remarkable – beautifully trained ten- to sixteen-year-olds – and the class would have been a pleasure, except there was no pianist, leaving me to sing and count. Class with the company followed and we ran through Act 1 of *The Magic Flute*, the forgotten scenes starting to come back, but we've a long way to go.

The performance has been sold out for some weeks, and we had to hold the opening for ten minutes to placate a hundred odd people who couldn't get seats. It was then well danced and it looks as if everyone is settling down. Maybe the jet lag is wearing off? We grabbed hamburgers to go afterwards and found the motel, the worst possible motel; covered in desert dust, next to the highway where the huge trucks park right up to the building, with their engines running all night, and the locks on the doors of our rooms didn't lock.

22 October

Another early start and we drove towards the coast through some stunning scenery to San Luis Obispo. The theatre is part of a college, but in a former army camp – this is on the edge of the college grounds, on the edge of town, miles from anywhere. We made a trip to the coast, which was shrouded in fog! We spent a couple of hours wandering around and then back to the motel – which was superb. However, we had just an hour before driving off again to the theatre. We spend (waste) so much time driving from the theatre, to the motel, to a restaurant – several times a day. Gary turned up again and the performance, with *La Ronde*, went very well – the audience reacted loudly and enthusiastically, getting all the jokes.

23 October

We tried to enjoy the comfortable motel room, with a view right over an equally pleasant pool – but no luck, as it was another 8 a.m. start. We drove inland to Visalia, and back into respectable America – quiet, wide streets, no cars, no sign of life, it was a Sunday, after all. A very nice theatre, but we were only just ready for the 4 p.m. performance after a marathon battle with an exceptionally outdated lighting board. Graham was not dancing, with a shoulder injury, and Philip banged his toe (once again), fortunately at the very end of *La Ronde*, but screamed his head off, muffled, fortunately, by the loudness of the music of the finale. We drove on after the performance – to San Francisco, and a day off.

24 October

Gary booked us into a lovely hotel, with rooms around a huge courtyard, imaginatively furnished – such a relief after the monotony of the motel rooms. We could sleep at last, but got up at 9 a.m. and had breakfast in a nearby Vietnamese restaurant, an Asian version of an American breakfast. The hotel is in downtown San Francisco, but it appeared to be a rather rundown area, predominately Vietnamese. We were warned not to walk the most direct way to the centre of town, as this is a bad area. Without knowing quite what was meant, we skirted around the forbidden area and came across the opera house (most impressive and a very good imitation of a nineteenth-century European opera house), as well as museums and civic buildings which are all grouped together along a large avenue.

We turned into Market Street, San Francisco's main street, and soon hit the bad area: dossers, junkies, some very drugged, black, white, Hispanic, littering the pavement or wandering around aimlessly. Some had supermarket trolleys packed with their belongings, some had just a bedroll, quite a few had a cat! They were frightening, we were jostled and shouted at, but fortunately we arrived at the good end of Market Street and everything changed immediately – big luxury shops, which seem to be very recently built, the traffic thin and well organised. The buildings are all only two or three storeys high and there is a prevailing feeling of small-town 1950s here, as in so many towns and cities. We continued with frequent stops for coffees and snacks, as we were feeling decidedly delicate.

Following the shops, we came across Chinatown – more touristy than London's but pure Chinese – and we had a good noodle soup in a very small and simple restaurant where the menu was only in Chinese. Outside again, the streets were empty but there were security men perched on all the rooftops – apparently Michael Dukakis (the Democratic presidential candidate) was about to come through. Chinatown ends abruptly and Little Italy takes over, leading us down to the waterfront and a view of the Golden Gate Bridge, and Alcatraz. We could also get a real espresso, at last. Gary invited us all to dinner at his home, which is also his office – a very pleasant evening and it was decent of him to arrange this day off for us in San Francisco.

More Impressions

I feel very strongly that the USA is a two-tier society; there are those who live in comfort and with considerable wealth, and the majority who have to struggle just to survive. We meet people every day who are holding down two and three jobs in order to make ends meet – some of these work in the theatre in the evenings. We have learned that working as a cashier in Walmart, for instance, brings in the basic pay of $3 per hour – as does waiting in a restaurant or a similar job. As far as theatre is concerned, this appears to be organised for and by the elite. Without much government involvement, the theatres and the universities, where many of the best theatres are found, have been created by the trusts and foundations of wealthy benefactors – who also give their names to the buildings and organisations.

The majority of the residents in these middle- and small-sized towns do not know that there is a theatre in their town, and have certainly never attended a performance. The theatre/music/arts societies which run these organisations, mostly voluntarily, are made up from an elite and these same people make up the audience. Only once, somewhere in the South, did we see a black couple in the audience, and very rarely does one see black students in the universities. Of course, we have not yet been to New York, Chicago, Washington – the major cities – where doubtlessly the situation will be different. But these places where we are performing make up the heart of America.

A very nationalistic, patriotic country too – with the stars and stripes fluttering from flagpoles in most front gardens and the young people kept busy every day after school, and university, with organised activities. The girls practise their cheerleader rituals of marching, batons swirling, singing and shouting, and the young men play sports seriously and train in what appear to be military youth organisations. We can't help thinking that, while the dictatorships of Eastern Europe force people to take part in activities to support their regimes, sing the praises of their countries and swear oaths of allegiance to their leaders, people here do this happily and apparently voluntarily. Our biggest shock: a group of men at the side of the road, digging with pickaxes, with chains around their ankles – a chain gang, prisoners in shackles, in America, in the twentieth century!

The dancers are enjoying the tour immensely – they feel rewarded, naturally, by the success of each performance and the fuss which is made of them at every reception. Playing to one or two thousand people is certainly challenging and tiring, but most of them are now coping with this, as well as with the travel, and the inevitable time differences which throw one's body clock over and over again. However, they do sleep a lot. The coach is so big that we each have a row to ourselves and they can stretch out with some degree of comfort. This way, most of them slept through the vistas of autumn colours in Michigan, missed the cotton fields and the mangrove swamps of the South and even ignored the Gulf of Mexico and the Pacific Ocean. However, they are dancing well.

My daily diary ends at this point, although I did keep occasional entries during this two-month tour and the years ahead. The 1988 tour continued on the other side of the US, in Pennsylvania, Connecticut and even included a performance in the Tropicana Showroom in Atlantic City. In Scranton, Pennsylvania, we performed in a Masonic temple, an extraordinary mishmash of architecture, partially Egyptian temple and partially medieval castle, with a bit of art deco thrown in. But it was here that we had our only experience of the more dangerous undercurrent which does exist in American cities. We were all waiting in the hotel lobby one morning, when Darius James (a dancer who had joined us this season and was to prove a valued member of the company for several years) came rushing in from the street, gasping and sweaty. He had made an early walk through the downtown area, and only narrowly escaped being mugged, but was forced to make a desperate sprint back to the hotel, closely followed by a posse of young men. We had been warned, almost every day, not to leave the motel on foot, not even to the diner on the next block, never to go out in the dark or to venture in the downtown areas. It all seemed over-dramatic to us, perhaps too much TV, and we had not taken much notice – this was a good warning to be more careful.

Back in London we had just three days to rehearse and to pack up the new scenery and costumes for *The Magic Flute* before setting off for a five-week tour of Germany, Austria and Switzerland. This was made easier with a brand new Mercedes bus, excellent new sound equipment and Dabney, who had flown over from the States to join us for the Continental tour. We were also able to replace one of the bumpkins with our favourite technician, Colin

Publicity photo for *The Magic Flute* by Anthony Crickmay with John Broome as Papageno and Caroline Heming as the Queen of the Night. (These costumes were not used.)

Small, who arrived backstage during one of the first performances in Germany to be startled when I left the 'prompt corner' to leap towards him with a warm embrace! The new production, *The Magic Flute*, was a complete contrast to the lightweight *A Midsummer Night's Dream*, but the original libretto for Mozart's opera, by Emmanuel Schikaneder, is almost Shakespearean in the complexity of its plots and subplots, its cast of colourful characters and the fantasy world of its setting.

This time we decided to call in assistance with the costume design and commissioned Julie Read, whose work, mainly for children's theatre, we found bold and original. Alexander had decided from the start to set the ballet in the world of science fiction allowing Julie to stretch her imagination in creating some fantastical and outlandish costumes which suited the other-worldly characters of the production perfectly. As with the *Dream*, Alexander did not use the existing music, in this case the opera, but chose other music by Mozart, believing that the impression of 'miming' to a recording of the opera would be too simplistic. We did wonder if this might prove to be controversial, remembering the outrage caused by John Cranko's production of *Onegin* in Stuttgart in 1965, when he decided to use alternative music to that of the opera by Tchaikovsky. However, the success of this ballet, still in the repertoire of numerous ballet companies around the world, proves Cranko's decision was a wise one.

The premiere of *The Magic Flute* was in Wesel, a small town in northern Germany with a good-sized theatre and a lively annual programme of performances. We had known the director for several years so he felt confident enough to storm into Alexander's dressing room in the interval demanding to know what right he had to make changes of this magnitude. It took all of the interval and half an hour after the performance to justify the use of different music, mostly by insisting that Schikaneder's libretto existed of its own right, while it would be almost ridiculous, for instance, for the dancer performing as the Queen of the Night to attempt to imitate the vocal acrobatics of the soprano's coloratura arias. It is true that *The Magic Flute* holds a very special place in the German music lover's heart; it is usually the first opera a child is taken to see and there is almost a sense of priority about it – it is obviously considered as untouchable. The director remained unconvinced, but placated presumably by members of the audience, and the press, he did invite us back to Wesel.

The tour included a return visit to the International Congress Centre in Berlin where the production was well received, but we did encounter more protests from theatre directors about the choice of music during the tour. Despite the problems we had experienced with the rehearsals on the US tour, the dancers did settle into their roles and proved to be well cast: Caroline Heming won much praise for her portrayal of the Queen of the Night, as did John Broome as Papageno and Mark Longthorn as Tamino. Nicole Walmsley, recently arrived from Australia, was a beautifully warm and lyrical Pamina, and Charlotte Sibley cheeky and bright as Papagena.

We spent much of 1989 touring in the UK, as well as making a return trip to Malta. Perhaps unexpectedly, *The Magic Flute* was very successful in the UK, and proved to be so for several seasons. Among the theatres we visited in the spring of 1989 was the Gordon Craig Theatre in Stevenage, a venue which figured regularly on our itineraries. It always seemed a little curious that such a colourful figure in the theatre world should have been born in Stevenage, but the theatre has been named in his honour. Gordon Craig, born in 1872 (well before the construction of the less-than-colourful Stevenage new town), was an illegitimate son of the great actress Ellen Terry, and became a leading, and often controversial, figure in the world of the theatre himself, as an actor, designer and director, as well as being the most famous of Isadora Duncan's lovers. The theatre, based in the Stevenage Leisure Centre, is a very pleasant one with a good-sized stage and regularly attracted good audiences.

However, we were surprised by the apparition of a stocky, rather ruddy-faced man, dressed in a full-length African kaftan and matching hat, who swept into the dressing rooms following our performance of *The Magic Flute*. He introduced himself as Malcolm Williamson, and I then recognised the Australian-born composer, then Master of the Queen's Music. I also knew that he was a prolific composer, but was notorious for not completing important commissions, including the Australian bi-centenary, the London Proms, and most seriously, the Queen's Silver Jubilee celebrations. Malcolm had written a ballet score which he was intent on having choreographed and performed, and he courted us assiduously in attempting to succeed with this. He invited Alexander and me to his charming home near Stevenage. This was the cottage Rook's Nest, formerly the home of E.M. Forster, the setting for his book *Howard's End*, and which had been used shortly before our meeting for the film of the book. However, it was obviously a comfortable, if somewhat cramped, home for Malcolm and his partner, and publisher, Simon Campion, packed with books and scores.

Completely covering one huge table was the score of the most recent composition he was working on, a concerto for seven cellos! Over lunch, and for some hours afterwards, we listened to CDs of some of Malcolm's huge output – symphonies, concertos and a wonderful string quartet – after which I made a major faux pas in comparing it favourably with the work of Benjamin Britten. Apparently, Malcolm had a major feud with his former friend and colleague and didn't welcome such comparisons. We had another meeting at North House, when although we fell under the spell of his charm and likeability it was clear that a collaboration would be fraught with problems. What we did not know at that time, was that Malcolm was in dire financial straits, and desperately needed commissions, but his constant problems with alcoholism had made him a persona non grata in the musical establishment. It is a great pity that he almost faded from view, as he is undoubtedly an important figure in twentieth-century music.

In October we returned to the USA for another tour, seven weeks and twenty-five performances long, taking in places as diverse as Alaska, Michigan, Iowa, Georgia and Long Island, New York. From the cosmopolitan, over-crowded, multi-national density of Europe's towns and cities, it is difficult to imagine the isolation of the American Midwest, where we again spent a good deal of time. In Idaho, Iowa, Missouri or even Ohio or Michigan it is as difficult to find a copy of *The New York Times* as it is to buy *Le Figaro* or the *Frankfurter Allgemeine*. Press, radio and TV are all locally produced and distributed; the big stories are of local factories and politicians, beauty queens and football games. One incident remains an interesting reminder of that insularity of American life.

We had arrived after a long day's drive in a medium-sized town in Idaho, or Iowa, and were lodged, as often was the case, at a roadside motel on the interstate highway. There was no sign of the town where we were to perform, nothing but a cluster of twenty-four-hour diners and an endless vista of the highway rolling towards the horizon and that immense American sky. Around 8 a.m. the next day we wandered from the motel to the nearest diner, fairly quiet at this hour; a couple of lorry drivers were discussing the detours and roadworks encountered the day before, a group of farm workers were wolfing down outsize plates of waffles heaped high with bacon, eggs and maple syrup and a few glazed-eyed travelling salesmen were starting the day studying their files of papers. The waitress was a woman in her thirties, typically pretty with curly, shoulder-length hair, a neat uniform and a trim figure. She wore an expression of deep weariness and indifference. Like so many, she was probably finishing an all-night shift to bring in family income, or more likely, she was a single mother struggling to manage and holding down at least two jobs. She sidled up to us with the obligatory glasses of iced water and silently awaited our order. We were halfway through the tour and I thought I'd mastered it pretty well:

'I'll have two eggs, sunny side up, wholewheat toast, dry, with butter on the side, and coffee, please.' Incredulity brightened her face and she now studied us with some interest.

'You folks from outa town?' she asked, now positively curious.

How could I tell her that I was born in Australia, have lived in London, Paris, Berlin, Frankfurt, Amsterdam and have also worked in Hong Kong, Taiwan, Malaysia and have recently been in Ecuador and Colombia; that my husband comes from behind the Iron Curtain, that we married in Amsterdam, having met in Spain, etc. No, I couldn't do that. 'Outa town' meant the next town, or the possibly the next state, perhaps even Chicago – but not seriously outa town!

'Well, we're just here for a day, we're from London. London, England,' I added.

She didn't really believe me, but she replied, 'You'll find it kinda quiet here.'

We would probably have found it quiet if we didn't have a performance to put on. There was a nine o'clock fit-up ahead, possibly in a two thousand, or perhaps even a four thousand, seater auditorium, on a stage which might be a standard 15 metres wide and 10 metres deep, or it might be 10 metres wide and 6 metres deep, or perhaps circular, or triangular. There could be a highly skilled crew of professional stage technicians, but there might just be half a dozen unwilling high school kids and a harassed teacher trying to cope with what was his first professional visiting company. Our own stage manager would, understandably, be treating this once-in-a-lifetime tour as an adventure holiday and would probably have been up most of the night, boozing and watching blue movies on TV, or even discovering the recently opened new clubs with table dancers or pole dancers. Of the company dancers, some would also have chosen to live by night and sleep by day, whether this was while travelling or during breaks in rehearsals. Other dancers would be pining for lovers or spouses left behind, nursing ailments or injuries, or suffering the depression of jet lag. Alexander and I would spend a fifteen-hour day cajoling and humouring them, while assuring that evening the sponsors and the theatregoers of this special town in Iowa, or Idaho, had a first-rate performance; an attractive stage set, magical lighting effects, fault-free sound and a group of talented professional dancers giving their all in freshly washed and pressed costumes. Following the performance, inevitably a sell-out, and hopefully an unequivocal success, the last hour of that day would be spent at an after-performance reception. With hastily repaired make-up, or a change of clothes, the two of us would chat with the local dignitaries, smiling unflinchingly, while sipping warm, sweet punch. At the same time, we would be aching to sit down, to eat a grilled steak with a glass of red wine and then to get to bed before the exertions of the following day became a reality. Kinda quiet, it won't be.

My diary entries continue for parts of this tour :

7 October 1989

It was a good start to this new, six-week tour with a really enjoyable performance yesterday in Springfield, Illinois on a huge, well-equipped stage and where every request was greeted with 'no problem'. There was, however, something of a problem in that we performed *Dream* with the local orchestra who played perfectly at rehearsal, but much too slow for the performance. Rossini needs to be sprightly. Today we are in Batavia, Illinois at the Fermilab National Accelerator Laboratory – or at least, at their very pleasant theatre. The accelerator is clearly visible in the grounds, a large pipe which runs in a circle, containing, apparently, millions of atoms (or proton beams?) which rush around and collide – if I have understood correctly. Around the pipe were a herd of bison, their huge necks lowered while they munched the very green grass around them, unaware of the scientific breakthrough taking place right next to them. But apparently they are placed there as a symbolic presence, 'on the frontier of physics and its connection to the American prairie'.

24 October

Day off, the only one so far, and this in Alaska! Yesterday was a travel day, and a half. We set off from Atlanta, Georgia, flying to Los Angeles where we had a three-hour wait for the onward flight to Seattle. Sitting in the restaurant area, which was charmingly divided by boxes of plants and flowers, against which the benches and tables were built, we soon became aware that these boxes were occupied by hundreds of tiny mice, scuttling busily around. Some-one must have noticed? From Seattle we flew on to Anchorage, Alaska, land-ing with a perfect view of an aurora borealis, a glorious backdrop of emerald green and vermilion; from there we flew on to Fairbanks, arriving around midnight.

Fairbanks is in the very centre of Alaska and there is oil here – hence its very existence – and there is also a very good, large theatre here. The local arts association, run by a German woman, is well run and welcoming. They arranged for Donata to see a physio and organised a bus tour for the company to visit the oil rigs. We ventured outside after breakfast when the sun was shining on the brilliantly white hard snow which covers everything. Despite being dressed in multiple layers of clothing, the cold bites through one's body, and cheeks and nose feel as if burned. It was −40°C and we hurried into a department store to buy fleece-lined jackets so we could explore a bit further.

25 October

The flight from Anchorage had been in the dark, so we saw nothing of the country, but the return flight in full daylight displayed an extraordinary land-scape of snow and mountains cut through by the occasional ribbon of a road. The shapes formed by nature are extraordinarily beautiful in beige and white.

29 October

A tough day at Boise State University Theatre, in Boise, Idaho, with a matinee of *A Midsummer Night's Dream* and an evening performance of *The Magic Flute*. I'm not sure what was the more difficult – organising the costumes and scenery changeover, the stamina challenge for the dancers, or getting the lighting focused, and plotted (twice) in time for the performances. Why did anyone agree to this?? But there may be a reason for such an ambitious idea in that the director of the local ballet company is Paul Russell, former principal dancer with Dance Theatre of Harlem, an international star who competed with Nureyev for a time. Possibly, he just wanted to see both programmes?

An African–American, Paul Russell trained with the Russian ballerina Natalia Dudinskaya, on a scholarship to Russia, and no doubt this explains his virtuoso technique. It is stated that he was the first African–American to dance the purely classical role of Siegfried in *Swan Lake*. No longer dancing, here he is, in the backwoods, running a school and an affiliated company. It seems strange that he should have virtually disappeared. Sitting in a cafe in downtown Boise the evening before, we noticed that the plate glass window next to us had been pierced by bullets from a high calibre gun, which makes Boise an even less attractive place to settle in. (PS: Paul Russell died of AIDS shortly after; perhaps he had deliberately sought out a quiet place?)

9 November

The tour ended with a week around New York, in New Jersey and on Long Island. We arrived in New Jersey after a long flight from Albuquerque in New Mexico, via Dallas to Newark, and then a bus drive to the Holiday Inn in Somerville. We must have eaten in the hotel and it was around midnight when we put on the TV; it is unusual to see news of Europe on American television, and it was extraordinary to see pictures of the Berlin Wall, to see people scrambling up onto the wall, hugging each other on the top of it, and even breaking off pieces of cement to throw to the ground. It took some time to realise that it was not a movie and that the impossible had happened; people power had brought down the Iron Curtain.

13 November

Our last day in the US and as the flight did not leave until the evening we were able to spend part of the day in New York – our first glimpse of the city. First impressions were favourable; a lively, bright and friendly city. We only had time for the Rockefeller Centre with the winter skaters, Fifth Avenue, Times Square, and obviously we saw more from the bus as we headed for the airport. MW has been with us again this tour as a touring manager and he sat in front of me in the bus. I noted with alarm a ring of purple spots around his neck and that he was flushed and sweaty in the air-conditioned bus. I have seen these signs before – I think he may be HIV positive… This illness has decimated the American dance world, directors, choreographers and dancers, and many more as well in all walks of life. I hope for the best.

Once back in Europe, we continued, as in the previous seasons, with a tour of Germany, and also included performances in the Netherlands, Austria and

Switzerland. The spring of 1990 was a busy one in the UK, followed by a tour of France and visits to L'Aquila in Italy and to Geneva, completing one hundred performances in the eight-month season. Alexander had made a big decision during this last tour in the USA, and handed over his last dancing role, that of Bottom in the *Dream*. He had danced it literally hundreds of times and felt a special fondness for the role, but Mark Longthorn (who had been with us since 1986, dancing a number of major roles) was quick to jump into his shoes (and to fit into the donkey's head), bearing an almost eerie resemblance to Alexander.

For the following season, we found new rehearsal premises, just at the end of the road, in the Central School of Speech and Drama at Swiss Cottage. We had outgrown our own ballet studio several years before and had moved around London's West End and the Covent Garden area from one studio to another, according to availability. The old Dance Centre in Floral Street offered the best studios, but this was soon to close after our last season there in 1988, when we prepared *The Magic Flute*. It was a period of intense work, when once again there was a big turnover, but when we acquired a number of talented new dancers.

In preparation for the many styles which the choreography for *The Flute* would demand, we asked William Louther to give the company contemporary dance classes. Bill Louther had danced with Martha Graham Dance Company, but became a world star during his time with Alvin Ailey American Dance Theatre where he was an incomparable interpreter of Ailey's exciting choreography. Coming to England, he was a founder member of the London Contemporary Dance Theatre and when arthritis brought about the end of his dancing career he directed companies in Israel and in Wales, before teaching for several schools in London. Bill was a hard taskmaster, and although he was no longer able to demonstrate (he brought with him an excellent student to do this) he was an inspiring person to have involved with the company.

We had, over the years, invited a number of first-class guest teachers to the company, including several from The Royal Ballet – Maryon Lane, Eileen Ward, Nancy Kilgour, and Keith Rosson, who retained his connection with the company for some years. Once we were on tour, Alexander and I gave the daily company classes, something we felt was essential to prepare the dancers for the demands of the choreography, as well as personally taking into account the varying problems caused by such extensive touring; be it those caused by the weather, the amount of travelling, the stage, or just the general mood.

The 1990–91 season followed the pattern of the previous years with tours in the USA and Germany in the autumn, and a lengthy tour of the UK in

Stephen Brennan and Darius James rehearsing at the Dance Centre (then called the
Fitness Centre) in Covent Garden in 1989.

Alexander rehearsing with Graham Woodward at the Fitness Centre.

the spring. We were also happy to get a good tour in France where *The Magic Flute* was well received and where the more contemporary dance style and costumes suited the taste of the French audiences better than the more conservative *Dream*. In May 1991 we made our first venture into the former German Democratic Republic, now part of a reunited Germany, with a performance in Meiningen, a city with a good reputation for theatre. It was over twenty-five years since we had toured in the GDR with our concert programme, *Soirée de Ballet*, and the country had, over those years, almost wasted away with neglect and hardship. The streets of what had been an attractive town were potholed, the buildings dirty and even crumbling, and the theatre looked and felt like the 1950s. However, we were overwhelmed with the welcome at the theatre, where we must have been the first Western company to visit there since the re-unification, and the performance of the *Dream* was rewarded with twenty-five minutes of applause. The resident stage manager breathlessly told us they had never experienced anything like it; but, of course, the audience was not just applauding our company, they were also expressing their joy in the fact that a company from England could now perform in their theatre, as they could now also cross what was once an impassable border, and travel to wherever they wished.

During the 1990 US tour, we were saddened to have to send MW back home, as it was obvious that his illness had overtaken him and he was unable to continue working. It was another nationwide tour, with venues in California, North and South Carolina, Georgia, Tennessee, Ohio and Illinois. In Las Vegas, where we played in the excellent University Theatre (and not on the strip!), we found Vassili Sulich, whom we had known from Paris where he was a member of Milorad Miskovitch's company in the 1960s. The very good-looking dancer had become director and choreographer of the local ballet company and was obviously enjoying the good facilities and comfortable life in Nevada.

For us, this year marked a watershed; with neither of us now dancing, and new productions only practical and possible every two or three years, it was no longer a life dominated by creation and performing. The company was more successful than it had ever been; it was on a better financial footing than it had ever been, but it had become a 'business' of which we were the observers, if also the directors. Things had also reached a period of general change internationally; the boom years of the 1980s were over, unemployment soared, and the British government was in crisis. Several well-known drama companies folded while many theatres lost essential funding. Things were no better in France or Germany, with cuts affecting theatres and funding organisations, and even in the USA sponsors were becoming more cautious. As far as dance was concerned, the floodgates now opened from Eastern

Europe, which brought forth a plethora of quickly assembled new dance companies with almost fictional names – Russian National Ballet, St Petersburg State Ballet, Moscow Festival Ballet. They were snapped up by Western agents, as they were cheap and easy, and they performed *Swan Lake* and *The Nutcracker*, foolproof box office successes.

All the same, life continued as normal for us – there were more US tours scheduled and bookings in the UK remained healthy. The reunification of Germany meant a whole new market became available to us, and we were keen to take advantage of this and were fast to do so; Alexander had plans for new productions and there were always dancers keen to work with us. Once again, the advantages of independence seemed to assure us of a healthy future.

chapter
thirteen

Winding Down 1991-1994 and 1998-1999

Many directors are happy to send their company off on tour with a ballet master (or mistress) and a company manager, while they remain in the home town, possibly planning new productions or future seasons. This is something we could never have considered; the company was still our creation and although we were no longer performing, it seemed essential, and natural, for us to be involved and to be present at every performance. There have always been directors for whom this was the norm; notably Georges Balanchine and Maurice Béjart (both director–choreographers), who were always to be found backstage during a performance, in fact almost on stage, just inside the proscenium arch in the downstage wing. Alexander and I continued to supervise all the daily preparations for the performance. He was always busy with rehearsals, while I generally gave the daily ballet class, but was happy to find there was still a way to actually take part in the performance; on those lengthy one-night tours I could supervise, and even run, the lighting during performances. In the US, and in most of the German theatres we visited, the lighting boards were still manual ones, allowing one a good deal of freedom to make subtle changes during the performance – heightening the atmosphere or compensating for technical problems on stage, or even catching a dancer who had wandered out of the light. Being personally in charge also saved several hours of work on one-night stands, when otherwise the technicians would need to plot the lighting effects for each performance. However, there were occasions when I, and sometimes both of us, did dare to spend the performance in the auditorium, among the audience, although we always found it nerve-racking.

For the 1991–92 season Gary Lindsey decided to change our annual tours of the US to the spring, so we could visit Florida and those Southern states where hurricanes and storms made the autumn season too hazardous. However, the season commenced with a visit to Vichy, the still elegant French watering hole with its famous theatre, where the Diaghilev Ballets Russes gave their final performance in 1929. We gave an all-French programme of *Coppélia*, *Le Boeuf sur le Toit* and *La Ronde*. The autumn was then spent touring in the UK, performing *The Magic Flute*, ahead of a particularly promising tour of the USA, with additional visits to Canada, Aruba, the American Virgin Islands and Caracas, Venezuela. One of the first performances was in New Jersey, where we were amazed to find a dance critic from *The New York Times* in the audience, which won us a half-page review in that prestigious paper.

Among the many towns we visited on that tour, and one which stands out in my memory as an example of the contradictions which are part of American society, was Youngstown, Ohio, a city once in the centre of the steel industry boom, but now somewhat forgotten and forlorn. On arrival at the hotel, we were given the usual instructions; above all, we should not walk the few blocks to downtown. Although there didn't appear to be anything particularly ominous about Youngstown, we found, on reaching downtown, that the stores and offices on the main road were all connected by corridors and passageways, so there was no need to venture out into the danger zone at all!

The local ballet teacher drove me to her studio, where I was to give a class to her pupils, and apologised that the route would take us through some bad areas. And indeed, once we had left the good area where our hotel was located, we drove down some suburban streets full of sadly dilapidated houses, the front gardens overgrown and scattered with litter, and where the residents lolled around on battered sofas on the front porches, probably unemployed, and possibly suffering the effects of drink and drugs. A couple of blocks further we were back in 'respectable America' where the white weatherboard houses were surrounded by immaculate green lawns, sporting a flagpole from which the stars and stripes proudly fluttered.

Our performance took place in the original Warner Brothers Movie Theatre, an art deco palace with 2,300 seats, a huge stage and an old union technical crew, who were exceptionally cooperative. After the performance we were given a dinner in the dress circle foyer, while the very glitzy guests at the reception milled around below us in the palatial gilded lobby. It was obviously an important social event, but it appeared that the members of the audience were now either unaware of or disinterested in us and our contribution to the evening, as we remained curiously isolated and ignored, grateful, all the same, to be able to enjoy what was a very good meal.

Travelling from Ohio to Florida, we found a different world; white sand beaches, pelicans and palm trees, and in towns such as Palm Beach, Fort Myers, Orlando, Daytona Beach and Boca Raton, good theatres, almost making us feel that we were on holiday. Florida is traditionally a haven for retirees, and audiences tended to be quieter and more reserved than elsewhere. We were assured that this more restrained response was normal, due to their age or their health. We spent three days in Key West, which we imagined was little changed since the days when it was a favourite haunt of people like Tennessee Williams and Ernest Hemingway. Now it had become a world mecca for gays, who gather there, filling the hotels, the bars and the clubs at any time of the year. Following brief visits to Aruba, and to Saint Croix in the Virgin Islands, we flew into Caracas to take part in the International Theatre Festival which is held there annually.

The final part of our tour proved to be more dramatic than expected, and my diary entries can take over:

7 April 1992

South America, and there's revolution in the air, again. Our arrival at Caracas airport was uneventful; we were met by an arty-looking young man from the International Theatre Festival organisation and bussed into central Caracas. Not the best entrance to a major city; the long uphill drive from the airport leads past miles of barrios, the squalid shanty towns hugging the sides of the bare hills, dusty and breathless in dry weather and awash with mud during the wet season. These settlements, built of mud-bricks, corrugated iron, plastic sheeting and general debris, are also choking in the pollution brought by the smoking fumes belched out by thousands of climbing cars and buses.

We are staying in the Hilton Apart-Hotel, a huge multi-storey block in what appears to be the city centre and is walking distance from the impressive Rios Reyna Theatre. On arrival we were asked to call at the festival office to receive the per diem cash payments which are stipulated in our contract. The office was packed and chaotic but no one was prepared to talk to us, or to give us anything. However, on producing the contract we were asked to wait, and this we did on the only available spot, spending an hour sitting on the steps leading up to the office from the street, awaiting the cash.

We had a day off, so were able to do a company class in the theatre, and also had time to wander around Caracas. The city is modern, noisy and busy but there are older quarters to be found, quiet tree-lined squares where elderly people sit silently on the low walls and benches. During the afternoon the saucepans started – people living in the high-rise blocks of the city centre leant out of their windows banging saucepan lids together, creating a suitable cacophony to herald a revolution. The tactics changed as dusk fell, and the lights from hundreds of apartments flashed on and off throughout the city. The theatre staff told us that the technical crew may go on strike – which means we may have a performance, or maybe not. It's a long way to come not to have a performance. However, this evening's performance by the French company of Philippe Genty went ahead.

8 April

A long day in the theatre during which the crew kept disappearing into their offices and doubts remained as to whether the performance would take place, which left me wondering why on earth we had considered coming back to South America at all, even more so after the endless and often frustrating exchange of faxes and letters with the organisers. (This performance was our own addition to the tour; the organisers had contacted us and, as we were already in the Caribbean, so close to Venezuela, it seemed to make sense…) Towards evening everything did settle down, and with just a background of the saucepan lids banging – which even has a special name, *'cacerolada'* – we performed *Dream* to a packed house, with hundreds of students filling the aisles and sitting on the steps. At least, the students were present for Act 1, but most disappeared during the interval – either because they were bored or, more likely, because the events out in the streets were more interesting.

9 April

We had an early start to get to the airport, and were to be escorted there by the same young man who had met us two days earlier. With no sign of him, no one we could telephone, and not much time left, we searched the streets around the hotel and found a bus with a dour and uncommunicative driver, who finally admitted that he was there to take us to the airport. The scene there was not much more encouraging – the check-ins packed, and the flights so overbooked that it looked as if we would not all get away. Once again, at the last possible minute, we did make it onto the flight to San Juan where we were to board a flight to Miami. (A minor revolution did take place that day and we had got away, again, as in Quito in 1987, on the last flight out of the country. This was Hugo Chávez's attempted coup, but he had several more years to wait before he took over power.)

Two extra performances in Miami had been added to the schedule after our arrival in the States, and although we, and Gary, were happy to include these in the tour, the problem of our US visas running out on the day we flew into Miami had not been solved. I think we all thought that a couple of days shouldn't make any difference and, in any case, we would get into the States without trouble. We should have all been more careful, as on arrival in San Juan (Puerto Rico) it was necessary to go through US immigration; half of us had passed through without trouble, but when one of the dancers was asked amiably by an immigration officer what he was intending to do in Miami, and he replied that he was looking forward to the performances we were to give, all of us were rounded up, our passports taken away and we were incarcerated in a glass-walled room. Several hours of telephone calls followed, hampered by the fact that Gary, in San Francisco, was several hours behind Puerto Rico time. At the same time, the promoter in Miami was furious with him, with us, and was threatening to sue.

Finally, our passports were stamped 'deported from the USA', but we were allowed on to Miami, where we were to spend the following day under house arrest, in the hotel, while things were sorted out. Fortunately, Dabney was with us again for this tour, and she was left to cope with the string of telephone calls which continued throughout that long day. It was only by evening, when news came that we should all go to the immigration office, which was working after hours, that the extension of the visas was made. I asked the promoter how he had managed to do this: 'What do you think, Christina?' he replied, 'Bucks.' At least it wasn't our fault…

Following the two performances at the huge Jackie Gleason Theater, despite everything Alexander was presented with a 'Proclamation' and a medal from the city of Miami for cultural services. Back in the UK, the company immediately gave a performance in Abergavenny, in Wales; 'Miami to Abergavenny' made a good headline in the local press.

The following season was a rewarding one and brought us a new full-length ballet, *Figaro, Figaro*, based on the play *The Marriage of Figaro* by Pierre-Augustin Caron de Beaumarchais. This was set to music by the eighteenth-century composers Jean-Philippe Rameau and Luigi Boccherini. *Figaro* was a theme which suited Alexander's talents perfectly – drawing inspiration from the *commedia dell'arte*, Figaro's exploits with the other characters of Count Almaviva's household are full of fun, yet beneath the frivolity are glimpses of the revolution only a few years away. However, it was a production we had to mount on the proverbial shoestring, as ever increasing costs and diminishing income from badly cash-strapped theatres left us without spare funds for a new production. But, we did have a storeroom full of costumes collected over thirty years, some not much used, boxes of silks and rayons from Bombay, as well as a bale of curtain material picked up on a street market some years earlier. From this Alexander concocted four palace doorways to form the stage set, while I designed the costumes, reutilising those from *La Favorita, Castles in the Air, Le Boeuf sur le Toit* and even Keith's jacket from *Swan Lake*. In the end we did have to buy ten pairs of tights.

The season opened with a short tour of eastern Germany, visiting Gera, Dessau and Görlitz. Much had been done to renovate these towns of the former GDR, repairing and restoring, but they remained dull, grey places, with empty streets and little traffic. In Görlitz, which had been spared damage in the Second World War, the facades of the old houses were literally crumbling and potholes remained along every pavement. It was obvious that it would still take a number of years before these eastern parts of Germany could catch up with the West.

Our tours continued in Germany and throughout the UK, and in January we returned to Malta to perform *Figaro, Figaro*. We had not performed in central London for some years as a suitable theatre for our size of company was just not available, but in February the company played the newly restored Richmond Theatre in the London Borough of Richmond. This Edwardian theatre had recently been brought back to life with a massive programme of renovation and modernisation, and despite the small stage, we felt comfortable performing the *Dream* there, and enjoyed a full house.

The highlight of the 1993 American tour was a week's season at the opera house of the Brooklyn Academy of Music in New York. This 1890s opera

Gina Long and Stephen Brennan photographed in Anthony Crickmay's studio for
Figaro, Figaro in 1992.

house with 2,500 seats has a sumptuous auditorium and is one of New York's
best and most prestigious. Our visit was part of a subscription season for
schools and local residents, requiring us to perform at ten o'clock in the morning. Gary was diffident in offering us this booking and was prepared to
arrange evening performances in Manhattan as well, but BAM insisted on
their exclusivity, and we were happy enough to perform in New York, at any
time! Performing at this hour meant leaving the hotel at 7 a.m. to battle our

way across Manhattan with Armenian taxi drivers, who seem to have a monopoly, but unfortunately very little knowledge of the city and its districts. On arrival at the theatre, we would be welcomed with huge trays of doughnuts and steaming coffee – the essentials of American backstage life – and then with packed houses of lively and voluble young people who hooted with delight at Bottom's transformation into an ass, and cheered Puck (Gina Long) like a pop star.

Our stay in New York was complicated by the arrival of a blizzard which swept across the eastern states bringing ice and snow, half a metre high in some places. In the worst conditions for nearly a century, people were killed, power lines brought down, train and road travel were in chaos. Some streets in Manhattan were cleared just enough to allow the intrepid Armenian taxi drivers to work – but very few other drivers dared use their cars. The entire city was blanketed in snow, mounds of it covering parked cars and banks of it on the pavements, but life did go on. Families skated and skied in Central Park, while some office workers even made their way to work on skis along the almost silent and deserted streets. Fortunately for us, our performances carried on as scheduled.

Starting so early meant we had the rest of the day for sightseeing, visiting art galleries and museums and attending performances every evening. It was only after a couple of days we realised that most of the dancers were not venturing outside the hotel, apparently frightened of crime on the streets, as well as the weather. We did see a lot of characters on the streets of New York – beggars, drug addicts and eccentrics of every kind – while during the night the wail of police sirens and even the sound of gunshots could be heard from our hotel. With a new mayor, New York has been cleaned up since the 1990s, but then one did need to be streetwise and avoid certain streets and certain districts. Nevertheless, we managed to persuade some of the company to forego the takeaway pizzas in their hotel rooms to see something of the great city, as well as taking advantage of the Times Square ticket booth to get cut-price tickets for evening performances. Fortunately, the weather improved by the time we were to leave, but the company toured for another five weeks through snow and ice in 1993, and I can still remember on one occasion trying to cross a parking lot in New Jersey, battling against an Arctic blizzard, snow and ice pelting my face, and thinking I really might not make it!

The tour finished with a four-day visit to Trinidad where we arrived in the middle of a record heat wave. On arrival at the airport we were greeted with a traditional 'Trini welcome', with two steel bands keeping us standing, and nearly melting, in the afternoon sun while photographers milled around. But we could only feel relief at the warmth of the welcome and the promise of some sunshine. The following day was a day off, which the company, naturally enough, planned to spend by the hotel pool; much as I didn't want to spoil their hard-earned day off, I was anxious, and made my way around the pool warning everyone that this equatorial sun was not like a European one, and could be dangerous. After ten minutes in the sun, when we could already feel the heat grilling our faces, Alexander and I set off to explore the town, meeting the company again that evening while we waited for transportation to the British high commissioner's residence, where a reception had been arranged for us. The results of a day in the sun were plain to see; the girls had piled on make-up to cover seriously burned faces and backs, while the men walked with a curious stiffness and sat down tentatively. While I was discussing the following day's schedule with Frank, our stage manager, his gaze became seriously glassy-eyed before he tipped gently sideways and slipped to the floor unconscious. Frank missed the reception, but fortunately recovered from sun stroke by the next day.

We gave two days of performances in the partially open-air theatre, battled with an eccentric and unpredictable local organiser, but enjoyed the audiences dressed in their Sunday best – frilly white dresses, the little girls with ribbons in their hair and their mothers in flowery hats. A final free day allowed us to see some of the rest of the island, gloriously wild and tropical, before boarding our flight back to the UK.

Since the beginning of the 1990s our seasons had been getting shorter with slightly fewer performances each year. We were being more cautious, and more demanding of the terms of our contracts; the costs were carefully calculated before travelling more than a few hours from London, and it was often necessary to decide, reluctantly, that certain performances were simply not feasible. There were cutbacks in subsidies for theatres and cultural organisations across Europe, not only in the UK, but the squeeze was also being felt in the USA, with sponsors becoming less generous and organisers reducing their annual programmes. By the 1993–94 season, we gave just fifty-two performances, split almost equally between the UK, the US and Germany, with the odd sortie to France or Switzerland. It was an enjoyable season with a group of good, experienced and mature dancers like Alexander Sinelnikov, a former soloist from Kiev, and long-term members such as Emma Payne and Anne-Marie Cox. These were dancers who formed the heart of the company, receptive and sensitive to Alexander's choreography and always ready to lead rehearsals and to assist generally.

Once again we spent the autumn and winter in Europe and set off for the US in February 1994 after a sell-out return visit to the Richmond Theatre, this time performing *The Magic Flute*. After a marathon flight from London to Los Angeles, performances in California, Tennessee, Florida and Arizona went by in something of a rush. In Nashville we enjoyed some real country

A company photo for the 1993–94 season. Alexander Sinelnikov is seated centre, Anne-Marie Cox is sitting on the floor at the right and Emma Payne is in the back row, on the right.

and western music, and in Key Largo we spent three days in a luxury hotel with a private beach. Unfortunately, the performances in Key Largo, organised by an over-excitable Bulgarian tenor, took place on a small platform erected in a tennis court in the super-elite Ocean Reef Club. The stage was fitted with multicoloured disco lighting, which, if over-used, would blow the fuses, plunging us into darkness, but we had fun under a starlit sky and did not complain.

We then made our first longer tour in Canada, mostly through British Columbia, where we travelled by coach; long, long trips of hundreds and hundreds of miles through forests and mountains, often encountering, and needing to avoid, elk and moose on the roads. We missed a grizzly bear, but found his footprints all around the roadside cafe where we had made a stop and innocently wandered through the snow to a nearby lake. The towns were small, the theatres also, with names such as Grand Prairie Regional College Theatre or the Trail Community College Theatre. But the dancers enjoyed the country and the scenery and there was always assistance from the ever friendly organisers, and willing, helpful staff. We had a day off, I believe it was in Prince Rupert on the Pacific coast, where the only thing to do was to wander around the fish canning factory, and to sit by the sea in the early spring sunshine.

Looking at each other, Alexander and I said almost simultaneously, 'What are we doing here?' We had a touring manager and a competent stage manager, Richard Jarman. Richard was one of our favourite technicians, always reliable and good-humoured, essential qualities on tours such as those to the USA. The company dancers were in good form and rehearsals were hardly necessary, leaving the two of us to spend hours travelling and more hours waiting around on performance days. It no longer seemed to make sense and we knew it was time to do some serious thinking and possibly to make some major decisions.

Back in Europe, we had a two-week tour in Germany, where we raced down the autobahns now packed with huge trucks criss-crossing from Eastern Europe to the West. This ever-increasing onslaught of heavy traffic was making me more and more nervous as it already had done in the UK, where motorways like the M1 were groaning with heavy traffic twenty-four hours a day. I feared for our drivers, I feared for us and for all the company, knowing that accidents had already happened to other touring companies. Those leisurely trips through France, the rediscovery of Germany and the tourist-like adventures in Italy and Switzerland were things of the past, as were the trips back to London at midnight when the motorways would be quiet and clear of traffic.

In producing new ballets, our first thought had to be: 'Will this sell well?' After so many years of forging a path to produce works which were both individual and original, the problem of compromising ourselves was a very real one. Was it possible that the particular life we had chosen, made up of dance and travel, where we had succeeded through hard work and determination, really had no place in this new world? We could continue, the contracts and the offers were still there, but it seemed to make no sense to carry on purely in order to make a living for ourselves, and for the dancers. After thirty years, we decide to take a break, a pause for a year or two to take stock of things, and to see what other companies, and other dancers, were doing. It was difficult to break the news to the company, but it was also with a great sense of relief when after the final performance in Frankfurt we opened a couple of bottles of champagne backstage.

Alexander and I spent a month on a small Greek island, without a telephone, newspapers or television, and almost forgot the outside world. We slept in a tiny whitewashed bungalow, just feet from where the water of the Aegean lapped the shore. We walked for miles through the stony hills, aromatic with the scent of thyme and rosemary, and met no one but herds of goats, bells jangling at their necks. Emerging, as if from some kind of therapy, we returned to London to clean up some of the mess left from twenty years of touring – times when one throws things into a corner to be dealt with at a later date, when one might have more time. (We had then been at North House for twenty years.) I packed up the files and the papers and moved into a smaller office while the builders moved in to convert most of the basement to an apartment. As they hacked away at the walls of what had been the office – and I imagined they were chipping away at the spirits of twenty years of dance – I became the tea lady for the insatiable British workman.

Our escape to a Greek island in 1994.

We revelled in the luxury of having time for ourselves, to go to the gym, to meet friends and to go to the theatre. (It seemed that, despite all the problems in Britain, this was a lively and stimulating time in the theatre, and we spent many enjoyable evenings at the English National Opera, the National Theatre and with the Royal Shakespeare Company.) Visiting dance companies were rare in London at that time, and The Royal Ballet was performing new productions of ballets such as *Swan Lake* and *The Sleeping Beauty*. These were sumptuous productions, the staging appearing to compete with the most lavish of the West End musicals, but it left the dancers struggling for space on a cluttered stage, while coping with lavishly over-decorated costumes. The millions of pounds spent on these productions did not come from government subsidies, but, fortunately, from other sources – donations from generous patrons, both personal gifts and business sponsorship. Perhaps this money could have been better used…

Alexander had often joked that our days off were 'cleana da shoppa' days, after seeing a TV interview with a hard-worked Italian shopkeeper, who cheerfully admitted he had no time off at all, and Sundays were just for 'cleana da shoppa'. So, on waking every morning, it took some time to get used to the idea that the day ahead was just for us.

Early in 1995, we made a trip to Germany, visiting friends and colleagues and catching up with dance and drama performances. We saw dance performances in Stuttgart, in Mannheim (where three of our dancers had settled), in Frankfurt and Berlin. All these theatres are highly subsidised, all have opera, dance and drama companies, and offer their dance directors almost carte blanche to build the companies and to create the works they wish to. In Stuttgart the performance started fifteen minutes late, keeping the audience locked out of the auditorium and with no explanation or apology for the delay. From a seat in the centre of the stalls, our view of the stage was almost totally obscured by the heads in front of us. The performance of Maurice Béjart's *The Magic Flute* (which we finally saw while standing by the exit doors) was one of Béjart's showy pieces, danced to taped music and relying mostly on the effects of movement performed by beautiful, scantily dressed bodies, but the subscription audience applauded dutifully. However, the following evening at a performance of several short contemporary ballets, only half the ballet company were to be seen, and then in uniform black costumes on an almost totally blackened stage. In Mannheim, the company splashed around on a stage filled knee-high with water, and in Frankfurt, the acclaimed company directed by William Forsythe appeared to have abandoned dance for what used to be called 'performance art'. This was a particularly darkened and depressing evening, perhaps due to the recent tragic loss of the choreographer's wife.

These last three performances, played to half-empty houses, once an unthinkable happening in theatregoing Germany, brought to mind a recent discussion we had attended, at the Barbican in London, between Adrian Noble, then director of the Royal Shakespeare Company and the director of the Drama Theatre in Düsseldorf. They discussed the differences between their two countries – the continuing struggle for the British companies to obtain sufficient funding in contrast to the security and comfort enjoyed by the German theatre. Adrian Noble asked his counterpart whether this could not lead to a certain complacency on the German side. 'What does that mean?' she queried, and even after further translation, she could not understand the sense of his question.

If these dance performances showed considerable self-indulgence on the part of the choreographers, and the withdrawn, unresponsive manner of the performers could be seen as a breakdown of the need to communicate with the audience, the standard of the dancing was an eye-opener. At each performance, the dancers were not just exceptionally good-looking and well trained, but they tackled the heavy demands made upon them, both in classical or contemporary choreography, expertly and skilfully. In fact, the physical demands were so great that one feared for their limbs torn into contortions, with positions and movements resembling acrobatics more than dance. It was all the more a pity that these dancers appeared to have become anonymous – their names were just listed alphabetically in the programmes, there were no photos in the programmes or the foyers by which one could identify them, and on stage they were costumed almost androgynously, and often left in semi-darkness. (This trend, or fashion, continued into the next decade, and spread from Germany to much of the dance world.) In contrast, it was then something of a relief to find an enjoyable production of John Cranko's 1969 ballet *The Taming of the Shrew* at the Berlin State Opera House, but it certainly left us wondering what was the future of the art form which had dominated our lives, and which had given us so much.

In Stuttgart we had also found work for two of our dancers with a small, contemporary group, and in November Alexander mounted *Voices* for the company. We were happy to be working again and there were discussions about future collaboration with the company. Further queries about guest productions came from around the world, the USA, South Africa, Estonia and Albania among them, but as negotiations dragged on we sensed that this path was not something we wanted to pursue. Alexander had already worked as a guest choreographer with companies in London, Amsterdam and Antwerp, and found choreographing for a company of dancers he did not know, with limited rehearsal time, always difficult and often frustrating. In the meantime, I was teaching professionals in London, and had even booked a tour of the UK for a colleague who ran a folk dance company. I was approached by several companies asking for assistance with bookings, but becoming a theatre agent was definitely not something to be considered – all the work and little of the pleasure!

In 1997 a call came from Gary Lindsey with the news that Columbia Artists, the major American agency, wanted the company to tour the US in the following year for their Community Concerts wing, with the production of *Alice* which had been under discussion in 1995. A week or so later, we received a query from a German agency wishing to organise a tour, also in 1998. The idea of a ballet around the theme of Alice and Lewis Carroll had interested Alexander for some time, and now with 1998 the centenary of Carroll's death, it was the perfect time. It seemed as if fate was nudging us into action.

It didn't take long to get the 'machine' back into motion; Alexander had little trouble finding reference material about Alice, and her creator, as the ballet was not to be a simple translation of the books, but to involve Carroll, as well as the real-life Alice's mother, Mrs Liddell, in a dreamlike work, surreal as the style of the original stories. In the office we were soon busy, and pleasantly surprised to find that we had not been forgotten; bookings flooded in, especially in the UK. This was just as well, as the US tour did not materialise – the expenses involved in bringing a foreign company had become a problem, not only because of cuts to the promoters' budgets, but also with increased fares, nationally and internationally. We found a designer who produced a versatile, attractive set and some interesting, stylised costumes, and started the search for suitable music. It had to be a British composer; Elgar was too heavy, Lord Berners too light, Britten's copyright arrangements too complicated. Then we found Malcolm Arnold, and a somewhat neglected treasure trove of scores.

We contacted all our former dancers who we thought might be available, but only three of them could rejoin for the rehearsal period, which started in the summer of 1998. This gave us a nucleus of dancers familiar with Alexander's style, and we were able to engage several more excellent, versatile dancers in time to set to work. We were also fortunate in having Nicholas Johnson, former principal dancer with both Royal Ballet and English National Ballet, to give company classes. Nicky had already worked with the company before our break, and was able to bring that very special Royal Ballet discipline to classes, helping to forge a new company in limited time. At that time, Nicky was also busy with a one-man show, based on Nijinsky, which he performed successfully in London and in New York. At that time, it was unthinkable that he, so full of life and energy, would be fatally ill within a few years, joining an ever-increasing number of losses among friends and colleagues, as well as most of our mentors – Sonia Arova, Paula Hinton, Rosella Hightower, Job Sanders, some of a long list.

Of the new dancers to the company, Alex Rose, a contemporary-trained dancer, was a convincing Lewis Carroll and, with a transformation scene, an intriguing White Rabbit; Anne-Marie Cox was a perfect Mrs Liddell, whose relationship to Carroll was perhaps more complicated than is known (she also performed the Queen of Hearts); and Emma Payne and Emma Brunton were both excellent as Alice. Stephen Brennan, who had been with us since 1989, and was an irresistibly engaging Figaro in 1991, took over a number of roles, including the Dormouse and the Ugly Duchess, with panache.

ALICE – Dreams and Wonderland was premiered on 2 October and performed at a series of venues around London, before we set off further afield. The major surprise of the season was the number of new, or successfully renovated, theatres right across Britain. Lottery money had been used for this very good cause, and finally we had a chain of theatres with modern technical equipment, good-sized stages and pleasant backstage conditions for a company of our size. With two tours to France and Germany we completed the season at the end of the year. If we had been somewhat unsure about the ballet's success in Germany, where Carroll's stories are less part of the country's culture than in the UK, we needed not have worried.

As has always been the case, the reviews were thoughtful and well informed: 'Alexander Roy has created a series of magical scenes full of fantasy. The dream world of Alice is well supported by his collaborators – Marsha Roddy's set and costumes and Christina Gallea's lighting. *ALICE – Dreams and Wonderland* looks into the double life of the Reverend Charles Dodgson and the struggle with the 'alter ego', Lewis Carroll. The transformation from the melancholic, frustrated Carroll into the lively White Rabbit is a wonderful moment in Roy's choreography, which also includes characters such as the Mad Hatter, Tweedledee and Tweedledum, the Queen of Hearts and the Cheshire Cat, all in fantastical and colourful costumes.' (*The Cologne Advertiser*) 'It is impossible to separate dreams and reality in *ALICE – Dreams and Wonderland* – where a series of surreal and colourfully amusing characters fill Alice's dreams.' (*Westphalia Newspaper*.)

We had only planned for a three-month season and had made no

The image for the poster of *Alice, Dreams and Wonderland* in 1998; Emma Payne is in the air, with Emma Brunton.

decisions about the future, but the enthusiasm of the dancers for a return season in 1999, and the number of possible bookings, which we had not been able to squeeze into the 1998 tour, seemed to make this good sense. There was also considerable overseas interest in *Alice*, with negotiations still underway with promoters in Beijing, Tokyo, Tel Aviv, Bahrain and Athens, as well as old contacts in Malta and Taiwan. So another season was underway for

317

the autumn and winter of 1999. As so often happens, and it was understandable in view of the months between the seasons, several of the dancers dropped out – one returned to Australia, another married, another could not resist a well-paid job in the West End – and negotiations for the elusive and exotic foreign engagements dragged on and on.

But we did have another three-month tour in the UK, Germany and France, which would have been easy enough to be enjoyable, had an accident not occurred to Alex Rose two days before the opening of the season. This left the roles of Carroll and of Bottom, in the revival of *A Midsummer Night's Dream*, to fill. Alexander had not performed for ten years, but there was little choice but for him to jump in – and to be grateful for the fact that we had both spent several weeks doing a daily ballet class before commencing the new season. Fortunately, after ten performances, but just when he was beginning to enjoy them, Stephen Brennan, who had been working in Ireland, returned to fill the breach. It was a successful season and we especially enjoyed the last performance of *Dream* in Bordeaux, which won us, unexpectedly, a true ovation, as well as a string of performances of *Alice* around Britain in the brand-new performing venues, thanks to the National Lottery.

Despite what could be considered as two successful seasons, a decision had been made not to continue the company's activities after 1999. After all, we had achieved all we set out to thirty-four years earlier – and much, much more. It had been an extraordinary adventure, foolhardy, no doubt, and if the workload had often been almost unbearable, the rewards had been many. We could feel that for many years, our tours and performances had fulfilled a service, or a purpose, in providing dance performances in towns and in countries where there was otherwise almost no other professional dance to be seen. On the other hand we had performed, and been successful, in many of the major cities of the world – London, Paris, Berlin and New York among them. We had given ourselves an outlet for almost unhindered creation, sometimes experimentation, and in doing this formed our own very individual style.

It had also been of great importance to us to pass on a legacy of all we had learned as young dancers from an unbeatable array of teachers, and the experience we had gathered as dancers with directors and choreographers in international companies, to those dancers who then worked with us. It is gratifying to see so many of our former dancers now running their own companies, or schools, or leading fulfilling lives in new, but related, professions. It was not clear exactly what we would do in the future, but it seemed a good time to start again. Neither of us wished to continue as teachers, and after another long trip, this time visiting ballet companies right around the world, Alexander knew he would not want to pursue a career as a guest choreographer for other companies.

First of all, the storerooms were emptied. We gave away and sold as much as we could – costumes, scenery, lighting and sound equipment, office equipment, stationery, etc. This all ended up in colleagues' dance companies, in dance and drama schools, and in small drama companies scattered in and around London. There followed a difficult time when we lost both our mothers, who had contributed so much to our careers, and an unexpected and dramatic event whereby we nearly lost North House as well. Following a lengthy legal battle we finally became the freeholders of the house, only to decide that we couldn't continue to prop up what was in danger of becoming an elderly, even decrepit house demanding constant care and repair. It was also becoming clear that we didn't really need to live in London any longer. North House was put on the market.

The estate agents were ecstatic, full of optimism and marketed the house forcefully: 'an unequalled opportunity', 'a spectacular residence', 'a magnificent Victorian mansion', and so on. The potential buyers flocked in, and all bemoaned the lack of off-street parking; an Irish racehorse owner complained at the lack of an atrium, while an American peered from a third-floor window mystified that there was no direct access to the garden – from the third floor. All ignored our efforts to entertain them with the history of the house, and most muttered disgruntledly: 'It's so big.' Then came the developers; they planned demolition, division, partitions and sub-divisions. We couldn't let the house go to them, so we waited.

Another year brought a new launch and one cold, rainy afternoon a youngish American woman came to inspect the house. Alexander led her to the pièce de résistance, the 40-foot drawing room on the first floor, our former rehearsal room, and right on cue, the sun broke through the clouds, piercing shafts of light through the tall stained-glass windows, bringing the American to reach for her mobile: 'Michael,' she called her husband, 'you've got to come over here right away.' The couple lost no time getting planning permission to turn the house back into a family home, with the large rooms being perfect to house their formidable art collection. We were delighted to pass on North House to this couple and to see it revert back, not only to a family home, but to remain a centre for art.

Alexander and I had always sensed that we would move permanently to France one day, a country which had always been a second home, and which had played a major part in our lives. On the day the keys were handed over to the new owners of North House, we set off, the car packed to the roof, and with a removal van to follow shortly after us. We took the usual route, the way we had set off from Swiss Cottage hundreds of times to reach the Continent, with a truck and a bus in tow, but this time alone – through the West End, past Buckingham Palace, across Vauxhall Bridge and then on and on, Camberwell, New Cross, Lewisham and the M20 to the Channel Tunnel. Would it be for the last time? For the first time in our adult lives we were free from a commitment to a demanding profession, and from responsibility to what had become a complicated way of life. In the new millennium, it seemed a good time to start again, in a new house, and in a new country.

On tour during our last season, 1999.

chapter
fourteen

Conclusion

When Job Sanders watched Madame Nora's class in Paris that summer of 1959, looking for a dancer for American Festival Ballet, I was not the only one who caught his attention. One other dancer seemed a possible candidate. Older than me, she was a competent, very experienced dancer – and three inches shorter. When Job telephoned the company director Renzo Raiss that evening, asking for his advice, the reply was, 'Take the taller one.' And so my fate was sealed. Had I not joined the company that year, Alexander and I would never have met and none of the subsequent adventures would have come about. It seems as if fate has often played a role in my life; chance encounters, unexpected offers and pure luck have made so much possible that I should probably consider the astrological explanation to this, and believe that Sagittarius is the 'lucky' sign of the zodiac.

We have both been lucky, too, in having our careers at the time we did, allowing us to work with teachers and choreographers with direct links to the Imperial Russian Ballet and with the subsequent Ballets Russes companies in Europe and in America. We worked with teachers, dancers and choreographers who were at the forefront of dance in Britain, Alexander with those who had brought about the rebirth of dance in Germany after the war, and we then had the opportunity to work with choreographers and in companies, European and American, when huge and exciting changes were taking place in dance. Our own independent path would probably be impossible today for all sorts of practical reasons, and I also wonder if dance, as we knew it, has come to the end of an era.

Dance as an art form, and most importantly as a theatrical performing art, is changing to become something more abstract, more physical, even athletic or gymnastic. This may be inevitable in this technological age; where music is replaced by sound, painting and sculpture by form, dance is in danger of becoming just movement. While the nineteenth-century classics, and even the new full-evening productions, are mounted to resemble West End shows, dance as a means of expression, of emotion, of communication or even of entertainment, is not in fashion among many of today's leading choreographers. Some of these even opt for what has become known as 'non-dance', rejecting any similarities to either nineteenth- or twentieth-century dance.

The works of Balanchine, Ashton and MacMillan are zealously administered by their official guardians, but little remains of Fokine, Massine, even Robbins, and almost nothing of Tudor, de Mille, of Gore and Jooss, and so many other passionate dance makers and contributors to twentieth-century ballet-theatre. Obviously there are ballets, and choreographers, who do not stand the test of time and these will inevitably fade from sight, as the title of this book intimates. Possibly this would not matter if there were exciting, original and interesting creators to replace them. We can hope that this is a period of transition out of which new ways to create dance works will evolve, which will re-establish ballet and dance as part of a long and treasured tradition, celebrate the skills acquired through a lengthy and demanding training, and recreate the magic of a theatrical performance.

Alexander and I were lucky to have witnessed and to have taken part in a period in which dance was a flourishing and thriving art form, but most of all, we were fortunate, and privileged, to spend all those years in a chosen profession – something one could not call 'work', but a very special way of life.

AFTERWORD

When I found out that Christina was writing a book about the companies, International Ballet Caravan and London Ballet Theatre, which she and Alexander Roy had directed, I wanted to say something about them. Having spent almost twenty years in The Royal Ballet organisation, starting as a student and becoming a principal dancer, I have been fortunate in working with some of the most important choreographers of the day and in partnering the company's leading ballerinas, not only Dame Margot Fonteyn, but also Nadia Nerina, Svetlana Beriosova, Deanne Bergsma, Dame Monica Mason and Dame Beryl Grey. I left the Royal Ballet to work abroad, first as principal dancer in South Africa and then as ballet master to the Minnesota Dance Theatre in the USA. Returning to London in 1975 to continue my dancing career, I met Alex and Christina, by chance, in a professional ballet class in London's West End, and accepted their offer to join what was then *International Ballet Caravan*.

We performed in a huge variety of theatres, large and small, with a lively, multi-talented group of dancers, touring throughout the UK, Europe and even to the Far East. I also had the opportunity to attend classes in Paris with great teachers, such as Madame Nora. Alex had a special talent to create works, and as with all good choreographers, could draw out and develop his dancers' talents. His *A Midsummer Night's Dream* was wonderful, and proved to be a huge success. Working with Christina, and dancing Alex's ballets with her, was always enjoyable, and enriched by a mutual understanding and easy rapport. The company also gave opportunities to a number of dancers, notably to Prue Sheridan, to learn and perform major roles – chances they may not have had in a larger company.

Credit must also go to Alex and Christina for their entrepreneurial and organisational skills. In addition to their artistic contribution, there were so many other details to consider with the extensive travelling the company undertook, as well as technical problems, and sometimes personal dramas. On behalf of all dancers who worked with them over the years I was involved (at different periods between 1975 and 1981) a heartfelt 'thank you' to Christina and Alex, for all that they did, and what they achieved.

Keith Rosson,
Jávea, Spain, July 2011

Photo Acknowledgements

The author acknowledges the kind permission of the following to reproduce their photographs on the pages listed. Every effort has been made to trace the holders of copyright for photographs. Where this has not been possible, anybody having information should please contact the author.

Suzanne Board 297 (both); Roland Bond 97, 99; Camera Press London/ Anthony Crickmay 289, 307, colour plate section 2: 8 (top right); Anthony Crickmay ©Victoria and Albert Museum, London 31, 50, 230, 231; Jan Dalman 57, 60, 70 (both); Mike Davis 75, 136; Foto Dönitz 11; Dabney Forest colour plate section 2: 2 (all), 3 (both); German Dance Archive, Cologne, photo Jürgen Simon 9; courtesy of Harry Haythorne 37; Geoff Howard frontispiece, xii, 126 (below), 141, 149 (both), 159 (below), 196, 202 (below), 204, 206, 208, 227, 228, 234 (both), 235, 236 (both), 243, 310, colour plate section 1: 1, 2 (both), 4 (all except bottom right), 5 (all except bottom right), colour plate section 2: 1 (bottom left); Peter Isaac front cover, 86; Lara 106; ©MAI/Maria Austria 40, 55; ©MAI/Henk Jonker 13, 52, 54 (both); Duncan Melvin 25; National Library of Australia 3 ('Ballets Russes Collection', NLA), 16 (Walter Stringer), 17, 19; Linda Rich colour plate section 1: 6 (middle), 7 (all), 8 (all), colour plate section 2: 1 (top), 8 (bottom); courtesy of Keith Rosson 186; Roy Round 73, 203 (top), 203 (below), 213 (both), colour plate section 1: 3 (both), 6 (top and bottom); Charlotte Rudolph © Adagp, Paris 2011 6, 7; G M Siewert 8; Robert Smithies 150; Peter Teigen 317, colour plate section 2: 6 (top and middle), 7 (bottom); Jennie Walton 74, 143, 202 (top).

Those photos not listed above are from the author's private collection.

Index

326